FOLLOWING FARAGE

FOLLOWING FARAGE

ON THE TRAIL OF THE PEOPLE'S ARMY

OWEN BENNETT

Biteback Publishing

First published in Great Britain in 2015 by
Biteback Publishing Ltd
Westminster Tower
3 Albert Embankment
London SE1 7SP
Copyright © Owen Bennett 2015

ISBN 978-1-84954-869-4

10 9 8 7 6 5 4 3 2 1

A CIP catalogue record for this book is available from the British Library.

Set in Stempel Garamond

Printed and bound in Great Britain by
CPI Group (UK) Ltd, Croydon CR0 4YY

To Eric, for instilling in me a love of politics,
and to Alessandra, for having to put up with it.

CONTENTS

ACKNOWLEDGEMENTS

FOR THOSE OF YOU looking for a forensic analysis of the successes and failures of Nigel Farage and the United Kingdom Independence Party, I apologise. This book is not it.

But for those of you who want an idea of what it is like to report on, drink with, laugh at, and even, at times, defend the People's Army and its seemingly indestructible commander-in-chief, please read on.

In place of expertise, I offer you anecdotes. In place of objectivity, I offer you the opinions of a hack struggling to get to grips with a world he has always wanted to be a part of, but is slightly unsure of what to do when he gets there.

My journey on the trail of the People's Army saw me develop many friends both inside and outside the party. The ones inside shall remain nameless for obvious reasons, but those outside deserve my thanks.

Robert Hutton was far too generous with his time, Philip Cowley was far too generous with his ideas, and Christopher Hope was far too generous with his patience. John Stevens, Laura Pitel, Rowena Mason, Tamara Cohen, Mary Turner and Michael Deacon deserve special mention for their roles as supporting artists in this tale, as do Matthew Holehouse, Alex Wickham, Giles Dilnot, Dan Hodges and Isabel Hardman.

My colleagues at the *Express*, Alison Little, Martyn Brown, Macer

Hall and Jackie Murray, all deserve special thanks for their advice and tolerance. The same goes to Jason Beattie, Kevin Maguire, Jack Blanchard and Ben Glaze at the *Daily Mirror*.

Special thanks, and an apology, go to Alessandra Pino, who heard more about Nigel Farage over the course of writing this book than can be healthy.

And, of course, thanks to my family, who know what they'll be getting for Christmas this year.

PART I

SKIRMISHES

'We were written off as a party, we were cranks, gadflies, fruit flies, extremists, and the Prime Minister even called us "closet racists", so we've had to put up with a bit of stick over the years to get to where we are.'

Nigel Farage, 3 April 2013, in Lydney,
Gloucestershire, during his 'Common Sense' tour

CHAPTER 1

FROM HODDESDON TO ETERNITY

11 APRIL 2013

'DEXYS FUCKING MIDNIGHT RUNNERS,' he spat out with venom. The group's biggest hit 'Come On Eileen' was blaring out of the pub's speakers.

'Not a fan?' I asked. (Us journalists can pick up on subtle hints like these.)

Nigel Farage sniffed before replying: 'Honestly, I would ban music in pubs.'

He took another gulp of his ale.

I didn't really know what to say to that. I've got nothing against Dexys. Granted, 'Geno' is a far superior tune to 'Come On Eileen', but I don't think it was Kevin Rowland's musical shift from a Northern Soul-influenced New Wave act to chart-topping pop star that had annoyed Farage.

Despite the anti-Dexys – or, rather, music in general – proclamation, Farage looked relaxed. Of course he was. He was in his comfort zone – drinking warm ale in a pub after spending an hour working up a thirst by canvassing. He was relaxed now, but the day hadn't started off smoothly.

The UKIP bus had broken down, making him late. An hour and a half before our lunchtime pint, I had been with a small crowd of UKIP supporters gathered by the clock tower in the town centre waiting for Farage's arrival. There were no more than thirty of them, but they stood out. To be honest, any group of people gathered together in Hoddesdon town centre on a damp, grey morning in April is going to stand out. The Hertfordshire town is not known for its hustle and bustle. The purple balloons attached to a table, complete with a giant UKIP banner tied between two bollards, added to the spectacle.

But still, it was only thirty people. I certainly didn't look at them and think they were a 'People's Army'. But this was April 2013, before all the 'People's Army' rhetoric. Before the UKIP fox was in the Westminster hen house. Before defections.

Farage was well known, but still seen by many – especially in the media – as an eccentric. Some felt he was dangerous; some felt he was comical; most felt he was irrelevant.

UKIP had a handful of MEPs, but they kept defecting, getting sacked or saying ridiculous things such as all Muslims should sign a declaration promising they weren't going to become terrorists.

The party seemed destined to be on the political fringes. Even after successes in the European elections in 2009 and 2004, UKIP had failed to win any seats in the Commons in the following years' general elections. It only had seven local councillors across England, and support for the party was erratic – its polling fluctuated between 10 and 17 per cent in the first eleven days of that April alone.

Farage was coming to Hoddesdon as part of that year's local election campaign, and it was to be my first of many encounters with him.

Margaret Thatcher had died earlier that week, and suddenly everyone was a Eurosceptic Tory again. Good old Maggie, she wouldn't have taken any of this nonsense from the EU. She would have controlled immigration. She would have defended our high-powered vacuums. She wouldn't have voted to keep us in a single-market union in 1975. Well, maybe not the last one.

I was working for the *Hertfordshire Mercury* and, although Hoddesdon wasn't my patch – I had recently been given the much quieter beat of Buntingford – I had been sent down to report on Farage's visit.

I had already begun shifting on the *Daily Express* website at weekends, and, in a few weeks, would be leaving the world of local news and joining the *Express* permanently – hence the *Mercury* editor's decision to relegate me to the trainee beat of Buntingford to serve out the last few weeks of my notice.

Farage was running late and so, notebook in hand, with a pen slotted into the wire rings at the top, I paced around.

I had already done my vox pops, picking out a number of supporters to get comments from – the youngest, the eldest, anyone who looked vaguely interesting.

No one had said anything too remarkable – 'too much immigration', 'sick of Europe', 'down with this sort of thing' – and I knew, even as I spoke to them, their comments probably wouldn't get in the piece. Vikki, the paper's photographer, was taking some pointless snaps. She knew they were pointless but, like me, wanted to look busy. It was all very different from what the local UKIP organiser had promised in his press release: 'UKIP leader Nigel Farage will parade through Hoddesdon in a branded bus as part of his tour of the county ahead of the local elections next month.'

I was expecting an American-style, open-top election bus, complete with a loud hailer bellowing out into the streets of Hoddesdon that everyone must 'Vote UKIP' in the upcoming election.

I was expecting a carnival atmosphere; a swarm of people descending on the town centre, all hoping for a glimpse of their Dear Leader – all hoping for a wave from the man with a cigarette in his mouth, a pint in his hand and St George in his heart.

I was expecting too much, clearly.

As it was, with the grey April sky overhead threatening rain, I, like the others, was waiting to see if Farage would arrive at all.

UKIP's local organiser, a market-stall holder called David Platt, chatted with members of the crowd before he bounded up to me. He cheerily told me the UKIP bus had broken down near Norwich, and Farage and other party members were on alternative transport.

I quipped that I hoped it wasn't a plane, bearing in mind Farage's near-death experience while campaigning in 2010. For a publicity stunt, he had decided to fly in a light aircraft pulling a 'Vote UKIP' banner over Buckinghamshire on the day voters went to the polls in the 2010 election. The banner got caught in the plane's propellers, forcing it to come crashing to the ground. Farage was lucky to escape serious injury, although he was plagued with a back problem after the incident.

For commentators and headline writers it was a dream – UKIP's campaign literally coming crashing to earth just a year after a successful European election campaign.

David Platt just looked at me, and thankfully the awkwardness was broken by his phone ringing.

Three years on from the plane crash, and Farage, who had stood down as UKIP leader to unsuccessfully fight the Buckinghamshire seat, was back in charge of the party.

I glanced down Hoddesdon high street, which, like most small towns these days, operates a confusing one-way system. Trundling up the road to the clock tower where we were all stationed was a plum-coloured minibus, with bright yellow writing on the side. From a distance it looked like a retirement bus from a care home for Ribena berries, but, as it got nearer, I recognised the distinctive yellow pound-sign UKIP logo.

An American presidential motorcade convoy this was not.

The van pulled up next to the clock tower, and out stepped a man wearing the most disgustingly coloured trousers I had ever seen

– mustard yellow. The trousers were matched with a wax jacket, and the look was topped off with a felt trilby.

You can say what you like about Nigel Farage, but he certainly made an impression.

The combination of the trousers, his broad grin and the fact he had finally arrived appeared to send the gathered crowd into a very British kind of excitement. Everyone seemed to want to shake his hand, pat him on the back and have a picture with him, but they were aware this was not quite what you did in Hoddesdon to a man with mustard-yellow corduroy trousers on.

It was by now 11.30 a.m., and as Farage had been wearing the trousers for at least five hours in places where similar displays of colour, personality and uniqueness are equally frowned upon – my home town of Bishop's Stortford just 20 miles north, for example – he was used to the reaction.

In true politician style, he worked the room – or square, as it was. He shook hands, he posed for pictures, he flashed his Cheshire Cat grin. He thanked everyone for their support, seemed deferential to those older than him, acted like a cheeky uncle to those younger, and greeted those of the same generation like long-lost old friends.

With his supporters and a few curious members of the public gathered round, he gave a quick speech: 'I want UKIP councillors to expose the amount of money wasted on translation services, climate change officers and diversity officers. Somebody has got to stand up and oppose the building of these hugely expensive wind turbines which are spoiling the countryside.'

It was hardly the Gettysburg address, but as he couldn't really mention the EU – it was a local election, remember – he didn't have a lot to go on.

With that, he dived off into town for a walk around and to meet the great British public.

But town was empty. It wasn't market day. The weather was a bit cold and there's not much in Hoddesdon.

Unbowed by the indifference, Farage went into shops along the high street. The butcher, estate agent and, of course, a few pubs all got a little visit from the UKIP leader.

I followed him into one boozer and approached him at the bar. It was by now about 12.30 p.m., and as he lifted his pint of ale to his lips he saw me and smiled.

'Been looking forward to that?' I asked.

After a large, loud gulp, Farage turned to me and said: 'Oooh, yeah – life on the road.'

It was only half past midday.

We sat down at a table together and I asked him how he thought the day had gone. After offering his opinion on the pub's music policy, I told him I was off to the *Daily Express* full time in a few weeks. The paper was a big supporter of many of UKIP's policies, and within a year its chief political commentator Patrick O'Flynn would be working for the party as its director of communications before becoming an MEP.

Farage nodded approvingly, and reserved special praise for the pub opposite *Express* HQ in London's Lower Thames Street (The Walrus and The Carpenter).

He finished his pint and continued on his walk of the town with his band of followers.

I left the Ukippers to it, and surveyed the few people who were in the town centre for their views of Farage and his party. Each person gave me one of two responses: 'Never heard of him' or 'Love him and I'm going to vote UKIP from now on'.

Back in the office, I phoned the leader of the local borough council, a Conservative called Paul Mason.

Knowing I was leaving in a few weeks, I decided to wind him up.

'How was Farage then?' he asked.

'You're fucked, Paul, everyone's going to vote UKIP!' I replied.

'No! You're joking?! Really? REALLY?'

'Seriously! Stand down now, Paul, they're coming for you!'

In the election on 3 May, UKIP won 147 council seats across England. The party's share of the vote was 22 per cent – higher than the Liberal Democrats.

However, luckily for Mason, I was wrong about UKIP's popularity in Hoddesdon – in fact, UKIP didn't win a single seat in the entire county of Hertfordshire.

But this was just the beginning for Nigel Farage and me.

CHAPTER 2

A BLOOM TOO FAR

UKIP ANNUAL CONFERENCE, WESTMINSTER – SATURDAY 21 SEPTEMBER 2013

AFTER ITS LOCAL ELECTION success, the country seemed to wake up to UKIP. Well, much of the media did anyway. A party that, for all intents and purposes, was nothing more than an anti-Brussels pressure group suddenly had a sizeable representation in town halls across the UK.

Perhaps people cared more about translation services, climate change officers and wind turbines than we – the media – had previously thought. Of the thirty-five councils that were up for grabs in the elections, UKIP had representation on twenty-four of them – giving it 147 councillors in total.

It was most successful in Kent, where it picked up seventeen councillors, in Lincolnshire, where it won sixteen, in Norfolk, where it got fifteen, and in Cambridgeshire, where it secured twelve.

The question for UKIP was what to do next. The summer was spent pondering that very question.

Not by me, however. I wasn't that bothered, to be honest, and was instead focused on my new job at the *Daily Express* online. A work

day consisted of re-writing what was on the newswires, or slightly
changing news agency copy lifted from local papers, adding a couple of pictures and putting it up on the website. It was a world away
from being a local journalist, where you have to actually leave the
office and find stories, build up contacts and work a patch. After a
few months of copying and pasting articles written by other journalists on to the website, I was desperate to get out of the office, and
realised the party conferences would be the perfect opportunity to
find some stories of my own.

It was too late for me to get accreditation to the Conservative,
Labour or Lib Dem conferences, but I was able to get on the list for
the Green and UKIP meetings.

My editor wasn't too keen, but when I explained I would be going
in my own time and not missing a day of uploading to the web, he
agreed to fund my travel and pay me for the work (I was still technically a freelancer, so was paid by the shift).

First up was the Green Party conference in Brighton, held from
13–16 September.

I went along on the second day, and was one of only a few journalists present. Held in the huge Metropole hotel by the seafront, the
conference saw chilled-out environmentalists from across the country ponder the most important question of the age: why aren't we as
popular as UKIP?

After much soul-searching, the conclusion was that people don't
like being told not to use their cars, not to take cheap flights and not to
expect cheap heating bills. But people do like a man with a cigarette and
a beer saying how everything will be better once the UK leaves the EU.

The Green Party officials were all very nice to me, even though I
was from the *Daily Express* (hardly the paper of choice for them,
I imagine), and I even got an interview with leader Natalie Bennett in
the small press room next to the main conference room. In the evening, bowls of pasta were handed out at a quiz night, and some locally
brewed ale was on tap.

It was nice. Everything was nice. The food was nice. The people were nice. Nice. Nice. Nice.

The next week, I went to the UKIP conference. It was not the same.

The People's Army had organised what would be its biggest meeting yet, right in the heart of Westminster, at the Methodist Central Hall. The hall was built in 1911 and, over the years, has played host to speeches from Sir Winston Churchill, Dr Martin Luther King and Mahatma Gandhi.

It was the venue for the first United Nations General Assembly meeting in 1946, and in 1966 the World Cup trophy was stolen from the hall while it was on display ahead of that year's tournament. And now, in 2013, it was playing host to the UK Independence Party.

The hall is in full view of the House of Commons, meaning Kippers could pretend for a couple of days they were part of the Westminster elite which they so hated.

As with the Green Party conference, I missed the first day. But, unlike the Green Party conference, I actually missed something that happened.

That first morning, Nigel Farage had given his keynote speech, in which he predicted UKIP would win the following year's European elections.

Other speeches at the event seemed to be gaining traction, with policies on fracking making it onto the lunchtime news bulletins. Could it be that UKIP were moving from a single-issue, single-person party? Was this the turning point when the media started reporting on its policies, not its gaffes?

No.

Later that day, a UKIP MEP hit a journalist.

It wasn't exactly a knock-out punch, but Godfrey Bloom's slap of Michael Crick with a conference programme would have got him sent off in a game of football. (With an additional ban for having a conference programme with him on the pitch in the first place.)

The farce began when Bloom was recorded at a fringe meeting, focusing on how to get women into politics, describing female UKIP members as 'sluts' for not cleaning behind their fridges. The recording was published, and Bloom was immediately confronted by a horde of journalists when he left the meeting. A perplexed Bloom explained he meant 'sluts' as in 'slovenly' and it was a joke. Ha ha ha.

He might have just about got away with that explanation but, perhaps sensing his time was up, he decided to really go out in a blaze of glory.

After Crick – one of the best wind-up merchants in the business – asked Bloom why there were no black faces on the front cover of the conference programme, just a sea of white ones, the UKIP man exploded.

In a complete misunderstanding of political correctness, Bloom called Crick a 'racist' for bringing it up and stormed off. As Crick followed him, Bloom hit him on the head with the conference programme he was holding, shouting 'disgraceful' at the same time. It was, of course, all caught on video and within minutes was all over the internet.

'UKIP MEP hits journalist' was blazoned across the news channels, the footage went viral, and UKIP were doing what they did best – screwing things up.

It was not the first time Bloom had caused embarrassment for the party.

A month before he hit Michael Crick and called him a racist, the MEP hit the headlines for decrying foreign aid going to 'Bongo Bongo Land'.

It was a bizarre turn of phrase, almost so comical it struggled to be offensive. It was as if Bloom had watched an old episode of *Love Thy Neighbour*, mistook it for a docu-soap, and decided to adopt its language.

On 7 August 2013, an unrepentant Bloom appeared on BBC Radio 4's flagship news programme, *Today*.

When asked what he would do if UKIP told him to 'mind your

language', Bloom replied: 'I'd say, "Right-o, sorry, sorry everybody if I've offended anybody in Bongo Bongo Land. I shall write the ambassador at the Court of St James's and apologise to him personally."'

After Bloom's latest headline-grabbing antics, Farage went into full 'I am a serious leader' mode, and removed the whip from his friend immediately. He took to the conference stage to tell delegates any media coverage of the conference was now 'dead'.

Farage said:

> The trouble with Godfrey is that he is not a racist, he's not an extremist or any of those things and he's not even anti-women, but he has a sort of rather old-fashioned Territorial Army sense of humour, which does not translate very well in modern Britain.
>
> We can't have any one individual, however fun or flamboyant or entertaining or amusing they are, destroying UKIP's national conference and that is what he's done today.
>
> I'm sad about that, but we can't tolerate this.

Suffice to say, when I woke up the next morning to go to the conference, I was in a slightly more apprehensive mood than the week before when I was travelling to see those lovely people in the Green Party.

I had visions of the People's Army staying up long into the night, plotting their revenge on the media for provoking dear old Godfrey. Perhaps they had created a giant wicker man in the image of Michael Crick, which they would herd journalists into and set ablaze outside the House of Commons. I considered making a big sign that proclaimed 'Don't worry! I work for the *Daily Express* and we agree with your stance on the EU!' in the hope of being spared.

Or maybe: 'Nigel, I agree! Dexys Midnight Runners ARE shit!'

Having got my affairs in order, shared a tearful goodbye with my girlfriend and sent a letter to my solicitor to be opened in the event of my death, I boarded the Tube to Westminster.

Walking up the entrance to the Methodist Hall, there seemed to be no obvious signs of hostility. A handful of men in suits with purple rosettes were smoking outside the hall, but they paid me no attention as I entered the building. There was no holding pen full of journalists, Michael Crick's head wasn't on a spike and, if there was a wicker man, it was well hidden. I found the press accreditation desk and, without even showing proof of who I was, I was given a media pass.

The corridor outside the main hall was full of Kippers, perusing the stalls stacked with UKIP badges, mugs and copies of Farage's autobiography.

I noticed the table selling the conference programmes had rebranded them as 'fly swatters'.

The hundreds of delegates were pretty much what I expected: almost universally white, middle class and southern. They were, in the main, smartly dressed, and the conference had the feel of a rugby club inviting back old boys and their wives for a celebratory event.

There was some commotion over by the staircase that led up to the floor I was on.

Kippers were gathering round someone I couldn't quite see, and a camera crew was filming as they posed for pictures with the individual in question.

I pushed forward, assuming it would be the main man himself: Nigel Farage.

I was half right – it was the main man, but today that man was Michael Crick.

One by one, Kippers were remonstrating with him for stitching up dear old Godfrey, before politely asking him to pose for a photo with them. Far from being shackled, Crick was being indulged.

As I looked on, I realised that I was standing next to two of the few Kippers other than Farage I actually recognised: the disgraced former Tory MP Neil Hamilton and his wife Christine.

The words 'disgraced former Tory MP' could have been created just for Neil Hamilton.

Elected to the Commons in 1983, Hamilton came to wider public attention when he was accused of taking money from Harrods owner Mohamed Al-Fayed to ask questions in Parliament. Hamilton began legal proceedings against *The Guardian* over the 'cash-for-questions' allegations, but then dropped the case and settled out of court.

A parliamentary inquiry in July 1997 concluded Hamilton was guilty of taking cash for questions, but it didn't need to boot him out of Parliament – the voters had already done that.

In that year's general election, held two months before the inquiry published its findings, Hamilton lost Tatton – the fourth-safest Tory seat in the country – to former war journalist Martin Bell. Bell stood as an independent, and Labour and the Lib Dems decided not to contest the seat to allow the anti-corruption campaigner a free run at Hamilton.

Since leaving Parliament, Hamilton had lost a libel case to Mohamed Al-Fayed, and became something of television personality by appearing on chat shows and, along with his wife Christine, a Louis Theroux documentary.

Christine Hamilton had also built up a media profile, taking part in reality TV shows such as *I'm a Celebrity … Get Me Out of Here!* and *Celebrity MasterChef*, sitting in dictionary corner on *Countdown* and even having her own short-lived chat show on digital channel BBC Choice.

As character witnesses go, I'm sure Bloom wouldn't have picked Hamilton, but I decided to ask him his views on the previous days debacle.

'Godfrey is a good friend of mine, but he did behave in an idiotic fashion,' he said. 'He shouldn't have reacted to Michael Crick as he did. His conduct was indefensible. He shouldn't, at his age and with all his experience, have blown up as he did. Crick is an irritating little squit, there's no doubt about that, and I'm sure he's just as complimentary about me.'

With a handshake, Hamilton was gone.

I sent a message to my father: 'You'll never guess who I've just met! Neil Hamilton!'

His reply: 'Make sure you wash your hands.'

Fair point, I thought.

I ventured into the conference hall itself to see if anything approaching a news story was about to break out.

I sat down in the press area to the left of the stage, just in time to hear one particularly angry UKIP member launch into a passionate defence of his party and decry the treatment doled out to it by the media. Managing the impressive feat of shouting through gritted teeth, he angrily – and repeatedly – denounced Crick and his hateful employers, the BBC.

Except Crick was working for Channel 4.

The audience members twigged this, and every accusation laid at the door of the Beeb was met with cries of 'Four!' from delegates. The poor chap on stage was so caught up in his diatribe that he misheard 'Four!' as 'More!', and so rounded on the BBC again. All the journalists positioned stage left were joyfully tweeting out the confusion. The ranter still received a hearty round of applause when, like a hurricane, he eventually blew himself out.

So far, so UKIP.

By now it was mid-afternoon, and I was getting worried. I needed a story to justify me getting out of the office, and I had missed the main one by twenty-four hours.

A brief chat with the Hamiltons wasn't going to cut the mustard. What I really needed was an interview with Farage. I contacted the head of UKIP's press office, Gawain Towler, to see if there was any chance of a chat with the leader. Towler and I had spoken many times on the phone but never actually met, and he told me to come and find him in the next-door pub – the Westminster Arms. He said I would notice him by his red trousers and, by Christ, he wasn't wrong.

Ukippers must get a discount on corduroy, as, like Farage in Hoddesdon, he was wearing hideously bright clothes made out of the fabric.

He was already holding court outside the Westminster Arms when I arrived, surrounded by numerous Kippers hanging on his every word.

If you ever get the chance to meet Towler, take it.

He comes across as a complete buffoon. Incredibly well spoken, and capable of a beguiling turn of phrase, but he still often acts like Tim Nice-But-Dim from *Harry Enfield and Chums*. Except he doesn't look 'nice'. With his foppish hair, angular features and scar running down one of his cheeks, he has the air of a Droog from *A Clockwork Orange*. At any moment, one senses, he could break out into ultraviolence.

Of course, he is not dim – well, not all the time. But he does have a mischievous edge. He was co-editor of a Brussels-based satirical magazine called *The Sprout*, which lampooned the EU on a monthly basis. His personal blog was a mixture of diary pieces from Brussels and personal diatribes. There were a bizarre few weeks when he just posted poems by Enoch Powell, and another occasion when he claimed a male Tory had vowed to destroy him after he rejected the man's sexual advances when the pair were at university – although this post was taken down almost as soon as it had gone up.

I went to the bar to order a pint of beer and overheard the barman explaining to two Kippers that they couldn't have any Spitfire ale as the pub's supply had been drunk dry.

'Ah,' said one, who was in his early seventies, 'in which case I'll have a pint of … Asahi.'

'You don't want that!' said his friend – or possibly twin brother – 'That's Japanese beer!'

'Crikey, good point. I best have something British – pint of Foster's, please.'

Inwardly laughing at the misunderstanding of the origins of lagers aside, I found myself enjoying my time with the Ukippers.

Gawain was holding court outside the pub, and his audience was ever growing.

A steady stream of beer was finding its way into my hands, and talking to the party supporters was proving to be an interesting experience.

There were initial reservations when I was introduced as a member of the press, but after I told them I worked for the *Daily Express* I was considered a 'friendly'.

Men were dominating the conversation with their deep, plummy voices, and the few women who were there listened politely.

But one woman seemed at odds with the men around her, and not just because of her gender.

She was a schoolteacher in her late thirties, and something of a rarity – a former Labour supporter.

Unlike the boorish accents of the voices swirling in the September air outside the pub in the centre of Westminster, her tone was much more in keeping with the comprehensive education I had received. I and Andrew Lowry – a freelance journalist I had teamed up with for the day – immediately realised that, among all of the normal Kippers, she was the most interesting.

We asked her about UKIP, and why she had joined the party. She looked unsure whether to answer, but we assured her that even though we were part of the nasty media, we weren't trying to trip her up, catch her out, or trick her into hitting us.

She explained how she felt let down by Labour, and didn't feel comfortable with the changes in the community in which she lived.

It was a perfectly reasonable point, devoid of anything particularly inflammatory.

Lowry and I asked if she would repeat it for the benefit of our tape recorders – the several pints we had both gleefully imbibed meant our trusty shorthand was a no-go. It was at this point that the two men flanking her began to look uneasy.

'I'm not sure about that,' said one.

'Why, what are you planning to do with it?' said another.

'Well, it's a really interesting point that you are making,' I said, addressing the woman who had been speaking to us, 'and the fact that you are a former Labour supporter that's joined UKIP is a change from lots of others here.'

The two men were not convinced at first, but then relented.

She repeated her points again, this time with two Dictaphones pointed towards her.

But when we started asking questions – UKIP's attitude to women, the complaints of racism and divisive politics – the two men stepped in. I mean they physically stepped in, forming a kind of shield around her.

She seemed to have no problem answering the questions, but the two men – who, from what I could gather, were just party members, not members of the press office – clearly decided the woman needed to be protected from the nasty journalists.

Or maybe they were protecting us from her! Maybe she was a loud and proud racist, ready to spew forth her neo-Nazi views at the slightest provocation. Perhaps beneath her smart blazer and white blouse was the beating heart of a violent, psychopathic homophobe, who spent her spare time planning an anti-gay killing spree. Maybe all she needed to set her off was a couple of questions from journalists about UKIP's attitude towards those people who aren't white British men. In which case, maybe those two gentlemen were actually specialist bodyguards, who were protecting Lowry and me from this crazed UKIP-supporting schoolteacher.

Or maybe they just didn't like two male journalists talking to one of *their* women. Maybe they thought she couldn't possibly justify her own views and beliefs under mild scrutiny. Maybe they thought that, as men, they knew best and had to protect the little woman in their midst.

Whatever the reason, they stepped in, she stopped talking, and we went and got another drink.

I was still on the ale, but Lowry was on the Asahi. 'Poofter!' was one Kipper's view on his choice of drink.

It was by now almost 6 p.m., and the conference was still going on in Central Hall. Not that anyone either in the pub or outside on the pavement seemed to care.

I asked Towler if he felt he should be in the conference centre, making sure no one had set fire to Michael Crick or organised a pitchfork-wielding mob with the plan of storming the nearby House of Commons or the BBC.

'I'm a press officer, you're a member of the press. I would say I'm doing my job!' he replied.

'Will I get to speak to Farage?' I asked, conscious that all I had so far was half an interview with a woman no one had ever heard of, a ranting Ukipper blaming the BBC for Channel 4's Michael Crick, and Neil Hamilton.

'Yes, yes, he'll be along shortly,' came the reply.

He was right. I discovered one of the rules of the universe that day: if you stay in a pub long enough, Nigel Farage will eventually show up.

I almost didn't notice him. I was expecting a media scrum to be stalking his every move, with paparazzi bulbs exploding incessantly.

I expected his disciples to be laying down palm-tree leaves in his path. I didn't expect him to just walk around the corner, by himself, save for his two bodyguards.

After someone had got him a beer and given him a cigarette, I approached him.

'Nigel, you probably don't remember me but I spoke to you in Hoddesdon about six months ago,' I said.

'You were going to work for the *Daily Express*, right?' he replied.

'Yes, well remembered!' I said. I was instantly flattered. 'Is it OK if I ask you some questions?'

'Of course, of course.'

I then proceeded to ask a series of terrible questions about Godfrey Bloom, views of UKIP and whether the conference could still be classed as a success. They were questions journalists had been asking for twenty-four hours. They revealed nothing new at all. But I didn't care. I was too caught up in the 'I'm-having-a-drink-with-the-leader-of-a-political-party-because-I'm-a-reporter-for-a-national-news-paper-so-I-must-be-very-important-and-wonderful-look-at-me-mummy-I'm-doing-so-fucking-well-for-myself' vibe. I even asked to have my picture taken with Farage. I was a fan girl.

No, that's wrong. I was a drunk fan girl.

Andrew Lowry was not so deferential.

'In your speech yesterday you said more people came to this country in 2010 than in the thousand years before it. How did you work that out?'

Farage tried to justify the figure, but Lowry wasn't having it.

He repeatedly questioned Farage on the claim. Farage repeatedly defended it.

Lowry was persistent, and I guess an afternoon of drinking gave his voice a slight aggressive edge.

The bodyguards behind Farage stepped ever so slightly closer to the UKIP leader.

No matter how often Farage tried to justify the claim, Lowry pulled his figures apart.

Hostilities paused for a split second, and the pair just stared at each other. Just for a moment, there was tension in the air, and I saw the bodyguards fixing their eyes on Lowry. But it was all over with a handshake, and Lowry even asked Farage to pose for a photo with him.

Day over, I made my way back to my home in east London. Drunk and somewhat slightly dazed, I berated myself. I should have grilled Farage on his immigration claims. I should have been touring fringe meetings trying to pick up further indiscretions by Ukippers. I should have been scrutinising policies emerging from the conference hall.

I shouldn't have tried to take Farage on in a pub – that's his battleground, and he'll always win there.

CHAPTER 3

DO YOU HEAR THE PEOPLE SWEAR THEY ARE NOT RACIST?

EMMANUEL CENTRE, WESTMINSTER – THURSDAY 8 MAY 2014

I N SEPTEMBER 2013, NIGEL Farage predicted UKIP would cause an earthquake in British politics by winning the following year's European elections. His prediction was derided by many, but, as the 22 May election day loomed nearer, it seemed the People's Army was on course for a sizeable victory.

One of the great ironies of UKIP is that it's a party that wants Britain out of the EU, yet it could not have survived without it. The only elections the party had achieved any success at prior to 2013 were the Euros, winning three MEPs in 1999, twelve in 2004 and thirteen in 2009.

Despite these European successes, the party was still considered to be on the fringes by many in the media and general public at large. But the local elections breakthrough, together with second-place finishes in five consecutive Westminster by-elections, meant UKIP was on the cusp of joining the political mainstream. Winning the European elections would confirm it. But, by raising the stakes, Farage also raised the scrutiny.

The media magnifying glass was turned on to the party, and it didn't take much detective work to discover a potential Achilles heel: racism.

The claim that UKIP was a 'racist' party was not a new one. In 2006, the then Leader of the Opposition David Cameron dismissed the party as a bunch of 'fruitcakes and loonies and closet racists'.

By 2014, the combination of more UKIP candidates than ever before and the seductive speak-your-brains nature of social media meant the press could find a rich seam of racist comments from people sporting purple rosettes.

It all seemed to kick off after Godfrey Bloom's comments about foreign aid going to 'Bongo Bongo Land' before the 2013 conference, followed by his bashing of Michael Crick.

But far from his expulsion from the front bench acting as a line in the sand for the party when it came to the race issue, matters just kept getting worse – and it was still coming from the top.

At the party's spring conference in Torquay in February 2014, Nigel Farage used his keynote address to say he felt 'slightly awkward' when he could only hear foreign languages being spoken on a commuter train leaving London.

Undercover journalists from the *Sunday Mirror* then revealed that a stand-up comedian booked to provide the entertainment at a £35-a-head black tie dinner had told numerous offensive jokes based on racial stereotypes.

The paper claimed Farage laughed and clapped as Paul Eastwood joked about the Olympics, and said: 'Poland did well. They took home bronze, silver, gold, lead, copper – anything they could get their hands on.'

He also said: 'Team Somalia – they did well, didn't they? They had to apologise. Didn't realise sailing and shooting were two different events.'

Someone call the police, Bernard Manning's been robbed.

In April, the party produced a slick, glossy political broadcast to show off its candidates and supporters ahead of the 22 May vote. Like all political broadcasts, it was pretty hopeless.

Deputy chairman Suzanne Evans standing in Piccadilly Circus, talking into the camera while people milled about her at double speed like she was some sort of Time Lord.

UKIP's deputy leader Paul Nuttall walking along a beach in a suit, looking as if he was about to do a Reggie Perrin because of EU trading regulations.

The party's event organiser Lizzy Vaid having her afternoon wine-drinking session with her gal pals ruined because of European judges calling for British prisoners to be given the vote.

Farage popped up at the end in an empty pub, as if he were the sole survivor of an EU-caused apocalypse who had stayed alive by seeking solace in a boozer.

But the controversy arose from the builder featured in the video, Andre Lampitt.

In the section of the broadcast focusing on the free movement of people across EU member states, Lampitt says: 'Since the lads from Eastern Europe are prepared to work for a lot less than anybody else, I've found it a real struggle.'

So far – so meh.

But a quick trawl through Lampitt's Twitter feed showed he had thoughts on a range of subjects. His view on Islam? 'Muslims are animals their faith is disgusting their prophet is [a] pedophile.'

The Zimbabwe-born builder also branched into the complex matter of African sociology with the comment: 'Most Nigerians are generally bad people ... I grew up in Africa and dare anyone to prove me wrong.'

People should 'get over' slavery, which was just 'an act of war' and 'inner peace will come when Aids does what it should and reduces African density'.

Labour leader Ed Miliband, who was born in Britain to a Polish mother and Belgian father, was apparently 'not a real Brit. I hope he never gets to be PM! He was only born here.'

After his views were splashed across the media, UKIP suspended Lampitt and a spokesman said: 'We are deeply shocked that Mr Lampitt has expressed such repellent views. His membership of the party has been suspended immediately pending a full disciplinary process.'

Just three days after Lampitt's suspension, a UKIP candidate for Enfield Council in London decided he too wanted to get involved in a bit of controversy.

After comedian Lenny Henry launched a campaign to see Britain's ethnic minorities better represented in the media, Henwood tweeted: 'He should emigrate to a black country. He does not have to live with whites.'

He later told the BBC: 'I think if black people come to this country and don't like mixing with white people, why are they here? If he wants a lot of blacks around, go and live in a black country.'

Henwood resigned his UKIP membership after the story broke – a UKIP spokesman said it was 'mutually agreed this would be the best course'.

As well as the comments of some party members, UKIP was also facing criticism for its billboard poster campaign. One featured the text '26 million people in Europe are looking for work. And whose jobs are they after?' next to giant finger pointing out at the reader.

Former Labour immigration minister Barbara Roche decided the best form of defence was attack and, in her role as joint chair of the Migration Matters Trust, blasted UKIP for running a 'racist campaign'.

She said: 'The party is practising what is, in effect, a form of "Euracism". They are deploying the same language and tactics used by openly racist parties like the BNP, but instead of targeting migrants from Africa and Asia they are targeting migrants from within the EU.'

On 29 April 2014, UKIP's director of communications Patrick

O'Flynn, who was standing as an MEP for the party in the upcoming election, appeared opposite Roche on *Newsnight* to defend the poster campaign.

But, for all UKIP's accusations of media bias against them, it was *Newsnight* host Jeremy Paxman who seemed to go into bat for the party.

PAXMAN: Let's look at this poster and you tell us why this poster – '26 million people in Europe looking for work. And whose jobs are they after?' – why is that racist?

ROCHE: Because it's an absolute nonsense, isn't it?

PAXMAN: It may be nonsense but that's not the same as being racist.

ROCHE: So there are 26 million people – it's alarmist – in Europe who are going to come here looking for work.

PAXMAN: That wasn't your accusation. Your accusation was it was racist. Why is that racist?

ROCHE: And I'll explain. If you substituted for the word Europe, you substituted people from Africa, or people from Asia are coming here to look for work, everybody would say that was absolutely racist.

PAXMAN: But it doesn't say that.

ROCHE: There's no reason at all why [because] it says Europe, that that isn't racist in exactly the same way. It's alarmist, it's nonsense and as [Conservative backbencher] Nicholas Soames says, it's completely divisive.

PAXMAN [TURNING TO PATRICK O'FLYNN]: Why do
you think your party does appeal to racists?

O'FLYNN: I don't think our party appeals to racists any more
than any other parties.
    What I do think is that we're under enormous media scru-
tiny, which I don't complain about.
    As [former Lib Dem leader] Ming Campbell said to me
yesterday: 'Welcome to Test match cricket.' Where there are
people who have expressed racist sentiments, we root them
out and we take disciplinary action.

Despite the protestations of O'Flynn – and others – that the party
was not racist, there were concerns within UKIP that the label would
stick and deter potential voters. The party decided to tackle the issue
head-on in that oh-so-British of ways: it organised a meeting. But
not just any meeting.

A 'We're Not Racist!' meeting.

They didn't name it that exactly, but the plan was to get as many
black, Asian and other UKIP members from ethnic minority backgrounds as possible together, stand on a stage and say, 'Look! Look
at us! Look at the colour of our skin! How can UKIP be racist if
we're in the party?'

On Thursday 8 May, the day of the meeting, I went to meet Nigel
Farage's former press aide Annabelle Fuller at the Loose Box bar on
Horseferry Road, near Westminster.

I had met Fuller once before, at an event at the London School of
Economics, where Farage had taken part in a debate on the importance of the upcoming European elections. Despite no longer
working for the party, she had arranged for me to meet Amjad
Bashir, UKIP's small business spokesman, and Steven Woolfe, the
party's economic guru. Both were candidates in the European election and both were non-white members of the party. Woolfe has

an Irish grandmother and an African-American grandfather on one side of his family, and a Jewish grandmother and English grandfather on the other.

He joined UKIP four years ago after leaving the Conservatives, and said any racism he had encountered since his move came from people outside the party, not from those within.

Woolfe said:

> I myself have been called an 'Uncle Tom', I have been called an apologist. We are not going to let the agenda be driven any more by those who are calling us racist or xenophobic when our party is completely the opposite. If anyone has a care to look at our immigration policy, they will see it is the most ethical immigration policy.

He said that night's meeting had been called for by UKIP 'members who are mixed race, Jewish, Catholic, Muslim, north and south, who are tired of being called racists, tired of being abused on the doorsteps'.

Woolfe was an impressive speaker who seemed a lot more coherent and rational than other UKIP members I had spoken to; in other words, a lot less barmy.

A trained barrister who then worked in the City of London, he came from a similar professional background to leader Nigel Farage.

But his personal story was different from Farage's private-school-educated childhood in Kent.

As Woolfe explained:

> I was born in Manchester, grew up initially in Moss Side and spent most of my life in Burnage. I grew up a few streets away from the Gallagher brothers [Noel and Liam, who formed Britpop group Oasis]. I was the only 'coloured' face – as it was then called, black face as we call it now – in my primary school, and I used to get a fair amount of abuse.

I asked if he had to justify his decision to join UKIP to his family.

'We had a dinner recently of family members who are from different backgrounds – my wife is from Winchester, so a middle-class family, and I come from a northern working-class family,' he replied.

> We were sitting there at dinner and they said, 'Why are you in UKIP allowing these people in?' The problem with it is we get frustrated as well. We bang our heads against the table when we see these people. But we do what other parties don't do. We find them when they are observed and we deal with them and get them out and that's our procedure because we recognise that there may well be bad people in all political parties but at least we are making an effort.

> We are going to review the systems we put in place after this week when we have seen one or two candidates. It will stop and it will get better because we don't want to face it any more and we don't want those bad apples ruining it.

> But the key point is no one turns round and says because you've got Muslim bombers in a different country that the whole of Islam is wrong. No one turns round and says, 'You've got a Catholic priest [who] is an abuser so all Catholic priests are the same.'

Woolfe left the bar to go and prepare his speech for the meeting, so I began talking to UKIP's small and medium business spokesman, the Pakistan-born but Yorkshire-raised Amjad Bashir.

I had caught some of Bashir's speech at last year's UKIP conference, in which he opened with the joke, 'I wasn't born in Yorkshire, but I came as soon as I could.'

The Bashir family moved to Bradford when Amjad was eight years old, attracted by the booming textile industry. Amjad Bashir made his career in restaurants, eventually owning two in Bradford and Manchester respectively.

Like Woolfe, he told me it was unfair to characterise a whole party based on what 'archaeologists' had dug up on Facebook and Twitter:

> Is it right that we demonise the whole of the Lib Dems for Cyril Smith being a paedophile? We don't say that about the whole of the Lib Dems, and the same [goes] for us.
>
> As a party, if there are a few nutters, as there are in all parties, we don't demonise the whole of the Lib Dems or Conservatives for that.

I asked for his views on UKIP MEP Gerard Batten, who, in 2006, commissioned a 'charter of Muslim understanding', which called on followers of Islam to sign a declaration rejecting violence. It also says that the parts of the Koran that promote 'violent physical Jihad' should be regarded as 'inapplicable, invalid and non-Islamic'. Despite the document being commissioned eight years ago, Mr Batten had said in February 2014 that he stood by the proposal.

Bashir, who is a Muslim, said he had never spoken to Batten about the 'charter', but it had been raised with him by members of his Islamic community.

He said:

> The views put forward by an individual at a time of the 7/7 bombings are not the views of the party as a whole. That party has dismissed these views, the party never subscribed to these views. The party believes all people, all British people, who live in this island are equal, and all religious beliefs are to be respected.

I found this slightly odd. If someone in a party I was in had a written a document saying that all Spurs fans had to sign a 'charter of understanding' (I'm not religious, so the closest thing I can draw a comparison to is my love of Tottenham – but, unlike those of faith, at least I *know* Spurs will let me down), I would be having pretty strong words with them.

Maybe Bashir thought it best not to cause dissent in the ranks of the People's Army.

With the interview over, Bashir, Fuller and I walked together to the Emmanuel Centre. When we were within 500 metres, we started hearing the noise of protesters who had gathered outside. The crowd of no more than 100 were booing and jeering people going inside. They were behind a metal barrier, and police were on guard in case any serious trouble should break out.

Using a loud hailer to whip up the crowd, one protester was shouting, 'We are the UKIP haters!' and, 'UKIP – no way! Immigrants – here to stay!'

The other protesters gleefully chanted along, with many brandishing placards proclaiming: 'No to UKIP's racist lies'.

I walked past them with Bashir, and he – and probably I, as well – was booed. Before slipping into the meeting, I went over to the crowd to try to talk to them.

'Why are you here?' I asked. I wasn't being confrontational, simply opening with an easy question. A young lad in the crowd, who was probably in his late teens, explained how he thought UKIP was racist and its policies divisive.

'But what about the fact that tonight is all about UKIP members from non-white backgrounds coming together to say the party isn't racist? Does that not undermine your argument?'

'Not all racism is about skin colour, and I would say some have been tricked and they are being used,' he replied.

I made my way inside and, instead of sitting in the designated press area, I decided to sit in with the UKIP members and public.

A white, well-dressed gentleman, who looked to be in his seventies, sat down next to me.

I assumed he was a UKIP member.

'So, young man,' he said. 'What are these lot all about then?'

'UKIP? Well they're an anti-EU party standing in the European elections,' I replied.

'Yes, yes, I know that, but all the people here – what's the meeting about?'

'They're trying to prove they're not racist.'

'Why are they having to do that?'

'Because one of their candidates said Lenny Henry should go back to a "black country". And another said Muslims are animals. And they go on about immigration a lot.'

'Oh,' he said, and thought for a while as he took it all in. 'So, are they racist?' he asked me.

Now it was my turn to think. 'I don't think Nigel Farage is. I don't think most of them are. But a few probably are. How come you're here, if you don't mind me asking?'

'I saw an advert for this in the paper so I thought I would come along and see what all the fuss is about.'

'Did you see the people outside?' I asked.

The gentleman nodded.

'Did it put you off coming in?'

'Not at all,' was his reply. 'Everyone is entitled to their view.'

The meeting began and various UKIP members took to the stage to proclaim the party was not racist.

Deputy chairman Suzanne Evans said how great the party was for women; Gravesend member Joshua Duroch said how great the party was for Asian Brits; and Bashir said how great the party was for everyone.

But, alas for the hippy-love-in vibe the party was trying to foster, there were some vocal dissenters in the audience.

A handful of protesters had managed to get round UKIP's highly polished and sophisticated security system by buying a ticket – and had positioned themselves in pairs and small groups around the hall. At seemingly random points during the speeches, a pair would leap up and begin shouting at the speakers before being bundled out by security. After the third or fourth such interruption, you could feel the atmosphere in the audience change.

It was predominantly, but not exclusively, young adults who were heckling, but at least one anarchist was an elderly gentleman, who waved his walking stick in the air as he berated UKIP.

People started getting edgy: 'Is the person next to me a double agent?' they were thinking.

'Sure, they may be wearing a UKIP rosette, and have a signed copy of Farage's autobiography on their lap and what seems to be an "I Love Godfrey Bloom" tattoo on their forearm ... but are they really true UKIP? They did stop clapping a second earlier than everyone else when Suzanne Evans finished speaking. And I'm sure earlier on I heard them say that arch-Euro-lover Ted Heath hadn't been that bad a Prime Minister. My God – I'm sitting next to a LEFTIE!'

Well, at least that was the vibe I was getting from the Ukippers as they looked nervously round at each other.

However, far from derailing the meeting, the protesters only made the resolve of the UKIP speakers greater, and added more poignancy to their speeches.

For example, when Steven Woolfe was describing his childhood in Manchester as a descendent of immigrants, two protesters leapt up and began shouting: 'Fake! You're a faker!'

I didn't get a chance to ask them what they were accusing him of faking (his heritage?) as security guards quickly dragged them out of the hall.

As they were being removed, Woolfe appeared on the brink of tears as he said: 'Let me tell you something – a five-year-old child having to go home and tell his mum he was called a nigger all day at school – that's not a fake.'

It was a genuinely emotional moment. If Woolfe is a faker, then he deserves an Oscar.

After numerous UKIP members had taken to the stage to dismiss the racism charge, decry the media for running a smear campaign and profess their love for the wonderful all-encompassing egalitarian dream that is the UK Independence Party, it was time for the main man himself.

I was unsure if Nigel Farage was going to appear. Perhaps the UKIP leader would think the limelight should remain solely on the party activists tonight in order to hammer home the inclusiveness message.

It would also help counteract the other accusation against the party – that UKIP is a one-man band that derives its popularity and support purely from the personality of its leader.

But it would be unheard of for Farage to pass up a round of applause.

So, with the stage full of black, Asian, white, male, female, young and old members, Nigel Farage entered the hall to a hero's welcome. He positioned himself smack bang in the middle of the stage, drinking up the applause. His UKIP disciples were behind him, many staring adoringly at their leader.

With his arms outstretched like Christ the Redeemer overlooking the beach in Rio de Janeiro, he spoke unto his followers:

> Let this picture, let this picture of me on this stage with these wonderful men and women from all their different backgrounds and their united belief in being British and being part of this country and wanting this country to be free and independent and self-governing and proud, let this be UKIP's Clause IV moment.

No, Farage was not comparing himself to Jesus Christ. He was aiming higher – he was comparing himself to Tony Blair.

With the proclamation delivered, Farage shifted into automatic and began tearing into those who attacked UKIP.

'They have decided that rather than going for the ball, they are going to go for the man,' he opined. The media had permeated 'very deep unpleasantness' in the course of 'defending their friends in the so-called main parties – or, as we prefer to call them, the legacy parties'.

We have put forward into the field this year 2,234 candidates for the local elections. While UKIP has professionalised, while UKIP has improved, while UKIP is better now at doing everything than it ever was before, and while UKIP has a membership form that says within it 'if you have ever been a member of an extreme organisation or you have views that are not compatible with the party you shouldn't join', and while every candidate is asked to sign a declaration to the same effect, there will always be, in any system, a few people who creep over the line and cause us embarrassment. I would rather the ten people out of the 2,234 who have said things that are either stupid or offensive in some cases, I would rather it hadn't happened.

'We asked them to fill in a FORM!' was his argument. 'How can we know if they are racist or homophobic or xenophobic if they filled in a FORM saying they weren't?'

Looking down the barrel of a television camera in the hall, Farage then made his final plea:

I don't care if you disagree with us, I don't care if you think we are better off being governed by Cameron or Clegg or Miliband. I don't care if you think uncontrolled immigration is good for Britain. I don't care if you criticise us for wanting to be a free, independent country and not under that flag and anthem and preposterous president whose name no one actually knows. I did a bit of marketing for him, didn't I?! I don't care what you call us – you can call us right wing, left wing, you can call us small-minded, you can call us whatever you like, I don't care what you call us, but from this moment on, please do not ever call us a racist party. We are not a racist party.

It was impressive. In a rant about the continuing false accusations of racism levelled at his party, Farage had managed to get in a dig at European Council president Herman Van Rompuy.

The audience lapped it up and carried on cheering as Farage hugged the members on the stage.

I turned to the gentleman next to me.

'What do you think of that? Do you think they're racist?' I asked.

'No, I don't think they're racist,' he replied.

'Would you vote for them?'

He paused and then emphatically said: 'This lot? No, not at all.'

Although Farage failed to win over the gentleman next to me, he had succeeded in demonstrating UKIP was not a racist party – at least to those in the hall.

The race issue died down for about a week.

On 16 May, Nigel Farage was asked in an interview by James O'Brien on LBC radio to explain remarks he had previously made about having Romanian neighbours.

> O'BRIEN: What about the line about not wanting to live next door to Romanians?

> FARAGE: I didn't say that. I was asked: 'If a group of Romanian men moved in next door to you, would you be concerned?'

> O'BRIEN: What about if a group of German children did? What's the difference?

> FARAGE: You know what the difference is.

> O'BRIEN: No, I honestly don't.

So much for the racism issue being put to bed.

Farage tried to explain his remarks away as being born out of tiredness after a long election campaign. He even took out a full-page advert in the *Daily Telegraph* in the form of an 'open letter'.

After claiming 92 per cent of all ATM crime in London is carried out by Romanians, Farage wrote: 'The vast majority of Romanians who have come to the UK wish to better their lives and would make good neighbours.' But the 'unpalatable truth' is that Romania has not made the transition to a full Western democracy, he said:

> We should not be in a political union with Romania, with an open door to all of their citizens. We must take back the power to stop criminals from entering our country by taking back control of our borders.
>
> When this happens, my answer to the question, 'Should people be concerned if a group of Romanian men moved in next door?' will be, 'No.'

When it came to UKIP and racism, the two couldn't leave each other alone.

Did it affect the European election? No.

UKIP came first, winning 4.4 million votes, 26.6 per cent of all cast. The party went from the thirteen seats it had won in 2009 to twenty-four.

In the local elections, UKIP secured 167 seats, building on the 147 it had won the year before.

Earthquake: delivered.

CHAPTER 4

DAMNATIO MEMORIAE

PARLIAMENTARY PRIVILEGE IS A weird and wonderful thing.

It means politicians can say whatever they like in Parliament without fear of being sued for defamation or held in contempt of court.

In March 2014, former UKIP MEP Nikki Sinclaire used it to accuse Nigel Farage of having an affair with party press officer Annabelle Fuller. Addressing the UKIP leader in an EU Assembly debate, Sinclaire said: 'With unemployment still a problem across Europe and indeed the UK, does Mr Farage think it is a fair use of taxpayers' money, namely his secretarial allowance, not only to employ his wife Kirsten, but his former mistress Annabelle Fuller?'

Farage didn't respond in the debate, but afterwards told the *Telegraph* the accusations were a 'cowardly and malicious act'. He said Sinclaire had been making the claims for eight years, and added: 'I have spoken to every national newspaper on this issue and the answer today remains the same as it was in 2006. The answer is no.'

As Farage implied, rumours of a relationship between the pair had long circulated the bars and pubs of Westminster and Brussels. Fuller was Farage's closest aide and confidante, and, as such, was seen as the 'gatekeeper' to the UKIP leader. She would often be the sole person to accompany him to events, would ghostwrite articles for national newspapers that appeared in his name and even ran his Twitter account. Farage and Fuller always denied any affair, and both adopted a business-as-usual approach whenever the rumours resurfaced.

But this latest intervention was something different. By making the claims in the EU assembly, Sinclaire ensured they could now be reported by the press without fear of legal action from anyone involved.

The comments came just as UKIP was gearing up to fight the 2014 European elections, which Farage had already predicted the party would win. Anything that would distract from that goal needed to be eliminated, and Fuller continuing to work so closely with Farage would be a distraction. If the pair were photographed together, for instance, the rumours would start up again, and so, just over two months before the European elections, Fuller was quietly eased out of the party.

It was a humiliating end for one of Farage's closest advisors. Fuller started working for UKIP in 2004, when she was just twenty-two years old, initially in the European Parliament before joining the national press team. She left the party in 2008 to move into public relations, but re-joined in 2010 for that year's general election. As well as the normal duties expected of a close advisor, Fuller did Farage's make-up before he appeared on television, went with him to physiotherapy appointments after his plane crash and made sure he did the exercises to help with his back pain.

She had become increasingly central to the UKIP press operation, and was part of the team that guided the party to second place in the 2013 Eastleigh by-election, a result that, for many, heralded UKIP as a serious force in British politics.

But while the economics graduate, who served in the Territorial Army before leaving due to a back injury, was highly thought of by Farage, she was not universally loved in the party. Some felt she held too much influence over Farage, while one former member of staff for a UKIP MEP called her a 'drama queen'.

Before the claims about her and Farage's relationship were made public by Sinclaire, Fuller had been involved in another set of allegations involving Tory MP Andrew Bridgen. The events of 8 June 2011 are vehemently disputed by Fuller and Bridgen, but both agree they were introduced to each other in the Marquis of Granby pub near the House of Commons, which was opposite Bridgen's flat. Bridgen invited Fuller and the civil servant who had introduced them to his flat for a drink. The evening ended with Fuller running from Bridgen's flat in her bare feet, clutching the MP's Blackberry and House of Commons pass as evidence of where she had been. A security guard called the police, and Fuller claimed Bridgen had groped her. Bridgen was arrested and strongly denied any wrongdoing. Fuller later withdrew the allegations.

Speaking to the *Daily Mail* three years later, Bridgen said: 'Those two and a half hours with Annabelle Fuller have ruined my life. The events of that night and the huge media intrusion of my wife and children that followed led to the end of my marriage.'

Despite this scandal, which gained increased media coverage after Fuller waived her right to anonymity to give an interview to the *Sunday Mirror* about the incident, Farage stood by her.

Three years later, and thanks to Sinclaire's allegations, the 32-year-old was no longer part of UKIP as the party headed for its greatest achievement to date – victory in the 2014 European elections.

On Monday 26 May 2014, the day after UKIP's victory had been announced, Fuller turned up for the celebrations at the InterContinental Westminster in central London, claiming she had been invited by Farage.

Her attendance did not last long.

Farage's wife Kirsten demanded she go immediately, shouting: 'I will have security drag you out by your hair if you don't leave.' Fuller then went to a nearby pub, the Feathers, instead, only for Mrs Farage to show up there and again call for her to leave.

Fuller, who had long battled depression, went back to her flat in north London, took an overdose of pills and slit her wrist.

Friends who had called her after the confrontation with Mrs Farage were worried, and when they were unable to get hold of her again, contacted the emergency services. Fuller woke up the next morning in hospital on a drip.

I know all this because she told me everything over a fish lunch in London less than a fortnight later. Fuller and I had known each other for fewer than six months. Like most journalists who dealt with UKIP, it was inevitable I would come into contact with her at some point. We got on quite well, and I always felt she understood what a journalist was after when it came to a story or getting a quote from the party. But I was still surprised when she sent me a text message the day after she ended up in hospital, telling me what had happened. I had only met her a few times, although we'd exchanged emails and text messages on numerous occasions. If you want to do well at the *Daily Express*, getting on well with the people around Nigel Farage is a good place to start.

My initial reaction was one of horror, which I made pretty clear to her. Then the story-grabbing journalist in me kicked in and I realised this was a hell of a scoop: the woman accused of being Nigel Farage's mistress tried to take her own life after the UKIP leader's wife threw her out of the party's European election celebrations. After not too long, the human part of me gained control and I realised what Fuller needed wasn't to be part of another story, but to receive medical help.

We stayed in contact, and I checked in with her every now and then with a text to make sure she was OK. Fuller seemed better very quickly, but was angry with the NHS for not providing sufficient care for her after her suicide attempt. She wanted to go on the record about the poor after-care she had received. I was reluctant, as I knew it would be seen as naked opportunism on my part, and I would be accused of taking advantage of someone who clearly was not well. I told her to think carefully about it, but she was insistent. I think she felt the story would break eventually, and if she went on the record first she could have some control over how it was reported.

Ted Jeory, one of my news editors at the *Express* online, was unsure. He had previously worked for the *Sunday Express*, and had been involved in its award-winning Better Mental Health Crusade (the *Express* titles run 'crusades' not 'campaigns'). After much discussion, we decided to go ahead with the interview – but would have to be careful with how we handled it. The focus would be on how someone with a mental illness can survive in politics, and her experiences of care within the NHS.

Fuller suggested meeting in Sweetings, a fish restaurant in the City of London near Mansion House. It was, appropriately, one of Farage's favourite restaurants from his days as a commodities trader, and he nearly ended up buying it at one point. I arrived at the restaurant on time, but Fuller was already there drinking a glass of something bubbly. The restaurant was busy with mainly men in well-cut suits, probably enjoying a well-earned lunch after a morning's hard graft in the City. We were shown to our table and, over the noise, I ordered half a Guinness – I was paying for the meal and was, as always, incredibly broke. It was hard to know where to start, so, taking the advice of Julie Andrews in *The Sound of Music*, I started from the very beginning.

'What was it like when you first met Nigel?' I asked.

It was when she began working in the European Parliament, she replied, 'I was scared because he was my boss. You have to earn his trust but he's never unpleasant at all.'

She went on to describe what it was like working with Farage, and how, despite being eighteen years younger than him, she felt like 'Nigel's mother'. Fuller claims she would often have to remind Farage to drink water and not just tea with his breakfast of kippers, as 'he wouldn't accept tea is a diuretic'.

'I defended him. I always said I would take a bullet for him,' she added.

I asked her about the Sinclaire speech, and whether she knew that meant her time with UKIP was over. 'I thought, "This is it",' she said. 'It was when people tried to link me to anything.'

Fuller denied the allegations outright, as she had done many times before.

'Why do you think these rumours kept persisting?' I asked.

'I don't look like the back of a bus,' she said. 'Simple fact: if you want to get on in politics as a woman you'd better be ugly, you better be thick-skinned or better have got married.'

I moved the conversation on to the celebration party. Fuller claimed it was Farage himself who invited her to the UKIP celebrations in Westminster, and she had no idea that his wife would react in such a way to her.

> I was escorted out in front of colleagues and friends I had known for years, and I knew outside there were a load of TV cameras and journalists. I was humiliated. I knew it had nothing to do with Nigel and I called him up he said, 'What the hell's going on?' He then comes along, he hugged me and I was in floods of tears – the floodgates opened like they had never opened.

Fuller said her former boss told her: 'I'm sorry.'

Despite the confrontation with Mrs Farage, Fuller said she did not blame her at all for her suicide attempt. Instead, it was losing the 'support network' of a job in UKIP. 'It was a desperate desire not to be unhappy any more after a bloody awful day,' she said:

> I had been waking up every morning for the past few months dreading the phone ringing, dreading checking my emails, wondering if there was going to be someone at my door – basically living my life in a veil of complete panic. No relaxing, no mañanas. Just everything hit all of a sudden. Then, after the

hospital, I thought, 'This isn't ideal.' The other awful thought, which no one should have to put up with, is, 'This could be a story: me being ill is a story.' One of the reasons I'm speaking now is sometimes it's easier to lance the boil yourself.

I suspected as much. I had no doubt that Fuller genuinely wanted to raise the issue of mental health support for those working in politics, but I also thought she wanted to break the story on her own terms.

'I'm really lucky with my GP, he has been excellent,' she continued. 'But my support network, which was work, has been completely taken away from me. What am I now? I've lost my identity, my social network, my *raison d'être*, I suppose.'

The interview, with these quotes, appeared on the *Express* website on Saturday 7 June 2014 after the *Sunday Express* decided not to run the story. I was never given a reason why it was dropped, but the stablemate the *Star on Sunday* had no such reservations, running the story the next day. The *Mail on Sunday* also liked the story, and ran it as a double-page spread.

I heard from Fuller intermittently over the next few months, and it was clear she was missing UKIP. But she was out in the cold. Fuller took a job at the right-wing news website Breitbart, writing under the pen name A. B. Sanderson. But, despite being a journalist, she rarely attended UKIP events, and, on at least one occasion, had the accreditation given to her by the party press office removed by her replacement at Farage's side, Raheem Kassam.

The pair remained in contact in the lead-up to the 2015 election, but she was very much outside the top rank of the People's Army. In January 2015, Fuller was interviewed under caution by the Metropolitan Police in relation to the Bridgen incident. A Met Police spokesman said: 'A 33-year-old woman attended a central London police station by appointment on Wednesday 14 January. She was interviewed under caution in connection with an ongoing investigation into a false allegation. Enquiries continue.'

In Farage's first autobiography *Flying Free*, originally published as *Fighting Bull* in 2010, he paid tribute to Fuller's 'perceptiveness and goodwill'. In *The Purple Revolution*, published in March 2015, he did not mention her at all.

Like in all the best revolutions, history is rewritten.

CHAPTER 5

DR FRANKENSTEIN WILL SEE YOU NOW

WINNING THE 2014 EUROPEAN elections put UKIP at the top of the political billing, and commander-in-chief Nigel Farage was going from strength to strength.

The man who had been on the fringes of political thought and discussion for fifteen years was now ram-raiding his way into the centre.

Questions flying around commentators and politicians were all focused on UKIP: How do the Tories defeat UKIP? How much should Labour fear UKIP? Are the Lib Dems still here?

I didn't want to defeat the People's Army (its progress was pretty much keeping me in a job at the *Daily Express*), but I was interested to know more about its leader, and where the weak points were in his armour.

Who better to ask how to defeat Nigel Farage, I thought, than the man who helped create him, UKIP founder Dr Alan Sked?

If Farage is Darth Vader, then Sked is very much Emperor Palpatine.

Dr Alan Sked is a professor of international history at the London School of Economics. In the folklore of UKIP, many things are disputed, but its birth is not one of them.

UKIP began as the Anti-Federalist League (AFL), set up by

Dr Sked in 1991. The good doctor was opposed to Britain's involvement in Europe and, in particular, the Maastricht Treaty, which had been drafted in December that year. That treaty created the modern-day European Union, and set the wheels turning for the single European currency.

The AFL stood seventeen candidates in the 1992 general election, all of whom lost their deposits.

After the Maastricht Treaty was ratified in the House of Commons in 1993, the AFL decided more direct action was needed.

At a meeting of the Campaign for an Independent Britain, held in Westminster, Dr Sked announced he was going to create a fully fledged party intent on getting the UK out of the EU.

Nigel Farage was at the meeting and, in his autobiography *Fighting Bull*, recounted that he and others were so impressed by Dr Sked that they made a beeline for him at the end to hear more about his party.

'Sked was persistent and persuasive. Every halfway personable enquirer was at once recruited to stand for his "Anti-Federalist League". These were the founding members of the General Committee, which soon became, and which remains, the national executive committee [of UKIP].'

Farage went on to describe Sked as seeming 'bright, sincere and affable'. That was pretty much the last nice thing Farage has ever said about Sked.

In *Fighting Bull*, he goes on to describe Sked as 'soft, unworldly and strangely spoilt', a man who 'did not listen to others or venture into milieux other than his own'. Farage also labelled him 'a potential liability': 'We needed thick skins where Sked's was shuddering and sensitive as a thoroughbred filly.'

He quoted another member from UKIP's early days, David Lott, as saying: '[Sked] wanted no rising stars. His invention was running away from him and he couldn't stand it.'

But whatever Farage thinks of Sked now, he clearly believed in him once. After deciding a change of name was needed to make the party more marketable, the United Kingdom Independence Party was officially born in a room at the LSE on 3 September 1993, with Sked as its leader.

No sooner had it come screaming into the world than baby UKIP did what babies often do – caused arguments.

Sked was seen as too much of an academic who didn't know how to talk to the masses. Farage was gaining support and profile as an accomplished speaker, but Sked was concerned that the party was being dragged to the right by young Nigel and his cohorts. Sked clung on as leader and steered the party through the 1997 general election, winning precisely no seats out of the 194 contested.

Only one candidate saved their deposit – Farage in Salisbury, who secured 5.7 per cent of the vote. After the 1997 election, Sked stood down. His final act as leader was to throw Farage out of the party. Since Sked left the party, he has not held back in his criticisms of it. Farage describes him as the 'lazy journalist's easiest source of a space-filling story about UKIP'. 'At every election Sked has re-emerged on air to accuse UKIP of right-wing extremism,' he added.

I wanted to meet Sked to find out what the party – and Farage – was like in those early days. I knew he didn't much like what UKIP had become now, and I wondered if he regretted starting the party at all.

I emailed him asking for a meeting, but he wasn't particularly keen.

'I have given many interviews and now fear repeating myself,' came the reply.

He added: 'Why were you chosen to write a book on UKIP? What are your credentials? Have you connections with the party? What is your angle? The previous "histories" of UKIP have been dire, biased, inaccurate, to say the least. Why should yours be any better?'

Wow, I thought, not even my publisher asked this many questions when I came up with this book idea.

I replied that this book would be less a history, and more 'focused on the various people who are part of the history of the party'.

And I offered to buy him dinner.

He responded with a 'yes' and suggested we meet in his private members' club Blacks in central London.

I had never been in a private members' club before, let alone one in swanky Soho. Blacks is opposite the infamous Groucho Club on Dean Street, but, on the outside at least, is more understated than its noisy neighbour. It looks just like a normal townhouse, and even if you knew the exact address of Blacks, you could walk past it four or five times before realising where it is.

So, on a rainy night in October 2014, having walked past it four or five times, I eventually realised where it was. The nondescript door was ajar, and I walked inside expecting to be greeted by burly security men. Instead, there was a young woman sitting behind a small desk. I proclaimed I was there to have dinner with Dr Alan Sked.

I assumed she would recognise the name and usher me to some secluded dining room, complete with old men in tweed suits stroking their beards and sipping the finest brandy known to man.

'Who is this young lad entering our oasis of snobbery?' they would no doubt think.

After an hour of them all simultaneously raising their eyebrows, looking down their noses and mumbling about the riff-raff in the duffel coat, I would stand on my chair and start shouting 'Anarchy in the UK' by the Sex Pistols and get slung out on my ear.

That was the plan, but I was feeling a bit ill and had taken a lot of flu medicine, so may have not been completely 'with it'.

(While I'm on the subject, flu medicine is as druggy as this book gets, so if you were expecting a *Fear and Loathing on the Trail of Farage* kind of book, you're going to be disappointed. Although later on, I do contemplate spiking Farage's drink, so you might want to keep reading for that bit.)

The receptionist didn't know who Dr Sked was and, according to the register, he hadn't arrived, so she let me go up the narrow staircase to the restaurant and wait for him.

Oh, what a disappointment. The inverted snob in me was

completely let down. This club wasn't full of sneering aristocrats at all!

From my table in the centre of the restaurant I surveyed the others in the room.

To my right was a pair of gentlemen talking loudly about their work and how one of them definitely deserved a promotion – a point with which the other completely agreed. Yuppies.

At the table in the corner was a man with shoulder-length, straggly hair who looked like he was on his way to a fancy dress party in a Russell Brand costume. He was crying into the arms of a young woman, who was dressed like Twiggy in her heyday. The couple had a good system – he was doing the crying, she was drinking the wine.

To my left was a long table with about ten people in their early twenties in T-shirts. T-SHIRTS! I was disgusted. What sort of snobby members' club was this? I was in my best suit and had even polished my shoes, and here was a bunch of practically children in T-shirts.

I don't know what Owen Jones has been going on about – the establishment is really letting itself go to the dogs.

After ten minutes of taking it all in, Dr Sked arrived.

He shook my hand, ordered some olives and garlic, and began telling me about his frail, elderly mother who lived in the Scottish Highlands. He seemed to be the only family she had left, and he was on a year-long sabbatical from the LSE so he could take care of her.

He spoke in a soft, mid-Atlantic, Glaswegian drawl, which was easy on the ear and oddly soothing.

Nothing he said came across as forced – instead he seemed very genuine.

With his soft tones and the hint of a regional accent, I imagined he would be very much at home presenting a show on BBC Radio 3.

I could see why a young Farage would have been initially drawn to him and then ultimately frustrated by him.

After talking about his family, and with a bottle of wine set on the table in front of us, the conversation moved to UKIP.

'I keep up to date with it, but most of it is nonsense,' Dr Sked said when I asked him his view on the party.

'How has it changed from when you were involved?' I asked.

'Well, we wouldn't go to the European Parliament if we won any seats. If our MEPs had to take the salary they would give it to the NHS.'

I asked him his views on Farage, although, to be honest, I already knew them. Sked had previously described Farage as a 'dim-witted racist' who 'isn't bright'.

He told me that when he knew Farage, young Nigel was often drunk, and enjoyed the company of women.

Sked said Farage was not much of a thinker, and during a discussion on expanding the fledgling party's policies beyond leaving the EU, young Nigel had not seemed too interested.

'We could always buy some policies from right-wing think tanks,' Sked remembers young Nigel saying.

Despite Farage's repeated and vehement denials that he is, nor ever has been, a racist, Sked claims young Nigel had a far more divisive attitude.

He said: 'He said to me, "We don't have to worry about the nigger vote; the nig-nogs will never vote for us."'

Farage has always strongly denied using such language and, when asked about those specific comments on LBC radio by James O'Brien, he said: 'As for the allegations as to what I said in a pub after committee meetings, you will not find a single other member of that committee who makes that allegation.'

Farage added: 'Dr Sked made the allegation. You know in politics all sorts of disappointments happen to people and they throw mud. It's as simple as that.'

When I put Farage's denial to Sked, he replied: 'He was half-pissed at the time, he wouldn't remember. He can't remember saying anything by about 9 p.m.'

Another accusation repeatedly levelled at Farage is his association with BNP activist Mark Deavin. Deavin was a student of Dr Sked's, who introduced him to the party's national executive committee in 1997. Dr Sked said he was not aware of Deavin's far-right associations, but had just written one of the best doctorate theses he had ever seen on immigration to Britain in the twentieth century.

After a BBC investigative programme outed Deavin as a BNP activist, he was expelled from UKIP.

A month later, and after the 1997 general election, Farage agreed to meet with Deavin.

UKIP were in the midst of civil war at the time, following Sked's resignation as leader.

The rancour stemmed from UKIP's non-association with Sir James Goldsmith's Referendum Party in the 1997 general election. The Referendum Party had one policy – to hold a national vote on whether Britain should remain part of the European Union. It was a natural bedfellow for UKIP, and a pact would have enabled the fledgling party to focus its limited resources on a few seats.

But no deal was struck. Farage claims Sked turned down an offer from Goldsmith 'to stand down his candidates in seventy-five seats where UKIP candidates would instead stand on "UKIP/Referendum Party" tickets', with Goldsmith 'willing to pay all costs'.

Sked denied such an offer was made, and said he had never met with Sir James.

At the general election, the Referendum Party won 811,849 votes, coming fourth overall. UKIP picked up just 105,722.

The Referendum Party – thanks to the bankrolling of its billionaire leader – was clearly the vote of choice for vehement Eurosceptics in 1997.

A month after the election, Sir James organised a lunch in Regent's Street, where it became clear that the Referendum Party was no longer going to continue to seek elected office.

Word that Sir James's pet project was reverting to pressure group status got back to Farage and others in UKIP, who immediately spotted an opportunity to recruit large swathes of the Referendum Party's membership.

(That opportunity became even clearer when, on 18 July 1997, Sir James died of a heart attack brought on by pancreatic cancer. Without its charismatic leader, and his hefty chequebook, the Referendum Party died as well.)

Farage and his cohorts invited the most successful candidates from both the Referendum Party and UKIP to a meeting in Basingstoke to discuss how to take the anti-European movement forward.

That same night, Sked held a UKIP meeting in London.

Farage claims this was announced in response to his Basingstoke meeting, but Mark Daniel, author of the 2005 book *Cranks and Gadflies: The Story of UKIP*, argues the London meeting was 'long-organised'.

(It is strange that Farage's autobiography *Fighting Bull* should differ from Mark Daniel's book on this point, seeing as they were both basically written by the same person. Mark Fitzgeorge-Parker, UKIP's first press officer, used the pseudonym of 'Mark Daniel' for *Cranks and Gadflies*, and ghostwrote *Fighting Bull*. Mr Fitzgeorge-Parker died on 3 May 2014, at just fifty-nine years old.)

Either way, at the London meeting an angry Sked took great issue with the actions of Farage and the other separatists. He subsequently expelled Farage and two others from UKIP, and the battle for control of the party began.

It was against this backdrop that Farage agreed to meet Deavin – now a known BNP activist – on 17 June.

In his autobiography, Farage claims he acquiesced to the meeting because Deavin told him 'he had valuable information about Sked which might help me in the battle'.

Farage was photographed with Deavin outside a pub in St Katharine Docks in east London.

Also in the picture was Tony 'The Bomber' Lecomber, a BNP member who had served jail time for stabbing a Jewish teacher and being caught with a range of explosives – including ten grenades.

To this day, the photograph is held up as proof of Farage's far-right leanings. He describes the meeting as 'the worst mistake of my political life' and 'that he had been right royally stitched up'.

He claims he agreed to see Deavin only to find out why he had betrayed UKIP, and what he knew about Sked. In July 1997, Sked resigned as leader as UKIP, appointing Craig Mackinlay as his successor.

Over his steak dinner in Blacks, Dr Sked told me had no idea Deavin was involved in the BNP when he first brought him into UKIP's inner circle. He claimed it was Farage who kept in contact with him, and the photographed lunch was evidence of that.

'Farage says he met with him to get information about you, which would help oust you as leader,' I said.

'But I had already resigned by that point,' came Sked's reply.

According to Mark Fitzgeorge-Parker/Daniel's works, Sked resigned after Farage met with Deavin.

I decided not to press the point further.

I wanted to know more about the kinds of people involved with UKIP when it first started.

Were they all like Farage, and was the party always going to travel down this anti-immigration route? Or did Farage just seize an opportunity to convert malleable people to his way of thinking?

But the conversation kept coming back to Farage himself. It was as if Sked's thinking on UKIP was attached to elastic rope, and every time he dragged his thoughts away from Farage, he was pinged back to the Nigel-shaped centre.

'Nigel wants a peerage. He would make a deal with the Tories and he'll go to the House of Lords,' was one of his assumptions.

He also said at one point: 'Would you want your daughter to marry someone like Farage?'

It was clear that even seventeen years on from resigning – or being ousted – as UKIP leader, it still hurt Sked. But surely he must have a grudging respect for Farage? Even I as a Spurs fan had to concede that

Arsenal had a half-decent team the year they won the league without losing a game. I don't like the Gooners, but you had to respect that.

Farage had taken UKIP from the edge of the political fringes to winning a national election. Surely Sked would agree Farage had shown impressive leadership?

No, Sked did not agree – at all.

'The electoral system for the European Parliament was changed in 1999. Before that it was first-past-the-post – that's how they got seats.'

And UKIP's rise in popularity in the past few years?

'Well the Lib Dems are now in government, so they are no longer the "protest vote party". The coalition has produced this policy of austerity. It's been borne by working people so they are looking elsewhere. It's nothing much to do with Farage and policy.'

'Even so, whatever the reasons for UKIP's increase in support, you must be pleased that it's bringing the founding aim of the party – your founding aim – of getting Britain out of the EU closer?' I asked.

Again, Sked disagreed.

'Support for staying in Europe is rising,' he said. 'The rise of UKIP – it's not helping with getting us out of the EU. It's backfiring.'

Sked spoke fondly of Gerard Batten, now MEP for London, but also one of the party's founder members. But he also questioned why Batten had signed up to the anti-immigration rhetoric so willingly, saying: 'Gerard has married a nice Filipino lady who has worked all her life – is she a foreigner taking a British job?'

As Sked puts UKIP's success down to outside factors – the European election voting system change and the Lib Dems going into government – he probably thought he could have led the party to the same levels of success it was currently enjoying.

Perhaps, he thought, even greater success. Sked is, after all, a thinker – a highly educated man. And that is the word that kept coming up in conversation – educated.

Farage is not 'educated'. The people at the top of UKIP are not 'educated'.

That seemed to be Sked's most damning criticism of his former party, the lack of an intellectual heavyweight in the leadership. But it seemed to me something far more basic than that: pride.

Dr Alan Sked, the intellect, the respected academic, was ousted from the party he created by a rag-tag bunch of political outsiders led by a non-university-educated City trader.

If UKIP were a rock band, then under Sked it was a prog-rock group specialising in twenty-minute-long guitar solos masterfully played by Dr Sked to no more than a handful of musos in the back room of a pub.

But under Farage, they went punk. Classically trained Sked was replaced by someone who had only bothered to learn four chords. UKIP were now playing to the audience's guts instead of trying to infiltrate their brain. Never mind Sked's intellectual bollocks – here's the Farage Pistols.

So while UKIP now plays arena tours, Sked rumbles along in sparsely attended blues clubs.

Having heard all of Sked's misgivings about UKIP, his views on Farage and his frustration about the fact that the party have managed to provoke a pro-EU backlash, I asked him the most obvious question imaginable: 'Do you regret starting UKIP?'

'No, I am proud of what I did,' he replied.

But then, after a pause, he added: 'I am Dr Frankenstein and the monster's gone amok.'

Perhaps that is why Sked had formed another political party, New Deal. He told me he wants it to appeal to those affected by the coalition government's austerity cuts, but will still focus on withdrawing Britain from the EU.

The Bride of Frankenstein, perhaps.

But New Deal seemed a long way off the success of UKIP. The party's website was only half-completed, and Sked admitted that he was unable to dedicate much time to the project because of personal circumstances.

The party stood no candidates in the 2014 European elections or the 2015 general election.

With the UKIP discussion finished, we spent the remainder of the dinner talking about his tutelage as a post-graduate under the well-respected historian A. J. P. Taylor at Oxford University.

We talked about the numerous European languages he had learned, and, as coffee was served after a hearty dessert, he enquired about writing some articles for the *Daily Express* – something I said I would look into. (I knew there was almost zero chance of getting someone so vehemently anti-UKIP into the *Express*.)

With a handshake, and an appeal from him to call him Alan, we parted company outside the club on Dean Street.

Dr Frankenstein, his hair white, his shoulders slightly stooped, disappeared into the central London crowd.

CHAPTER 6

THE STRANGE CASE OF MR CARSWELL

T HERE ARE VERY FEW genuinely surprising events in political journalism. Everything is leaked, briefed, counter-briefed,
inferred, implied and suggested long before it actually happens.
Spinners from the main Westminster parties amble through
the various media outlets in the Houses of Parliament, dishing out
and drip-feeding tit-bits of information to hungry journalists like a
mother bird does with worms to her chicks.

In the lobby offices, phones ring with ambitious MPs wishing to
tip off hacks in order to curry their favour – and vice versa. Twitter
is pored over by journalists, hoping to deduce something from one
MP's retweet of another MP's favourited tweet. Like panhandlers in
the Old West sifting for gold, precious little of any substance is found,
although occasionally a shiny nugget of news or scandal glimmers in
the muddy water of the internet.

And so it was on Thursday 28 August 2014. I arrived in my office
in Parliament having just returned from a summer holiday. In June
I had been moved from the *Express* web team to be a fully fledged
member of the paper's lobby team. That meant a desk in the Houses
of Parliament, working with some of the finest political journalists
in the country. I was delighted. Granted, my move had mainly been

engineered by my web editor Geoff Marsh because he was tired of my complaining ('Why can't I do more politics? Why can't I have a pay rise? Why can't I do more politics?'), but I didn't care. I was now working in the mother of parliaments.

That morning, my boss, Macer Hall, the political editor of the *Daily Express*, was preparing to go to a press conference called by UKIP in Whitehall.

The party had gone quiet since its European election win. The summer news agenda had been dominated by an outbreak of the Ebola virus in west Africa, the shooting down of a Malaysia Airlines passenger jet as it flew over Ukraine, and the World Cup in Brazil.

'Big donation?' I asked.

'They're not saying,' Macer replied.

We kicked it around for a bit. A fresh injection of cash from the party's major backer Paul Sykes seemed the most likely option.

Perhaps a celebrity endorsement – UKIP was always keen to parade its famous supporters, be it former chat-show host Robert Kilroy-Silk, DJ Mike Read or even sports presenter Des Lynam.

'Maybe Farage is going to stand down?' I suggested. He would be leaving on a high, and could focus his efforts on winning a seat in Parliament in the 2015 general election.

It seemed unlikely. Macer trudged off to the conference, and I took to searching for gold in the river of Twitter.

None of the journalists in the press conference knew what was about to happen. In fact, only a very few members of UKIP who were in the room knew. So when the Tory MP for Clacton, Douglas Carswell, took to the podium and declared 'Today I am leaving the Conservative Party and joining UKIP', it was met with genuine shock.

Only Farage, his wife Kirsten, and Mr and Mrs Carswell had known what the announcement would be prior to that morning. UKIP MEP and former *Daily Express* chief political commentator Patrick O'Flynn had only been told moments before Carswell took to the stage.

Not only was Carswell defecting, however, he was going to resign and trigger a by-election in his Clacton constituency in Essex to seek a mandate under a UKIP banner. Carswell was a known Eurosceptic and political maverick. But although seen as the most likely MP to defect to UKIP, no one actually thought he would. He had repeatedly claimed the only way to get the UK out of the EU was with a Tory government after the 2015 general election. But in his defection speech, Carswell hit out at David Cameron's plan for renegotiating Britain's place in the EU ahead of a 2017 referendum.

'His advisors have made it clear that they seek a new deal that gives them just enough to persuade enough voters to vote to stay in,' he said. 'It's not about change in our national interest. It's all about not changing things. Once I realised that, my position in the Conservative Party became untenable.'

UKIP had finally succeeded in keeping the momentum gained through a European election campaign going after the polls had closed. Even more than that, the party could soon see an MP elected to the Commons under a UKIP ticket for the first time in its history.

No wonder Farage's grin seemed even wider than usual that August morning.

I was pretty happy too. One of the local papers I had worked for before entering the Westminster bubble had been the *Clacton Gazette*, meaning I had that precious commodity – local knowledge. So, while lobby journalists and TV crews dashed from Westminster to London Liverpool Street station to get the train out to Clacton, I was able to write a colour piece from the comfort of my office.

As soon as Carswell announced his defection, the Tory press machine cranked into action. Every statement he had ever made decrying UKIP and urging voters to back the Tories if they wanted real EU change was sent out to journalists. The word was put out that all the Conservative voters in Clacton would be so angry at Carswell's defection they would turn against him at the ballot box and he would lose his seat.

In a piece for the *Express*, I pointed out how this was wishful thinking (and yes, I am about to quote myself at length – there is nothing wrong with a little vanity every now and then...):

> If Nigel Farage wants to truly deliver his 'earthquake in British politics', then towns like Clacton will need to 'go UKIP' at the next election. The iconic seaside resort, which like many others is sadly a long way from its heyday as a holiday venue, feels worlds away from the political bubble of Westminster.
>
> The town centre is made up of numerous charity shops, bookmakers and discount stores, and it still retains quintessential amusement arcades and a pier stretching out into the sea. Like numerous towns, there is a shopping outlet on the outskirts, and many of the retired residents enjoy traditional British entertainment such as bingo and the annual pantomime at the local theatre. But what it lacks in the metropolitan hustle and bustle of a big city, it more than makes up in community spirit. The residents have retained much of the east London spirit inherited from their ancestors who left the Big Smoke in search of pastures new after the war. It feels a very 'British' place when you walk through the town, and its people are friendly and jovial. It is exactly the kind of place in which UKIP will thrive during next May's general election.
>
> Douglas Carswell, who has represented the town (formerly included in the Harwich constituency) since 2005, has in many ways already been a UKIP MP. Get Britain out of the EU, reform the ruling elite, introduce fundamental changes to the financial sector, promote greater choice into the health and education sectors. These are all policies proposed by Mr Carswell which sit perfectly alongside UKIP's vision for the UK.
>
> And that is the reason why the Tories are so wrong if they think voters in Clacton are going to be up in arms about Mr

Carswell defecting. Those same Tories have always known that he believes these things. This is not a 'road to Damascus' moment for Mr Carswell, with him suddenly becoming a Eurosceptic after years of championing Brussels. Nor is this opportunism from Mr Carswell, jumping ship before the UKIP wave crashes his Tory boat. UKIP did not even stand against him in the last election, and it is unlikely they would have wasted precious resources trying to oust such a Eurosceptic MP in May's election next year.

Yes, some previous supporters will stay with the Conservatives, but many more will welcome Mr Carswell doing one of those rare things – behaving honourably. And that is a British value which is still rated very highly in Clacton.

However, there was just one problem with Carswell and his honourable decision to stand for UKIP in the Clacton by-election – the party already had a candidate in the constituency, Roger Lord.

Lord represented UKIP on Essex County Council and claimed to have known Nigel Farage since 1997. He had been selected as UKIP's candidate for the general election in Clacton in July, just a month before Carswell's defection. The *Clacton Gazette* even reported that UKIP's secretary in the town, Anne Poonian, had asked Carswell to defect from the Tories prior to Lord's selection.

'The *Gazette* contacted Mr Carswell about UKIP's claims, but he declined to comment,' wrote the newspaper on 29 July.

Lord was a local farmer and was very much old-school UKIP – not afraid to speak his mind, and certainly not about to stand aside for Carswell. As far as he was concerned, he was the true UKIP candidate in the by-election.

In a media blitz that Farage himself would have been proud of, Lord popped up on BBC News, Sky, LBC radio and even list-aggregating website Buzzfeed to decry Carswell's claim to be representing UKIP. He told Buzzfeed:

I've been through dangerous situations in Pakistan and South America, and you negotiate them: I've had a sixteen-year-old shove a machine gun up my nose in Nicaragua. I've faced bigger threats from real killers, and if they think they can walk up to me and push me then I'll push back. I've never run away from anything.

He insisted: 'Until they fire me, shoot me, or blow me out of the party for being a rebel, then I'm here.'

Like I said, old-school UKIP.

Alas for the Essex farmer, the UKIP rule-makers had seen a situation such as this coming, and had the perfect get-out-of-jail-free card: Lord was not the party's by-election candidate, just its general election one.

Carswell would be wearing the purple rosette, not Lord.

The veteran Ukipper dropped not-so-subtle hints that he might still contest the by-election after all, as Carswell had 'created a vacancy' in the Tory Party. This particular game of right-wing swapsies never got going, and so disgusted was Lord by his treatment at the hands of UKIP he resigned from the party and his position as an Essex county councillor – thus triggering a local by-election that would be held the same day as the parliamentary vote.

In a final fit of pique he called on his supporters to back the Liberal Democrats.

With all the relevant ducks in a line, the by-election was set for 9 October, and I was despatched up to the Essex town to cover the potentially historic event.

I hadn't been back to Clacton since I left there – if that makes sense.

I had worked for the *Harwich & Manningtree Standard*, based in Clacton, for nine months from 2011 to 2012. The paper shared an office with the *Clacton Gazette*, and both papers are part of Newsquest Essex. It was common that a story you were working on would cover both patches, so you would often write for both papers. All copy was also fed into the *Daily Gazette* in Colchester, another News-quest publication. So one story could potentially get three hits in a week – first in the daily, then in the *Clacton* on Thursday and finally in the *Standard* on Friday. Actually, you could get four hits, as News-quest printed an upmarket weekly paper – the *Essex County Standard* – aimed at the wealthy villages on the outskirts of Colchester and Clacton. Then, of course, your story would go online and, if particularly quirky or salacious, it would get sold to a national newspaper, where it would appear, with your quotes, your background, your hard work, under somebody else's name. Newsquest would get paid for this. The journalist receives nothing, except a hard-luck story to tell everyone about.

When I was working as an uploader to the web in my early days of the *Express*, I became one of those people – see a story on the wires, nick it, change the intro slightly, put your name on it. I hated it. I knew how it felt to be the journalist on the ground actually putting in the graft, tapping up contacts, double-checking facts, persuading people to be in photographs, only to see some web thief in London claim all the credit. But thems be the rules.

I had known Carswell from my time working in Clacton, and had caught up with him on a number of occasions since I joined the *Express*. He was a dream contact for someone working for a right-wing, anti-EU newspaper. He was an outspoken backbencher of a governing party, and was not afraid to attack his own side as well as the opposition.

When I met up with him in Parliament in September 2013 to renew our acquaintance, it was during the Tory Party conference, which he hadn't bothered to go to. He joked that with Parliament in recess and the majority of the government in Manchester, he had staged a coup and sold off the BBC. Our paths crossed numerous times in the next twelve months, including at a launch of a pamphlet he had written calling on Tesco and Google to run banks.

He was considered a maverick by those who liked him, and a

political loner by those who didn't. I always found him genuine in his beliefs and not someone to act rashly. Although he was happy to give you comments for stories, he would not be spun. Ahead of the 2014 Queen's Speech I asked him for a line on electoral reform policies – particularly those that had previously been blocked by Lib Dem leader Nick Clegg.

'Douglas, I've just been going over the comments you gave me, and I was wondering if you would say, "Cameron should hold a knife to the Lib Dem throat over electoral reform"?' I asked him.

'No, not my style,' came the reply.

So I was left with: 'Mr Cameron should stop being gentlemanly with Nick Clegg, as he wasn't gentlemanly when he reneged on the boundary changes. He should be absolutely ruthless now.'

All in all, Carswell was a good contact and, regardless of whatever political party he was a member of, I privately wanted him to win and stay a good parliamentary rent-a-quote. Prior to venturing back to my old stomping ground to write about the campaign, I called my former colleague James Dwan from the *Clacton Gazette* to get a feel of how the town was enjoying all the media attention.

'Oh, everyone is loving it, you'll see when you get here,' he replied. And he really wasn't wrong. The town was decked out in purple. Carswell's face, complete with his famous lopsided grin, was plastered on billboards, shop windows and buses. UKIP had hired vans, decorated with giant Carswell posters, that drove constantly round the town centre.

It felt more like an American mayoral election than a British by-election. It was clear that Carswell was being treated with much more reverence and adulation by his new party than he ever had been by his old one. When in the Tories, Carswell was just another player, one who rarely got in the first team. Now at UKIP, he was the star striker.

Even in more affluent, more socially conservative areas of the constituency, such as Frinton-on-Sea, Carswell's face still peered out at me from house windows and front gardens.

The Tories – who technically were fighting to hold this seat – had more of a presence in Frinton than in Clacton, with a smattering of posters suggesting not everyone in the area had enlisted in the People's Army. It was in Frinton where I caught up with Carswell. He agreed to have a chat with me outside a small café in a small shopping centre in the small seaside town. The last time I had sat down with Carswell it had been just the two of us in Westminster. Now he was the star of the show and had an entourage to match, with at least six or seven people milling around. A reporter from the *Wall Street Journal* was perched in the corner observing our chat, and UKIP's east of England press officer Michael Heaver watched over us during the interview.

Carswell was relaxed. He talked about how the by-election campaign had created a buzz in the area, how he was meeting people who had never voted before but were planning to turn out on Thursday. The Ukippers present, and Heaver in particular, swarmed around Carswell like worker bees protecting their queen.

He seemed enthused, energised and incredibly calm. He had a white shirt on but no tie, and leaned back in his chair as I asked him questions. He even started speaking in Italian to the Lombardy-born camerawoman who had accompanied me from the *Express* to record some footage for the website.

A weight seemed to have been taken off Carswell's shoulders, and his transition to a different type of politician seemed almost complete.

Two days later, and my next encounter with Carswell was outside the Clacton branch of McDonald's with Nigel Farage. For some reason he had been desperate to get the UKIP leader to eat a McFlurry. Politicians posing with food is always a risk – Labour leader Ed Miliband had been undone by a bacon sandwich a few weeks before. But Farage, who was more accustomed to a pint of beer than a tub of ice cream, dutifully went along with the performance.

It was polling day and, after a few hours' sleep in my hotel, I prepared myself for the long night ahead. After joining colleagues from other newspapers for dinner we all set off for Clacton town hall to take our seats for what would surely be a dramatic and historic night.

I confess, I was almost nervous with excitement. It was the first by-election count I had ever covered. In fact, it was the first parliamentary count I had ever been to. As a local hack I had reported on some council elections, but not a Westminster vote. In just a few hours I might be present when UKIP made history and won its first MP.

Just imagine if, after this victory, they went on to hold the balance of power in next year's general election, I thought. Imagine if, in a few general elections' time, they were the official opposition, or if, in the next twenty years, they were in government. Imagine if Carswell overthrows Farage as leader and becomes Prime Minister! I could say that I, Owen Bennett, was there when it all began. I was there when UKIP took its first faltering steps on its way to dominating UK politics.

'Look, little Owen Bennett III, that's your granddad in the background when President Carswell won the first by-election for UKIP. What's a "by-election", you ask? Oh, we used to have them before President Carswell appointed himself the unquestioned Master of the Universe. No, of course I don't miss them! Everything is so much better now – can you hand your granddad that little pill that makes all the feelings go away? Thanks, little Owen – now say your prayers to Lord Farage and go to bed.'

As you can see, my mind was open to the potential impact of this result and I was braced for a night of high drama.

But my oh my, how wrong I was.

Watching people counting bits of paper is just as adrenalin-inducing as it sounds, i.e. not at all. Us media people were positioned on a balcony overlooking the count. The three main parties had sent down representatives to appear in front of the various cameras – Priti Patel from the Tories, Chris Bryant from Labour and Sir Bob Russell from the Lib Dems.

Before Carswell and Farage turned up for the count, the only person of interest in the hall was former Lib Dem MP Lembit Opik. He was there advising by-election candidate Charlotte Rose, winner of the 2013 'British Erotic Award for Sex Worker of the Year'. Ms Rose was standing as an independent, and Opik was acting as a media advisor. Yet, despite the advice from the former *I'm a Celebrity … Get Me Out of Here!* contestant, (spoiler alert!) Ms Rose did not win the seat.

The press gang watched on as the counters sifted through the papers. Many of my more high-profile print colleagues appeared in front of the TV cameras to give their take on the events. Priti Patel, Chris Bryant and UKIP's Patrick O'Flynn were available for professional arguing.

You would see the three of them stand in a line in front of one camera on the balcony, then argue, interrupt and get angry with each other for a few minutes before being cut off by the interviewer.

The three would then shift along 5 feet to the next camera and have the same row again. And again. And again.

Sometimes, to break up the repetition, they would do it on the radio instead of in front of the cameras.

The print journalists were killing time by writing and re-writing the skeleton of their stories, which would file as soon as the result was announced. Most of us knew if we didn't get a result by 2 a.m. then it wouldn't make it into print, but thanks to the wonder of the internet age we would still need to have it ready for our websites. Of course, we all wanted to be the first to tweet out the result. The size of your Twitter following is now more important than the size of your newspaper's circulation, after all.

There was no excitement in the air because everyone knew Carswell was going to win. It was obvious and had been for weeks. The only question left to answer, as far as we journalists were concerned, was what would his majority be?

By 1 a.m., however, that stopped being the question. In fact, Clacton stopped being the story altogether. Another by-election was taking place the same night in Heywood & Middleton, Greater Manchester – and it was generating far more excitement than the one in Clacton.

That vote had been called following the death of Labour MP Jim Dobbin, and Ed Miliband's party was predicted to retain the seat easily. Polling carried out during the campaign gave Labour a nineteen-point lead over UKIP. Farage had talked up UKIP's chances though, claiming his party would 'park our tanks on Labour's lawn'.

In the days leading up to the election, Farage began to scale down expectations, privately admitting he did not think UKIP would be able to overturn Labour's 17,284-vote lead from the 2010 general election. When news of a recount in Heywood & Middleton broke in Clacton town hall, all the journalists cursed themselves for not being in Greater Manchester.

Thankfully – for us reporters in Clacton, at least – Labour won the seat by 617 votes.

With an upset avoided, the focus was back on Carswell.

Farage and Carswell, who both arrived while the drama in Greater Manchester was unfolding, paced the counting floor. With them was Raheem Kassam, a reporter from right-wing news website Breitbart. From our position on the balcony we could see the ballot papers being sorted into piles according to candidate. It was clear UKIP had won.

As the clock passed 2 a.m., the third and final edition of the *Daily Express* was put to bed, as it is known. The morning paper would not carry pictures of a jubilant Carswell celebrating his victory.

At 2.50 a.m., the result was finally announced. The candidates traipsed on to the stage before the returning officer took to the microphone.

On a turnout of 51 per cent (down from 64.2 per cent in 2010), Carswell won 21,113 votes. The Conservative candidate, former sit-com actor Giles Watling, won just 8,709.

Carswell had a majority of 12,404 – 336 votes more than his 2010 margin of victory as a Tory candidate.

There it was. After twenty-one years and a total of 1,726 Westminster elections contested, UKIP had its first MP. And the self-styled People's Army had done it with a private-school-educated former

Tory parliamentarian who had worked for the Conservative Party's Policy Unit in 2005 reporting to David Cameron.

There's your insurgency.

The victory was met with applause by the Ukippers in the hall. But it was hardly raucous. There were a few whoops and cheers but nothing like the tears and hugging I had expected. In my mind's eye I had envisaged wild celebrations reminiscent of the 'Portillio moment' when Tory Cabinet minister – and likely leadership contender – Michael Portillo lost his seat in the 1997 general election Labour landslide.

Yet the feeling in the room was more subdued. Carswell's victory had been so expected, and so emphatic, no one was surprised. So while the UKIP victory was entirely predictable, Carswell's acceptance speech wasn't.

He began with the customary thanking of everyone who had voted for him, supported him, believed in him, loved him, cared for him, worshipped him, blah blah blah.

But, after the platitudes, he said:

> To my new party, I offer these thoughts: humility when we win, modesty when we are proved right. If we speak with passion, let it always be tempered with compassion. We must be a party for all Britain, and all Britons, first and second generation as much as every other – our strength must lie in our breadth. If we stay true to that then there is nothing which we cannot achieve, nothing we cannot achieve in Essex and East Anglia, in England and the whole country beyond.

The journalists on the balcony looked at each other and began wondering: was Carswell already trying to remake the party in his own image? Would this message of inclusiveness play well with the UKIP faithful? Was this a leadership challenge?

We decided it was too late to really think about such things and retired to our various hotels to catch a few hours' sleep. The real fun would start the next day.

At 9 a.m., I was back in Clacton town centre, waiting for Douglas Carswell and Nigel Farage to undertake their victory lap.

Us print journalists had been promised a chat with the pair in the UKIP office at the top of the high street at noon. We were red-eyed and sleep-deprived, but knew today would be the day when we got the all-important colour pieces for our respective newspapers. Also, with the result coming through too late to get in that morning's editions, we all wanted to produce extensive copy to justify our journey and overnight stay to our news editors.

While the by-election result hadn't made the morning papers, one story concerning UKIP had. *The Guardian*'s Nicholas Watt, who was with us in Clacton, got hold of an interview Farage gave to Newsweek Europe, in which the UKIP leader had been asked what sort of people should be allowed to migrate to Britain.

'People who do not have HIV, to be frank. That's a good start. And people with a skill,' was Farage's response.

Cue outrage.

Farage appeared on BBC Radio 4's *Today* programme that morning to defend himself, but only made matters worse – in the eyes of his critics, at least – when he said Britain does not want 'people with criminal records and we cannot afford to have people with life-threatening diseases'. He added: 'We have leading cancer experts in Britain saying the burden now of treating overseas people is leading to huge shortages in the system. I do not think those [immigrants] with life-threatening diseases should be treated by NHS.' Farage also said anyone with a murder conviction should be banned from moving to the UK.

Dr Rosemary Gillespie, chief executive of the Aids and HIV charity the Terrence Higgins Trust, replied by saying: 'In bracketing those living with the condition with murderers, and suggesting there is no place for them in his vision of Britain, Mr Farage has stooped to a new level of ignorance. He should be truly ashamed.'

Regardless of whether you thought Farage was outlining a sensible set of proposals to manage migration into Britain, or scapegoating those with terminal illnesses, he had managed to hog the morning's news cycle on a day when it should have belonged to Carswell.

Come 11 a.m., when a black Land Rover containing the UKIP duo was driven down Clacton town centre's one-way system and pulled up just outside McDonald's, a bank of at least forty photographers, journalists and film crews was poised to leap on the pair.

As the Land Rover slowed down, the photographers and film crews formed an unstable, moving line on one side of the road, reminiscent of horses at the start of the Grand National. I watched as they hustled for position, the whole line swelling and contracting as one, but staying behind an invisible barrier.

A lone photographer was standing slightly ahead, and shouting at the others not to rush forward when Farage and Carswell emerged from the vehicle. But no sooner had Farage's foot hit the pavement than the starting gun was fired, and the pack broke free from its self-imposed containment, encircling the UKIP leader and its new MP.

It had become a scrum, a needless scrum.

If the photographers and cameramen had stayed in position they could have had hundreds, thousands, millions of pictures of the pair walking through Clacton toasting their success and meeting the public. But now the duo was trapped in this snapper frenzy, blinded by the flashes of dozens of cameras, deafened by the shouts of desperate photographers.

Even seasoned journalists – sleep-deprived seasoned journalists, it must be remembered – piled in and began shouting questions at the pair, mainly about the UKIP leader's views on HIV-positive migrants.

One of the delicious ironies about the story was that Carswell's father Wilson was one of the first doctors to identify HIV/Aids while working in Uganda in the mid-1980s. Wilson Carswell was a well-known and well-respected physician, and one of the inspirations for the protagonist in the 1998 book *The Last King of Scotland* – which was turned into a 2006 film starring James McAvoy.

Locked in the media scrum, *The Guardian*'s Nicholas Watt and Channel 4's Michael Crick pressed Carswell for his view on Farage's comments.

'We need an Australian-type immigration system with control over our borders,' was his response, before adding: 'I don't recognise *The Guardian*'s characterisation of this debate.' The words of a straight-talking politician who is sick of the Westminster elite failing to speak in a language the ordinary man on the street can understand, I'm sure you would agree.

Watt was not to be brushed off so easily. Yet, instead of asking a question, he just kept shouting what must be the most *Guardian*-esque heckle of recent years: 'Your father was a pioneer! Your father was a pioneer, Mr Carswell! Your father was a pioneer!'

Farage, on the other hand, had no such reticence in developing his views. Before Carswell had a chance to continue not answering the question about whether to ban people with HIV coming into the country, his new leader said: 'We can extend it. There's tuberculosis, there's many, many other diseases. And if you actually listen to what senior clinicians say about the pressure put on the National Health Service by foreign patients you will know what we're saying.'

After more snapping and shouting, Carswell managed to free himself from the scrum and made his way to the other side of the road. Now there were two media packs – and the journalists and film crews had to decide whether to follow Farage or court Carswell.

Bloomberg's Rob Hutton decided the story was still with the new man and followed Carswell. Hutton, who stands at an impressive 6 ft 6 in. tall, used his superior height to crane over the scrum and ask Carswell about Malala Yousafzai – the Pakistani schoolgirl who had been shot by the Taliban for advocating education rights for girls in 2012.

After the attempt on her life, she was brought to the UK to receive specialist medical care. Malala remained in Birmingham after she recovered and went on to become a global icon against Islamic fundamentalist oppression, even addressing the United Nations.

The same day that Carswell – a man who is proud to claim that he takes an internationalist view of the world – was in Clacton celebrating his victory, Malala was awarded the Nobel Peace Prize.

'Given Nigel Farage believes foreign patients are putting pressure on the National Health Service, do you think it was right for Malala to come to the UK for medical treatment, Mr Carswell?' asked Hutton. Carswell's response to Hutton's question was: 'I'm not familiar with that case.'

As Hutton later wrote in his article about the day's events: 'Carswell refused to say more, opting for silence and a smile.'

Carswell's silence was most likely down to him being separated from Farage – how could the UKIP MP know what his leader was saying across the road, perhaps on the very same issue?

Rather than risk a split, Carswell opted for faux ignorance, followed by silence.

Hutton tweeted the exchange – particularly Carswell's ignorance of the Malala case – and it exploded across social media like a firework in cyberspace.

I was watching the media scrum from across the road. It was a bizarre sight – and the perfect representation of the 'Westminster bubble' in action. Photographers, camera crews and journalists surrounding politicians, preventing them from getting anywhere near members of the public, as shoppers carried on regardless around them.

After about twenty minutes, Farage got bored of the whole debacle, clambered back into the Land Rover and was driven away. Carswell walked back to the UKIP office at the top of the road.

The journalist gang congregated outside McDonald's and, after receiving repeated assurances from Carswell's press officer Michael Heaver it would happen, marched en masse to the UKIP office for our noon interview with Carswell. The office was located just opposite

Clacton train station, allowing Ukippers to monitor which Tory big-wigs had arrived in the town from London, and how long they had stayed in the town for.

('My team was rather amused to see one minister arrive in Clacton on the quarter to train – before racing to get back on to the five past back to London,' wrote Carswell on his blog during the campaign.)

We gathered outside the door and peered in through the large windows of the former betting shop, waiting to be summoned in. I'm not sure what the collective noun is for a group of journalists (A gaggle? A lobby? A hack?), but it comprised: myself from the *Daily Express*; Matt Holehouse from the *Telegraph* – along with the paper's sketch-writer Michael Deacon; Tamara Cohen from the *Daily Mail*; Laura Pitel from *The Times*; Nicholas Watt from *The Guardian*; and Rob Hutton from Bloomberg.

We decided the best thing would be to work as a group – all of us would go in together and fire questions at Carswell. The first few would be some soft questions about how he was feeling today, where he would sit in the Commons, what reaction he expected from former colleagues etc. Then we would pull out the big guns. What was his view on Farage's HIV comments? How did he think his appeal for the party to broaden its appeal to immigrants would play with the grass roots? Does he want to be leader?

With the plan drawn up, and the questions divvied out, we prepared for battle. But the People's Army wasn't ready to engage. Michael Heaver wouldn't let us in.

We kept being told to wait. So we waited. And waited. And waited.

TV crews, local reporters, and even Sunday paper hacks were ushered in for their time with Carswell, but, for some reason, not us.

An hour went by, during which Heaver appeared at the door at irregular intervals to assure us we would soon get our slot.

Another hour passed – still no interview.

News editors were emailing, then texting, then calling their respective journalists to find out what was going on. It's humiliating to admit that you are struggling to get an interview with the most rent-a-gob party in the land.

It had now been over two hours since the agreed time for the interview. We were bored, tired, cold, hungry and, most importantly, our massive egos were dented.

Eventually, Heaver came to the door and said we were allowed in – two at time. Who the fuck did Carswell think he was – Noah?

We protested. We knew that by staggering it, and just giving each pair five minutes, Carswell would avoid a real grilling.

And we knew that he knew that. But the question was whether he knew that we knew that he knew that.

We never knew.

Laura Pitel from *The Times* and I went in first to soften him up. Carswell was as red-eyed and exhausted as we were. We bowled him some gentle questions about the result and what he planned to do in Parliament. He talked about how he wanted the 2012 Olympic spirit to permanently purvey through Britain, about how 'you will not get a campaign leaflet between my views and Nigel Farage's' on immigration, and how he had sought assurances UKIP was in no way a racist party before defecting.

That's pretty much what every reporter got. Carswell's plan to divide and conquer had worked.

Except Bloomberg's Rob Hutton.

After waiting for two hours, he was told he wouldn't be allowed to interview Carswell.

No reason was given, but a cynical person could draw a link between Hutton's tweet about Carswell's embarrassing non-view on Malala Yousafzai and his sudden lack of access.

Ousting local candidates in favour of established politicians, evading questions on controversial topics, 'not recognising the characterisation of the debate', banning specific journalists from media briefings – was this the 'new politics' of UKIP in action?

CHAPTER 7

HEART OF DONCASTER

UKIP CONFERENCE – DONCASTER, FRIDAY 26 SEPTEMBER & SATURDAY 27 SEPTEMBER 2014

EVERYONE REMEMBERS WHERE THEY were when Kennedy was shot, or when they found out Princess Diana had been killed.

I remember not only where I was, but what I was wearing, when I heard Tory MP Mark Reckless had defected to the UK Independence Party. I was in my pyjamas and dressing gown, on my sofa in my flat in east London, swearing very loudly at the television screen.

I was swearing not because of where I was, but because of where I wasn't: at the UKIP conference in Doncaster, where Reckless announced his defection.

Some sixteen hours earlier I had been there, covering day one of UKIP's annual conference. That was a Friday and, with the *Daily Express* not having a Sunday edition (the *Sunday Express* has a separate editorial team), my boss said there was no point in me staying up for the Saturday.

But I knew UKIP, and I knew something would happen on that second day. A few weeks prior to the conference, I asked the editor of the *Express* website, Geoff Marsh, if he wanted me up there for the second day at conference, covering it for the web. All it would cost him (well, not him, but his budget) was a hotel room for the Friday night, or my return train fare from London on the Saturday, plus my normal day rate.

He would be spending less than he normally sanctioned for pictures of a D-list celebrity with her bum out on a beach.

Marsh said no.

Even when I was up at the conference, I was asking around other hacks to see if they had a room they weren't planning on using on the Friday night so I could stay. The only rooms still available in hotels in Doncaster were priced in the hundreds – far too high for a hack such as me on a less-than-princely wage. Alex Wickham, from the Guido Fawkes website, was also up just for the Friday, and I tried to persuade him to split the cost of a room with me and stay for the Saturday. But Wickham was determined to go back to London that night as he reckoned he had a 'huge story' to finalise.

He wasn't bluffing. Conservative minister Brooks Newmark had sent a picture of his penis to someone he thought was young, attractive Tory activist called Sophie Wittams. Unfortunately for Newmark, Sophie Wittams was Alex Wickham, who had created the fake Twitter account after hearing stories about him. The Braintree MP stood down from government the next day, ahead of the scandal – although thankfully not the intimate picture itself – being splashed on the front page of the *Sunday Mirror*. Newmark subsequently announced he would not be contesting the 2015 general election.

After dining with colleagues in Doncaster town centre on Friday evening, I got the last train back to London, guaranteeing I would miss the next day's excitement.

Excitement was what I was hoping for when I arrived in Doncaster two days prior to the defection on a late Thursday afternoon. A year before, UKIP produced the conference story of the season thanks to Godfrey Bloom's slapstick reaction to Michael Crick, and I was of course hoping for more of the same this time.

It was a strange feeling, travelling north from London for something UKIP related. I had so often associated the party with the south of England. The previous year's conference had been held in Westminster, but this time UKIP were setting up camp on the border of Labour leader Ed Miliband's Doncaster North constituency. It was a blatant pitch by Farage and co. to move the perception of UKIP from comprising just disgruntled Middle-England ex-Tory voters to also include working-class traditional Labour voters who felt 'left behind' by modern Britain. UKIP's version of modern Britain is one of excessive political correctness, minority groups having a disproportionately loud voice compared to majority ones and a lack of fairness across the board.

After disembarking at Doncaster train station, I found myself in a taxi queue at least thirty people deep. For some reason, Doncaster taxi drivers had not realised the influx of people for the UKIP conference might provide them with some additional custom. Cabs were appearing at a rate of one every fifteen minutes, and the people who arrived on the train from London were certainly not used to the notion of waiting.

Eventually a shout came down the line that a gentleman was taking a cab to the Earl of Doncaster – the hotel I was staying at – and asked if anyone wished to share the ride.

'Earl of Doncaster? Yes, that would be great!' I said and rushed to the front to get into the black cab.

'Thank you so much for this, it was taking ages, wasn't it?' I said as I sat down, before looking at the man opposite me in the back of the taxi. It was multimillionaire Stuart Wheeler, UKIP's former treasurer, who had provided, and secured from others, vast sums for the party's coffers since 2009. Mr Wheeler had made his money through spread-betting in the 1970s and was known for his love of card games. He had reportedly played bridge with Lord Lucan two days before his disappearance and had also taken part in the world poker championships.

'That's OK,' he replied.

We exchanged small talk about the conference, Doncaster and whether the *Express* was going to come out and support UKIP in next year's general election, before arriving at the hotel.

The cab driver quoted us the fare, which was less than a tenner, and I was in a bizarre situation where I was trying to persuade a multi-millionaire to accept a £5 note as payment of my share. Wheeler wouldn't hear of it.

After checking into my room (double bed, wall-mounted television, small desk, kettle, cup and biscuits all present and correct) I wandered down to the bar to meet with Alex Wickham.

The hotel bar was a homage to art deco that even Liberace would have looked at and thought, 'Steady on.' Chandeliers dangled from the ceiling, the seat trimmings were shiny brass and rows of wine glasses were suspended above the semi-oval bar.

It was late afternoon and several Ukippers were already getting acquainted with the bar staff. We got ourselves a drink and were soon approached by a Kipper who knew Wickham: Emmett Jenner, UKIP's general election candidate for Bromley & Chislehurst.

With his slicked-back, black hair and slightly out-dated suit, he wouldn't have looked out of place on a City trading floor in the 1980s. He was clearly enjoying being in the bar with his comrades from the People's Army, and also revelling in having the attention of two national journalists. However, his air of sophistication was slightly undone when he knocked over the full glass of red wine he had rested on the bar, soaking one of those journalists in the process – me. Jenner looked sufficiently embarrassed and I assured him it was fine before scurrying up to my room to change clothes.

Now wearing a wine-free outfit, Wickham and I set off for the media drinks being held at the conference venue – Doncaster Racecourse. As we left the hotel we saw a group of anti-UKIP protesters who had positioned themselves across the street. There were about five of them, proudly displaying a large homemade banner calling UKIP 'racist'. I went over and spoke to them, and asked what about UKIP they objected to.

'They are racist,' came the reply from a young man who looked like he had come straight from a roller-skate park.

'The people or the party?' I asked.

'Both.'

'Which policies do you think are racist?'

'Well, one of them said Lenny Henry should go home to a black country.'

'True, but they kicked him out. Also, that's not really a policy. What policies do you think are racist?'

Another protester chimed in, trying to help his mate out. 'The immigration one,' he said.

'What about their immigration policy is racist?' I asked.

'Well, they want to stop people coming to the country,' he replied.

'Based on race?'

'Yeah.'

'But they don't, do they? They want a points-based system like the Australians operate. Do you think that's racist?'

'Oh, you don't think they're racist then? What a surprise! Typical journalist.'

'It doesn't matter what I think, you're the ones here with the banner which says UKIP are racist. I'm just trying to find out what about the party's policies you think are racist.'

There was no reply. I'm all for protesting, but surely you should know what you're protesting about?

We left the confused protesters alone and walked the 500 yards to Doncaster Racecourse.

UKIP had made a big play of the pre-conference media drinks, sending out numerous invitations and reminders to the press pack. At last year's event in Westminster, the press were an afterthought and weren't even given their own room to file copy from. As a result, journalists went rogue, leading to the downfall of Godfrey Bloom.

This year, there were cubicles set up for specific journalists, press officers on site to help with queries, and the racecourse itself provided a wonderful backdrop for the broadcasters.

The media drinks reception was an opportunity for the party to try to get the press onside – or at least find out early on who would be this year's troublemakers. Each UKIP policy spokesman had their own personal spokesman, who was working the room and giving little pre-briefings of the next day's speeches. We were all given sheets filled with contact details of everyone and anyone we would need to speak to. Some of the bigwigs themselves came along to schmooze, including MEPs Patrick O'Flynn, Amjad Bashir and Steven Woolfe.

But as far as the journalists were concerned, there were two massive problems with the reception. First, there was no food, apart from a few bowls of crisps. Second, there were no free drinks. At all.

I know, dear reader, I was as shocked and appalled as you are. The idea that a political party would organise an event for a press corps that had been almost universally derisive, condescending and hostile to them for a number of years and not reward them with free alcohol was baffling.

It took a while for us hacks to come to terms with the frankly shocking development that we would have to spend our own money, but there was no time to complain as Nigel Farage himself soon showed up.

I spotted him, unsurprisingly at the bar, and went over to talk to him before my colleagues noticed he was there.

'Bit of a change from last year,' I said, looking round the plush surroundings of the racecourse.

'I'd say!' replied Farage.

I asked him what he had planned for his keynote speech the next day, and he replied he had no idea because he hadn't written it yet.

'Really?' I asked.

'Absolutely. I'll work on it after these drinks,' he said, just as another pint was placed on the bar in front of him.

As he went to pick it up, he became slightly distracted by someone trying to get his attention. The pint glass was knocked over and, again, I was soaked in alcohol.

I could hardly kick off, so just had to act terribly English and insist it didn't matter and it was probably my fault anyway for standing there and of course it's no problem and let's face it smelling of beer at a UKIP conference is par for the course, wouldn't you agree, old chap? Ha ha ha.

By now the other journalists in the room had spotted Farage and soon we were both encircled by hacks wanting to get a tip-off about the next day's speech. Farage insisted he had yet to write it, and then Matthew Holehouse from the *Daily Telegraph* effectively proved the UKIP leader was telling the truth.

'Nigel, you holding this conference in Doncaster, right on the border with Ed Miliband's constituency, that's you putting your tanks on Labour's lawn, isn't it?' he asked.

The next day, Farage used that exact expression as the centrepiece of his speech. Holehouse had inadvertently pre-briefed the speech to a room of journalists without any of us, including himself, realising.

Farage made his excuses and was guided away to shake hands with other people. I continued to mingle, having chats with other Ukippers. No hint of any anger from anyone, no one looked ready to hit a journalist. Should I wind them up? I went over to O'Flynn, who I had briefly worked with at the *Daily Express* before he enrolled in the People's Army.

'It's all going well, Patrick. Everyone is under control and behaving themselves, I see.'

'Of course they are,' he replied with a smile.

'I'm disappointed, I thought someone would have hit someone by now!'

A bit obvious of me but, who knows, maybe being brazen would wind O'Flynn up.

'I could hit you if you like?' he said, forming a fist and pulling his arm back.

I thought about it. Obviously he wasn't going to actually hit me, but maybe I could hit him and claim it was self-defence. After all, he does *look* like he's about to hit me. I decided a journalist hitting a Kipper would more likely lead to my dismissal than his.

I just laughed. 'Maybe later!' I joked.

O'Flynn put his arm down. Did he looking slightly disappointed? Did he want to actually hit me?

I went on to the balcony to get some air. Farage was in the corner having a cigarette.

'Any more thoughts on the speech?' I asked.

'I'll tell you this,' he replied, 'I'm going to really let Labour have it over Rotherham.'

Farage was referring to the revelations in a report on child abuse in the South Yorkshire town by Professor Alexis Jay, which had been published a month before the UKIP conference. Professor Jay found that at least 1,400 children, some as young as eleven years old, had been sexually assaulted and raped between 1997 and 2013. The inquiry found examples of 'children who had been doused in petrol and threatened with being set alight, threatened with guns, made to witness brutally violent rapes and threatened they would be next if they told anyone'. Not only were the youngsters subjected to horrific attacks in Rotherham, they were also trafficked to other towns and sold for further exploitation.

The perpetrators of the attacks were predominantly from Rotherham's Asian community and Professor Jay clearly stated the ethnic make-up of the assailants prevented those in the local authorities from investigating allegations further.

The report read: 'Several staff described their nervousness about identifying the ethnic origins of perpetrators for fear of being thought as racist; others remembered clear direction from their managers not to do so.'

Denis MacShane, Labour MP for Rotherham from 1994 to 2012, admitted after the report was published that, although he had not been made aware of any specific allegations while in office, 'I think there was a culture of not wanting to rock the multicultural community boat, if I may put it like that.'

He conceded that despite being aware of 'the oppression of women within bits of the Muslim community in Britain ... as a true *Guardian* reader, and liberal leftie, I suppose I didn't want to raise that too hard'.

This was what Farage was going to use as a weapon against Labour, arguing this showed the party cared more about not offending other cultures than upholding British law.

'Do you not think you'll get some criticism for trying to make political gain out of such a horrific issue?' I asked.

'People will say this isn't political, well, you can bet your life it is,' was his reply. He finished his cigarette, went inside, shook a few more hands and left.

With the drinks winding down, the press pack decided food was a necessity. An Indian restaurant was Googled and booked. Taxis were Googled and booked.

The next task was trying to get some Ukippers to come with us. Without a word passing between us hacks, we all simultaneously began badgering whichever Kipper we were currently chatting to to join us for dinner.

The equation in everyone's head was: Ukippers + journalists x alcohol = stories.

But they were all being incredibly well behaved. Farage had gone, as had most of the other elected Ukippers, and the various press officers who were left were on their best behaviour.

Michael Heaver, who had left the main UKIP press office to take over the media relations for the east of England, appeared to be the most persuadable. He seemed keen, but every time he went to say 'yes' his eyes drifted into middle distance and he declined the offer. I reckon the press officers had been made to watch footage of Godfrey

Bloom hitting Michael Crick on repeat for hours, maybe days, with their eyes pinned open so they couldn't avoid seeing the moment last year's conference went belly up.

Every time a journalist spoke to them, the image of Bloom yelling 'Disgrace, you're disgraceful' as he clobbered Crick danced in front of their eyes.

Dinner with my journalist colleagues was perfectly lovely, but where was the scandal? Relax, I thought to myself, the conference hasn't even started yet.

After dinner, I went back to the hotel ready for a reasonably early night. But at the Earl, the party was in full swing, led by Master of the Revels himself – Nigel Farage.

It turned out the UKIP hierarchy was staying at the same hotel as me, meaning I was behind enemy lines, and they couldn't even throw me out because I was staying there!

Let the mischief commence, I thought.

Farage was out on the balcony holding court, unsurprisingly with a drink in one hand and a cigarette in the other. His wife Kirsten was also there, chatting away to fellow UKIP women.

After getting myself a drink I made a beeline for Farage. Maybe he would let me know a line or two of his speech so I could get the exclusive on the *Express* website. But no – he claimed he still hadn't written it, despite it now being nearly midnight. I decided alcohol was the way to go and offered to get Farage another drink. The UKIP leader is a serious drinker who can handle his booze, but maybe I could, well, not *spike* his drink exactly, but just give him slightly more alcohol than he was expecting.

Christ, I'm actually going to spike Nigel Farage's drink for a story, I thought. That's a new low, even for me. Luckily for Farage, and my career, the opportunity never arose as, no sooner had I arrived on the balcony, his wife took him up to bed.

The field marshal might have retired to his barracks, but there were plenty of other officers of the People's Army on the sauce. I went into the bar and was approached by a fresh-faced young Ukipper. If he had been sober, he would have come across as slightly aggressive, but he was quite drunk so, instead, had a big smile on his face. His name was Dan Jukes, he was eighteen and was active in the Thurrock branch of UKIP in Essex.

He spent a good while regaling me with how well UKIP was doing in his part of the world, how the party's candidate there, Tim Aker, was going to win the seat in next year's general election, and how Labour had parachuted someone in called Polly, who was rubbish.

Interesting, in a way, but not really a story.

After speaking to Jukes I noticed two mature women sitting at a table looking very glamorous, in a country-music-fan kind of way.

I turned to face them but they were already engaged in a conversation with BBC *Daily Politics* reporter Giles Dilnot. One of the women was telling him she played the banjo and performed at UKIP conventions and meetings. This sounded promising, but, alas, she didn't have her banjo with her. Dilnot was clearly gutted – she had 'quirky *Daily Politics* feature' written all over her.

As I was sitting there waiting for a UKIP gaffe to happen, a figure approached my table. It was none other than disgraced former Tory MP Neil Hamilton.

I had last seen him at the 2013 conference and, since then, he had tried – and failed – to be nominated as one of the party's MEP candidates in 2014.

'Mr Hamilton, how are you? I'm Owen Bennett from the *Daily Express*. Are you having a good night?' I said.

Hamilton swayed slightly, trying to focus on my face to see if he recognised me.

'You a journalist?' he asked, slightly slurring.

'Yes, for the *Daily Express*,' I replied.

He steadied himself, but still couldn't quite focus.

'Do you have an expense account?' he asked.

'Erm … yes.'

'Excellent, you can take me to lunch!' he exclaimed, then burst out laughing before falling forward slightly.

He steadied himself on the table and then wandered off. 'Neil Hamilton in drunk expenses demand'? Could work, but probably not, I thought.

By now it was nearly 1 a.m. and the bar was thinning out.

I looked around and contemplated trying to get Christine Hamilton to throw a glass of wine over me to complete the alcohol-spilling hat trick.

But even she had had enough and was walking off to her room. With no real scandal to report, I went to bed.

Friday 26 September, and the UKIP conference was getting underway. I arrived at the racecourse at just before 10 a.m. and set myself up in the designated media room on the third floor. The room was busy with journalists, camera crews, photographers, broadcasters and press officers. Not all the hacks had a desk, so some set themselves up outside the main media room – the overspill a sign that UKIP was now one of the big boys.

On that Friday, the House of Commons had been recalled from its summer recess to vote on whether to launch air strikes against the terrorist group Islamic State of Iraq and Syria (ISIS) in the Middle East. The vote meant the political editors of the papers remained in Westminster, but there were still journalists from all of the main players in Doncaster that day.

There were also commentators in attendance, such as Dan Hodges from the *Telegraph*, Rod Liddle and Isabel Hardman from *The Spectator* and Michael White from *The Guardian*. The Mainstream Media – as we are often desirously labelled by UKIP – were now paying attention to the party.

On the ground floor, more than a thousand Kippers were either sitting listening to the speeches in a cavernous, curtained-off area at the back of the racecourse stand or milling around the numerous stalls promoting a range of pressure groups and special interests.

UKIP clearly had its business hat on when designing the floor plan of the conference lay-out, as the first stall members came to once they had presented their ticket to security was heaving with party merchandise. UKIP-branded cufflinks, baseball caps, ties, bow ties and handkerchiefs sat along UKIP calendars, anti-EU books and, of course, UKIP fruitcake. One member had even constructed a small 'UKIP Closet', complete with a sign that popped up when you opened the door and read: 'There are no racists inside or outside this closet.' The merchandise and stalls meant that, despite the venue size, the conference still had a vibe of a slightly bizarre village fête.

The big UKIP hitters were down to give speeches on that first day – Steven Woolfe on migration, Amjad Bashir on community relations, Louise Bours on health, Patrick O'Flynn on the economy, all before Nigel Farage's conference address at 3 p.m.

I made my way behind the curtain and took a seat for the speeches. They were all fairly predictable. Woolfe talked about UKIP's 'ethical migration policy', Bashir about the need for immigrants to integrate into the communities they move in to, and Bours did her usual trick of spending twenty minutes trying to shout the NHS into submission.

O'Flynn got a huge cheer when he announced UKIP would scrap inheritance tax entirely, but he had journalists scribbling furiously in their notepads when he announced a proposed reform of VAT:

> I want it to investigate the feasibility of imposing a luxury goods rate of VAT. It makes no sense to me that VAT is levied at the same rate on budget items purchased by the hard-pressed as it is on premium ones that are the preserve of the very well heeled. And it seems to me that a luxury goods rate of 25 per cent could raise substantial extra funds from the wealthiest people. I would suggest such a rate be built around simple thresholds such as £200 for a pair of shoes, £1,000 for a bag or £50,000 for a new car.

The proposal received a lukewarm round of applause and several members of the audience turned and looked at each other with confusion on their faces. Hadn't O'Flynn just attacked socialists for targeting people's aspirations? Surely, in this consumer capitalist world we live in, which UKIP is supposed to wholeheartedly endorse, buying 'premium goods' is the most aspirational act a person can undertake?

Within minutes, hacks christened O'Flynn's proposal as a 'Wag Tax' and it was being tweeted out with a fair amount of scepticism and derision.

(Craig Woodhouse from the *Sun on Sunday* called it a 'Towie Tax', which I thought was much better, but Twitter had spoken and 'Wag Tax' it was.)

After writing up Comrade O'Flynn's leftist proposal, it was time for lunch.

Rumours spread that a Women in UKIP fringe event was laying on sandwiches.

Coincidentally, at the same time as we heard about the free lunch, myself, Wickham and a few others remembered we had always had a huge interest in the role of women in UKIP and, frankly, we would be letting ourselves down if we didn't go along.

We weren't the only ones who had come to show support to the UKIP women fringe event. A whole host of Kippers had turned up and were not holding back on piling their plates with sandwiches, and helping themselves to the free alcohol.

The women who had organised the event were surprised at the turnout, and more sandwiches were ordered to feed the hungry horde.

One Kipper tried to call the meeting to order, but no one really paid much attention and everyone carried on with their own conversations. The women who had organised the event were forced to move to the side of the room so they could be heard above the other Kippers who, by this point, it had become obvious to them were only there for the free food and booze.

I made my way over to hear the speakers who were trying to

address the meeting, but they were struggling without the aid of a microphone.

They each talked about how the party had won seven female MEPs in the recent European elections without such draconian measures as 'positive discrimination'.

There was then a bizarre moment when a young girl – no more than seventeen years old – was introduced to the meeting as she was a talented golfer, and a speaker waxed lyrical about how brilliant she was. The girl looked faintly embarrassed to be there, and I really couldn't work out what on earth this had to do with UKIP.

As the speeches went on, the background noise got louder and louder. Yorkshire MEP Jane Collins was starting to get annoyed, and she shouted over to the eaters and drinkers: 'Please, ladies and gentlemen, it is awfully rude to talk through the speeches.' No one listened, no one even looked up from their own conversations – including Kirsten Farage, who was gleefully chatting away. Collins was getting more annoyed, and shouted over again: 'The people at the back who have no interest in what we're doing, they're only here for the beer.'

The speakers struggled on and even though I was only a few feet away I couldn't hear what they were talking about. One woman finally had had enough and, standing up on her chair, shouted: 'The *men* up at the bar who aren't listening – why did they bother coming? For the free food!'

Well, I had come for the free food as well, but at least I was trying to listen to the speeches. Eventually the speeches came to an end and I made my way out. As I was leaving, I walked past UKIP's Scotland MEP David Coburn, who was positioned right next to the buffet table. A large guy, with a thick Scottish accent, he clearly had no idea what the meeting was for but was enjoying the grub. He turned to one of his co-eaters and said, 'So what's this then? The UKIP suffragettes?' before letting out a loud laugh.

By 3 p.m., all the Kippers and journalists were in position for Nigel

Farage's speech, which, apparently, as of midnight, he still hadn't written. He entered the room with extremely loud dance music booming out of the speakers and took to the stage.

A week earlier, Labour leader Ed Miliband had delivered his conference speech without notes, and was widely mocked for forgetting to mention the UK's economic deficit, despite it being in the draft of the address.

Farage would be performing the same 'no notes' trick, but it was unlikely he would be forgetting anything.

The standard Farage speech is: attack the media and Westminster elite; attack the EU; attack open-door immigration; thank Nick Clegg for debating him live on TV; make a few jokes about how he enjoys a beer or two; lead a call to get Britain back; and end.

Farage opened by praising UKIP members for helping to deliver the 'earthquake in British politics' at the European elections. Then came the attack on the media:

> Even people we thought were friends of ours, the Eurosceptic newspapers, said: 'Please, please, don't vote UKIP. Please maintain the established political order in this country.' You know the established political order I'm talking about, don't you? The Labour, Liberal Democrat and Conservative parties – parties that look the same, parties that sounds the same, parties between whom, frankly, on major issues of substance there is now very little difference. Parties that have all been committed to signing Britain up to the European project. Parties that have been wholly uncritical of open-door immigration. Parties that have contributed directly to a downward shift in living standards in this country over the course of the last decade or more, and I'm pleased to say that UKIP voters ignored the establishment, and ignored their friends in the media and they voted for one thing above all. They voted on May 22nd because they want change.

He followed that up with another jibe aimed at the 'mainstream national media', which 'like our political class rarely leave the confides of Westminster, or its restaurants. Or bars. Perhaps I shouldn't have said that myself but never mind.'

So far, so predictable, but the next section saw Farage dismiss the view – which I'm not sure many journalists actually held – that UKIP was only attracting Tory voters.

'We are tearing vast chunks out of the old Labour vote too,' said Farage, following it up with Matthew Holehouse's line from the night before: 'We want to signal to the world that we are now parking our tanks on the Labour Party's lawn.'

Farage continued his assault on Labour's 'one-party-state' style dominance of the northern towns and cities, and then went on a slightly surprising rant about postal voting. In an age of falling voter turnout, it seemed Farage wanted to restrict postal voting, a move that could see participation in elections fall even further.

Next up was Farage's attack on Labour over the child abuse scandal in Rotherham:

> Labour's failure in the north of England is even worse and even more serious than the postal-voting scandal. What we have seen in Rotherham in particular, although there have been other examples of it too, what we have seen within the one-party state of Labour, as a direct result of their national policies and as a direct result of their own political correctness at a local level, is child abuse that has taken place on a scale that I think is actually difficult for decent people to actually comprehend. I think it's just about one of the most shocking things that I have seen in my lifetime in this country and what we learn, and what's emerged, from the witness testimony of people in those councils, and even sitting MPs and former MPs, is that, because they were so scared of causing a division within the very multicultural society that they had created,

they were more fearful of being branded racist than they were
of taking on and tackling an evil that existed within that town,
and that is wrong and it shows why we need opposition. It
shows why we need a change in our political culture. And I
know that some people are saying to me, 'Nigel, it's wrong,
you shouldn't be saying these things, you shouldn't be making this political, this is simply a cultural problem.' Well, I'm
sorry, but if this isn't political, then what is?

The delegates applauded, but it was hardly the all-out attack I was
expecting. Farage was essentially regurgitating the comments from
Professor Jay herself, but adding a party-political bent to the analysis.
There was no solution offered, and he wasn't even calling for UKIP
to take control, instead saying Labour needed 'opposition'.

Farage moved on to the EU ('We love Europe but we hate the
European Union'), the rise in immigration depressing wages, and
joked about Miliband's gaffe the week before ('Yes, I nearly forgot
the deficit, that's right').

He said UKIP needed to tackle Labour's claims that his party 'will
privatise the NHS, that UKIP wants to charge you for GP appointments' by pointing out that Labour 'have done more than anybody
to actually bring private money into the health service and it's not
UKIP that will do it'.

The next section of his speech was either an example of either par-
anoia or perceptiveness, depending on your view of Prime Minister
David Cameron's attitude towards UKIP.

Referring to the House of Commons vote on bombing ISIS, Farage said:

There are those that will argue that today's conference for
UKIP has been slightly overshadowed by events taking place
in Westminster, and I'm not going to speculate on the tim-
ing of that. I don't find it unusual at all because I noticed

the day after Mr Carswell joined us we were told that the
nation was on a state of emergency. I kind of expect these
things to happen. If beginning the bombing missions was
that important, why couldn't they have met yesterday? But
never mind.

He ended with a rally against multiculturalism, a call for a round of
applause for Nick Clegg for debating him on television over the EU
and a claim that, after next year's general election, UKIP could hold
the balance of power.

The end.

Farage got a standing ovation, the dance music came back on and
camera flash after camera flash went off to get a picture of the leader
of the People's Army being cheered by his soldiers.

I went back to the media room trying to work out what the best
line was. Attacking Labour over the Rotheram scandal? The fraud of
postal voting? Deeply held belief that Parliament was only discussing bombing ISIS to take attention away from the UKIP conference?

Before I had a chance to sit down at my cubicle, however, Gawain
Towler came bounding in and told me Farage was holding a post-
speech press conference upstairs.

I and a few others went up the room and found Farage sitting at a
round table with an open bottle of red wine in front of him. He made
short work of the first glass before pouring a second.

We began questioning him about the speech. I asked him about
UKIP's plans for the NHS. In his speech he had attacked Labour
for introducing privatisation into the health service – does that mean
UKIP would definitely not do that if it found itself in government?

'Well, you heard Louise Bours's speech earlier, so there's your
answer,' he replied.

'Yes, I did hear her speech, but, to be honest, I'm still not sure what
the policy is,' I said.

UKIP's EU press officer Hermann Kelly aggressively interrupted:

'Why are you asking him? Why don't you ask Louise? She's the health spokesman.'

'Nigel's the party leader and he brought up the NHS in his speech, that's why I'm asking him,' I snapped back.

The questioning moved on to other areas of the speech, and behind me the room was filling up with journalists. The number had increased from about five to more than twenty, and it was clear Farage was not prepared for this.

After questions about his speech, Farage was asked about O'Flynn's proposed VAT reforms – the Wag Tax.

He explained he thought it was right that foreign shoppers should not be able to claim back the VAT on goods bought in the UK at the airport when they leave the country.

No, not that, the plan to implement a higher VAT rate on luxury goods.

Farage denied that was O'Flynn's policy. We assured him it was. He clearly hadn't heard anything about it.

Kelly brought the questions to a close, and Farage left quickly.

His keynote speech – his moment of glory in front of his fans after the party's European election victory no less – had been overshadowed by a proposal he knew nothing about.

The day was drawing to a close and I had been unable to find somewhere to stay that night. A group of us journos went out for dinner, during which the *Telegraph*'s Dan Hodges revealed an extensive knowledge of *Sex and the City*. I made a last round of calls to UKIP contacts to see if there was anything huge happening the next day that I was going to miss.

'No,' was the reply from them all.

The next day, after treating myself to a lie-in and lazy sofa day, I watched as Tory MP Mark Reckless announced his defection to UKIP at the conference.

If my life were a Hollywood film, this would have been the moment I threw my head back and shouted 'NOOOOOO!' while shaking my fist.

I didn't. I just swore a hell of a lot.

CHAPTER 8

SAVING PRIVATE RECKLESS

THE TORIES WEREN'T GOING to lose Rochester & Strood. They were determined. So determined, in fact, that, no sooner had Mark Reckless revealed his defection from the Conservatives to UKIP, they started getting nasty.

The day after Reckless announced his switch, Conservative Party chairman Grant Shapps put on his best serious face as he addressed delegates at the Tory conference in Birmingham. Standing on the conference stage, Shapps tried his utmost to make it sound like Reckless had essentially slept with the partners of everyone in the room behind their backs.

'Today, your trust has been abused. You have been cheated,' he revealed.

He went on to tell delegates: 'I share your deep sense of betrayal and anger. We have been let down by somebody who has repeatedly lied to his constituents, and to you. Who said one thing, and then did another.'

Staring, unblinking, into the crowd, Shapps claimed Reckless had 'lied, and lied, and lied again'.

The attempted ferocity of Shapps's attack was undermined slightly by having a bunch of young Tories sitting behind him, all decked out in blue T-shirts emblazoned with a Conservative-logo-shaped Union Jack worn uncomfortably over their shirts and ties.

It looked like Shapps was the leader of a religious cult and, after one member had escaped, he had rounded up all the children and put them behind him as if to say: 'If any of you other fuckers even think about leaving, I will personally execute every last one of these teenagers behind me.'

You could understand the Tories' frustration though. After Douglas Carswell's surprising/unsurprising defection earlier that summer, the party machine had really gone into overdrive to stop others from jumping ship.

Chief Whip Michael Gove had even taken Reckless out for lunch – that's right, lunch – as part of a master strategy to stop him defecting. But despite this high-pressured, well-thought-out campaign, Reckless went and did it anyway.

Honestly, if you can't trust a politician, then who can you trust, eh, Shapps?

(This is the same Grant Shapps who, before entering politics, wrote get-rich-quick books under the pen names Michael Green and Sebastian Fox, then claimed he stopped acting under those names since becoming an MP in 2005, only for it to be revealed he had continued giving advice as Michael Green until at least 2006. A man 'who said one thing, and did another' indeed.)

At Tory conference fringe events, David Cameron himself even attacked Reckless – or, more specifically, his 'fat arse'. The Prime Minister was reported as saying party volunteers had 'knocked on doors, stuffed envelopes, licked stamps to get his fat arse on the Commons benches, and this is how he repays them'.

The battle lines had been drawn – the Tories were determined not to lose Rochester & Strood to UKIP in the same manner in which Clacton went purple – i.e. by an absolute landslide.

The sense from the Tories was very much: 'Look, Douglas Carswell is Douglas Carswell, and he's always been a bit of a maverick. But Mark Reckless is a nobody. And we can't lose to a nobody.'

They were right – even the most dedicated lobby hacks didn't really know who Mark Reckless was.

If he had walked out on the stage at the Doncaster conference and said, 'I would like to announce … the café selling hot and cold snacks is now open, and, yes, we do accept payment by card,' nobody would have realised it was a Tory backbencher.

Obviously, I don't really know what the atmosphere in the room was like in those few seconds between him appearing on the stage and announcing his defection as I wasn't there (see previous chapter/rant).

All Reckless had really been known for before his defection was that he couldn't really handle his drink. In 2010 – just weeks after being elected to the Commons – Reckless had got so drunk in a Commons bar he hadn't been able to vote in the government's emergency Budget debate.

He claimed at the time he had decided not to take part in the 2 a.m. vote as, due to how much he had had to drink, 'I thought it would be inappropriate in the circumstances.' Others said he fell asleep on the Commons terrace, missed the vote, was unable to open a door as his own foot was in the way, and had to be bundled into a taxi to take him home.

I was looking forward to seeing how a man who can't handle his drink would survive in a party led by Nigel Farage.

Having missed Reckless's defection announcement at the UKIP conference, I was determined to get stuck into the campaign in Rochester as soon as possible.

Prime Minister David Cameron decided he wanted that as well – for himself, not for me. I don't think he really cared if I was there or not.

With Reckless making national news with his defection, the Tories decided they needed to hit back in the airwaves war as soon as possible. The party machinery held an 'open primary' so the voters of the constituency could decide who would challenge Reckless in the upcoming vote.

The two candidates on offer were local women Anna Firth and Kelly Tolhurst.

Anna Firth was a former medical negligence barrister who served on the nearby Sevenoaks council. One of her big concerns was the UK's immigration policy. At a hustings event during the open primary campaign she said: 'We had uncontrolled immigration for thirteen years, leading to – as we know – an extra 3 million people in this country.'

Her opponent, Kelly Tolhurst, was a businesswoman who served on Medway council.

One of her big concerns was also the UK's immigration policy.

On her website she listed her top priorities for the area, one of which was: 'Pressing the government and the council to get immigration properly under control – to ease pressure on services and make sure social housing is made available to local people first.'

What a choice for the voters of Rochester & Strood. Such diversity.

Cameron had committed to get his hands dirty in this by-election, and so it was that the leader of the United Kingdom of Great Britain and Northern Ireland found himself sitting at a tea-stained table in a draughty community centre hall in Strood on a cold October morning, with Kelly Tolhurst to his left and Anna Firth to his right – two women who appeared to disagree with his own party's immigration policy.

In front of him were no more than 100 people plucked from the local area, and, tucked into their own separate section way at the back, was a delegation of Her Majesty's Journalists (Westminster Division).

I was there, wearing my trademark duffel coat (if you knew me, you would know it is my trademark), wondering if we would get a chance to ask Cameron any questions. Around me were many of the same faces from Clacton, but this time the sketch-writers had turned out in force – Quentin Letts from the *Daily Mail*, Michael Deacon from the *Daily Telegraph*, John Crace from *The Guardian* and Donald MacInytre from *The Independent*.

The Clacton election had been difficult to make jokes out of because, for all intents and purposes, Carswell was doing an honourable thing, and the Tories had stopped putting up a decent fight long before election day.

But the Tories had to win Rochester to stop UKIP's momentum, which meant more visits from the PM, more negative campaigning and, frankly, more desperation. Desperation is funny, hence the sketch-writers.

Incidentally, that day I worked out the perfect way to cause panic among a group of sketchers. Prior to us being ushered into the main room for the hustings, the journalists were placed in a holding pen behind the community centre's kitchen. The reporters were all huddled together on one side, and the sketchers were all together on another.

I decided to venture over and talk to the sketchers – obviously bowing continuously as I went and staring at the ground so they wouldn't think I was challenging their natural dominance. Once I had been accepted into the group, I innocently asked what questions they would be asking Cameron today. I may as well have fired off a gun next to a group of chimpanzees, as the sketchers went from quiet musing to utter panic.

'"Questions"? What "Questions"? Are you asking a "Question", Quentin?'

'I don't know, are you asking a "Question"?'

'It depends. Should we? Should we ask a "Question"?'

'We could ask a "Question", couldn't we?'

'Ask a "Question"? Who wants us to ask a "Question"?'

I backed away from the sketchers, leaving them to grapple with the question of a 'Question'.

As it was, none of us got to ask any questions. Cameron chaired the hustings and took questions from the audience instead of the press.

Both candidates seemed keen to talk about how they wanted to control immigration, and Cameron tried to sound tough on what he wanted to get out of any renegotiation of the UK's membership of the European Union.

After the excitement of the hustings, I made my way into Rochester town centre to locate UKIP's campaign headquarters.

Rochester high street is not like Clacton's. The seaside town represented by Carswell has a more end-of-the-line feel about it. Pound
stores, takeaways and amusement arcades dominate Clacton, as do
charity shops.

Rochester has a lot of charity shops, but it's also home to independent book stores, vintage clothes outlets and artisan cafés. The visitor
centre in the middle of the town boasts about Charles Dickens's links
with the area – he spent much of his childhood in the Medway as his
father worked in the dockyard. There is also a wonderful cathedral in
the town centre, a few hundred yards away from a spectacular castle
that dates back to the Normans.

UKIP's headquarters was based in a quaint building on the high
street, next door to an Italian café and opposite the wonderful Baggins
Book Bazaar, which specialises in rare and second-hand publications.
The HQ itself was in a Tudor-style building, with the top storey jut-
ting out over the ground floor. Inside the office, giant maps of the
constituency covered the walls allowing the People's Army to see
the territory they needed to conquer.

Among the 'Vote UKIP' signs, mugs, tables, papers and posters
of Mark Reckless, there was a life-affirming slogan painted on the
wall, left there by the building's previous inhabitants, The Crystal
Butterfly. It read: 'When it rains look for Rainbows. When it's dark
look for the Stars.'

I'm sure that gave great solace to Farage and Reckless during the
campaign.

It didn't take long for us hacks to find a café that had the perfect
combination of tables and chairs, power sockets and free WiFi. The
Deaf Cat on the high street became the headquarters for Westminster's finest throughout the election campaign.

The staff – all in their early twenties – were wonderfully accom-
modating, even asking us what music we wanted on.

'You can have anything, we've got Spotify,' one of the café workers proclaimed proudly.

'How about some Miles Davis, *Kind of Blue*?' said Bloomberg's Rob Hutton.

'Never heard of it. Is that suitable for a coffee shop?' the youngster behind the counter replied.

'Put it on and if you don't think Miles Davis is suitable for a coffee shop, I will give everyone in here a million pounds,' replied Hutton.

A few minutes into the biggest-selling jazz album of all time, and Hutton wasn't exactly reaching for his chequebook.

After a few minutes discussing how to write up Cameron's latest attack on the EU ('His strongest signal yet?' asked one of us. 'Pretty sure we did that this morning.' 'Erm, toughened his stance?' 'Yep, that works.'), I noticed we weren't the only ones from Westminster in Rochester that day.

For who should be walking past our café but Tory Chief Whip Michael Gove and Tory Chief Wind-Up Merchant Michael Fabricant. The good people of Rochester & Strood would get used to the sight of politicians on their streets over the next five weeks.

An edict had been sent round by the Tory leadership that every MP was to visit the constituency at least three times during the campaign, with ministers instructed to go five times. Many Tories, especially those on the right of the party who were friendly with Reckless, simply ignored the request. Others went down to discover there was nothing for them to do except stuff envelopes, one Tory worker told me.

In the Conservative campaign office, located at the opposite end of the high street to UKIP's, MPs proudly wrote their names on the wall to show they had attended. The Tories had 302 MPs and, by the end of the campaign, there were not 302 names on that wall.

While others were wavering, Cameron was holding firm to his commitment to visit the constituency at least five times.

One of these was a typical Tory hard-hat photo op. Both Cameron and the Chancellor George Osborne loved nothing better than donning a high-vis jacket, putting on a hard hat and looking serious as they watched people build things. These people were generally men, and the things they were building were generally big.

On 4 November, the Prime Minister visited Chatham Dockyard and Chatham Segment Factory, which made huge tunnel sections for London's Crossrail project. Along with Kelly Tolhurst, who had won the Tory nomination by a fraction of votes on 23 October, he looked at huge slabs of concrete, nodded as he was told how important they were, and even watched as one piece was moved onto a barge. Exciting stuff, as you can imagine.

How this was meant to tackle the supposed fear in Rochester & Strood of mass immigration, I wasn't quite sure, but at least I got to watch the Prime Minister watching concrete.

In a question session with journalists afterwards, Cameron blasted UKIP for focusing on 'stunts'. He said: 'If you vote UKIP, it's not about you, it's about them. It will be about stunts and politics and trying to make a thing out of UKIP rather than trying to deliver for the people of Rochester & Strood.'

The Tory leader attacking an opposing party for playing politics in an election campaign – irony died in Rochester & Strood on 4 November.

Farage was also in the constituency that day, and UKIP had organised a town hall debate and invited us nasty media folk to come along to see him and Mark Reckless in action.

The open invitation to the town hall debate was a welcome contrast to a Tory hustings held during the open primary, which press were banned from attending.

After an afternoon filing copy from the Deaf Cat café, I made my way to the venue.

It was a dark and stormy night, as the cliché goes, when I arrived at the Hoo Village Institute. The building was divided into two parts. One side was the hall, complete with standard-issue plastic chairs and a bar that was only part open. The other section of the building was a mystery. Just a nondescript door with a man standing in front of it. In the hall side of the building, the press had gathered in a booth to one side of the stage, which had giant poster of Mark Reckless's face grinning down upon us all.

The hall slowly filled up with locals and, before long, it was standing room only. The vast majority seemed to be couples over the age of forty, but there were some younger families present and even the odd teenager who had been dragged along by their parents. It reminded me of my days as a local reporter when the borough or county council would organise a meeting to reveal where they were going to build thousands of new houses in the area. Most people turned up and simultaneously moaned about the lack of somewhere to live for their children, while opposing every new house proposed by a developer.

Also in the hall was Jolyon Rubinstein, one of the stars of the BBC Three show *The Revolution Will Be Televised*. The programme was a mixture of hidden-camera pranks, sketches and satirical interviews directed at politicians and others in the public eye. He told me he was now trying to make a serious documentary about politics to push back against the Russell Brand mantra that young people shouldn't vote.

Rubinstein's previous encounter with Farage was when he tried to get the UKIP leader to reimburse him for a coffee he had bought in Brussels for a UKIP MEP. In the guise of a Tory member looking to defect, he approached Farage on the street, presented him with the receipt and asked for the money on 'expenses'. Farage repeatedly said no, and told Rubinstein it has 'fuck all to do with me'.

Rubinstein was in Hoo to try to get a serious conversation with Farage. I thought that was ambitious, but wished him luck.

Before Farage took to the stage, Reckless addressed the hall, giving his reasons for defecting to UKIP.

At least, I think that's what he said. It's so difficult to concentrate whenever he talks. His voice never changes in pitch or tempo, it just ambles along at one speed. It's the equivalent to driving along the motorway late at night at a steady 70 mph while someone reads out the full terms and conditions of an Apple product. Dull in so many ways.

After the pound-shop John Major had sat down, Farage emerged – being the smart man he is he had hidden himself away during Reckless's monotone monologue.

He bounded onto the stage, lapped up the applause and gave us a greatest hits of Farage gags: 'I worked in the City of London for twenty years, and I worked damned hard up until lunchtime every single day.'

'How many people are not members of UKIP? Put your hands up? Virtually everybody. Right, we're going to lock the doors.'

While us jaded old hacks had heard these lines before, the audience were entertained.

One woman in the second row was reaching a near orgasmic state with every line that came out of Farage's mouth. At one point I thought she was going to stand up and proclaim, 'You are the Lord and I have been cleansed,' before drinking some poisoned Kool-Aid and offering herself up as a sacrifice.

(I spoke to her afterwards and she wasn't from Hoo. Or Rochester. Or even Kent. She had actually come all the way from Bournemouth to hear Farage speak. The force was strong with that one.)

After the speech – complete with an attack on the Lib/Lab/Con, jokes about Nick Clegg helping him to raise his profile and praise for the honour of Reckless and Douglas Carswell – the meeting was opened up to questions.

They were all fairly predictable, and mainly featured Farage laying into the EU, and Reckless laying into the Tories. Sometimes they swapped round, just to mix things up. But I was forced to wake up when someone asked about UKIP's defence policy. After years of obscurity on the back benches of the Tory Party, this was Reckless's chance to play at being a statesman.

With Farage nodding in agreement, he said:

> The politicians have cut back our armed forces to an extraor-
> dinary degree but they haven't cut back their ambitions to
> sort of strut their stuff and be self-important on the world
> stage. The main impact of the intervention in Libya, as I found
> out when I visited Calais about six weeks ago, is many of the
> people who are trying to get over to this country, many of
> them are coming through Libya, and whatever people can
> say about Gaddafi, one thing is he didn't allow those boats
> to come across; he had an agreement with Italy that stopped
> it. Since he's gone we have no idea what's going on in Libya;
> it's too dangerous for anyone to go there and tell us.

Good old Gaddafi. He may have ruled Libya as a dictator for forty-
three years, suppressed and tortured his own citizens, had his foreign
secretary executed then kept the body in a freezer in his palace as a
trophy, raped fifteen- and sixteen-year-old girls after forcing them
to watch pornographic videos so they knew what was expected of
them – but he did stop a relatively few people seeking a better life
for themselves in Europe.

After the question-and-answer session was over, we all crowded
round Farage to see if he would endorse Reckless's view.

'How many more hundreds and thousands have to die with us
pursuing our policy of removing people we may [not like],' he told
Christopher Hope from the *Daily Telegraph*:

> You could argue the same for Assad, you could argue the
> same for Saddam Hussein, you can make these arguments
> wherever you like. Yeah, they're bad guys being replaced by
> even worse guys and that's the point. We are going into what
> seems to be an endless series of foreign wars without really
> thinking through what the end consequences are.

I followed up by asking him why he wanted to increase spending on Britain's armed forces at a time of austerity, especially if he thought the UK should be scaling back its military ambitions.

'OK, Owen,' he said, jabbing his finger in my direction. 'Why don't you cancel your fire insurance on your house? Why don't you cancel that to save money, Owen, and see what happens when your house burns down?'

I couldn't remember him ever pointing at me like that before, or getting personal with his replies.

A few moments later, and another journalist was winding him up. Rubinstein decided to approach Farage as he was leaving the hall to ask him to appear on camera for his new show.

'No way, absolutely no way,' said Farage.

Rubinstein tried to explain that he was making a serious programme but Farage wasn't having it.

'I'll work with him,' he said, pointing to the cameraman, 'but not with you.'

Rubenstein looked disappointed, but he could hardly be surprised that Farage hadn't want to set himself up for another fall.

The hall was now almost empty, save for a couple of UKIP foot soldiers stacking chairs away and collecting empty pint glasses. I walked out into the car park and saw a few people ambling into the room on the other side of the building. I had already been told no press were allowed in, which made me absolutely convinced something amazing must be going on inside.

Maybe after a town hall speech like that, Farage relaxes Putin-style by having a wrestle in an unlicensed bout against a local champion. He had seemed pretty pumped, and I got the impression that when he was jabbing his finger in my direction he secretly wanted to throw a punch. A not unfamiliar feeling people have towards me, I am told.

Perhaps he goes the full Hugh Hefner after an evening attacking Brussels bureaucrats, and behind the door was a harem of women wearing UKIP-branded corduroy-yellow underwear.

Whatever was going on in there, I wanted to see it.

There was a security man on the door and I knew I would have to use all my journalistic cunning to get into the building. I walked up, ready to spin some tale that would baffle the bouncer into letting me past. The bouncer looked me up and down, taking in my duffel coat, satchel and (I later realised) notebook sticking out of my pocket.

'Alright, mate,' he said, and stepped out of the way of the door.

Blimey, I must have Jedi mind-tricked him without even realising, I thought to myself as I opened the door. I was in.

It was a pub.

Just a pub, showing the football.

The bloke outside wasn't a bouncer, he was just a guy having a cigarette.

There were no women in corduroy underwear, no wrestling matches, just people watching Arsenal throw away a three-goal lead over Anderlecht in the Champions League.

How disappointing.

I made my way to the bar, ordered a beer and looked round for Farage. He was at the back of the pub having an in-depth conversation with a woman I had never seen before. I asked a Kipper at the bar who it was.

'That's Nigel's first wife.'

'What's she doing here?' I replied.

The Kipper said: 'She lives nearby and wanted to come and see him in action. It is the first time she has even seen him doing anything like this apparently.'

Farage met his first wife, Clare Hayes, in 1985 after he was hit by a car while crossing the road, drunk, after a boozy day in the City.

The crash left the 21-year-old trader in plaster for almost a year, and there was, at one point, the very real possibility he could lose his left leg.

Clare was a nurse taking care of young Nigel and, in his first autobiography, he said: 'I fell in love with a warm smile, competent, jolly affection and Nature's guarantee of a future: my nurse.'

The pair got married in 1988 and, in January 1989, Clare gave birth to their first child, Sam. A second son, Tom, came along in 1991, but Farage said that by then the marriage 'was already dying'. 'How could it not be? I was never at home,' he wrote, and went on to talk about the seductive nature of working as a City broker as a 27-year-old.

'What on earth had made me suppose that I could be a devoted husband and father at that age when death or glory awaited me on the field of battle and companionable carousing with my comrades when at last the New York silver exchange shut its doors at 7.25 in the evening?'

The pair divorced in 1997, with Farage admitting it was 'amicable' as it 'made so little difference to our lives'.

I pondered whether to go and speak to the ex-Mrs Farage. I was well aware that Farage fiercely protects his private life, and it would probably lead to me being put on some kind of UKIP blacklist.

Before I had made up my mind, UKIP's head of press Gawain Towler appeared next to me at the bar. He was the one who had told me no journalists were allowed in. Before he had the chance to throw me out, I ordered him a pint of bitter.

'Ah,' he said, eyeing the frothing beer presented to him. 'Now you can stay, but just behave, OK?'

'Of course, Gawain. Absolutely.'

'Good.'

'So why is Nigel's ex-wife here?' I asked.

'Owen, I thought you were going to behave?' he replied sternly.

'I am behaving! I'm not going to go and talk to her!' I said innocently.

'Good!'

There was a pause as we both supped our ales.

'Unless, of course, she wants to talk, you know, and say how great Nigel is and even though they are divorced she still supports his political career. Would play really well with women voters, I reckon...' I trailed off as Gawain stared at me.

'No, Owen.'

Before I could start trying to persuade him, Farage himself came over. Out of the corner of my eye I could see his ex-wife disappearing out of the door. I could hardly give chase to her now, with Farage and Towler standing either side of me.

'Hello, Owen,' said Farage. Another beer was ordered. After the finger-jabbing moment earlier on I wondered if Farage had taken a dislike to me, but he seemed more than happy to share a beer.

'Did you enjoy tonight?' I asked.

'Yes, it was good fun, wasn't it?' he replied with a broad smile.

'Yes, people certainly seemed to enjoy it. There was one woman in the second row who almost threw her knickers at you,' I joked.

Farage laughed and carried on drinking.

I noticed a slight grimace on his face as he put his pint glass down on the bar.

'Everything OK?' I asked.

'I still have some problems because of the plane crash,' he said.

We chatted about his health, the back surgery he'd had just a few months earlier and how he was still in a lot of pain.

Just a few weeks later, while appearing on Channel 4's *Gogglebox* spin-off programme *Steph and Dom Meet Nigel Farage*, the UKIP leader dropped a glass of champagne due to a spasm in his hand – evidence that he was still suffering from the effects of the accident.

Maybe it was the beer talking, but I found myself telling Farage how impressed I had been with his performance tonight.

'I'll be honest, Nigel, I don't think Cameron, Miliband or even Clegg would be able to stand on a stage, speak to a room full of people without notes for fifteen minutes, and then take a host of non-prepared questions from whoever had just walked through the door. It's pretty impressive, but then, no offence, it shouldn't be, should it?'

Farage agreed: 'Exactly, I've never said I'm that special, it's just that the others are so useless.'

He was then accosted by a fan who wanted a picture with him, and my time with the People's Army field marshal was at an end. I watched Arsenal concede a last-minute equaliser and got a taxi to the station to go home.

Visiting Rochester became a regular occurrence, as did speaking to Farage. The trouble was that, working for the *Daily Express*, it was difficult to come up with new things to ask him.

Whatever your view of the *Daily Express*, it does have a very strong brand, and appeals to a significant number of people. In 2014, its January average circulation was 500,473 – more than *The Times* (384,304), the *Financial Times* (234,193), twice as large as *The Guardian* (207,958) and more than seven times the circulation of *The Independent* (66,576).

The paper is often mocked for its 'Diana, diabetes and weather' front pages, but these were clearly of interest to an awful lot of people.

When it comes to politics, the paper knows which side its bread is buttered – that's a loaf of Farmhouse English bread with British butter, of course. Anti-EU, anti-freedom of movement, anti-Labour. As an *Express* journalist, it didn't matter what my view was. My job was to write for the audience of the organisation that was paying my wages. When it came to UKIP, it was always a case of 'more of the same'.

Farage knew this, and he knew he got traction out of the *Express* that he wouldn't get from other papers. When I interviewed him in UKIP's Rochester headquarters on 17 October, he told me a million more migrants would come to the UK before David Cameron's proposed EU referendum in 2017. It seemed like he had just plucked the number out of thin air, and I pressed him on how he'd got to the million figure.

He said:

> At the moment it's a quarter of a million people a year. The referendum is in three years' time, and the eurozone is going down the pan as we speak, so the numbers coming can only increase. The situation in Greece today, in Italy, is very, very serious, so up to a million more will come before

that referendum takes place. So given that the argument is
about wage compression, lack of primary school places and
health-care provision and this process will last several years,
it simply isn't good enough.

'A quarter of a million over three years would still only lead to
750,000,' I said.

Farage again reiterated that it would be more than 250,000 a year
as the Italian and Greek economies were performing so badly.

He knew he was talking to an *Express* journalist; he knew it was
what my editor would love to hear, and he knew my scepticism of the
figures wouldn't make it into the copy. At least I was now grilling him
on his proclamations instead of watching someone else question
him while I took photographs, as I had done outside the Westminster Arms in 2013. Andrew Lowry would be proud.

The next day, the *Express* duly obliged, and his forecast was splashed
on the front page: 'IM MIGRANTS TO FLOOD BRITAIN'.

What was that about the media always being against UKIP?

Normal service was resumed, at least in the 'the media are always
out to get us' UKIP way, just two days before the by-election was
due to take place.

Appearing in hustings on *ITV News Meridian*, Reckless was asked
by an audience member: 'What would happen if we left the European Union? What would happen for instance to the Polish plumber
who lives in Rochester? Would he be able to stay, would he have to
go back?'

Reckless replied: 'Well, I think in the near term we'd have to have a
transitional period, and I think we should probably allow people who
are currently here to have a work permit at least for a fixed period.'

The presenter jumped in: 'Forgive me, if there's a Polish plumber
who, for instance, has got a house, got a family, got kids at a local
school, are you going to deport him and his family?'

Reckless said:

I think people who have been here a long time and integrated
in that way, I think we'd want to look sympathetically at.
But what we'd want to do is new people coming in [inter-
rupted by laughs from the crowd] … what we'd want to do
is to look at new people coming in and apply a consistent,
Australian-style points system and the same to people coming
from Europe as we do to those coming from, say, the Commonwealth, from Australia, Africa, India, the Caribbean.

He finished by saying: 'We shouldn't have a discriminatory system
which favours Europeans against people from the outside.'

This sounded dangerously liked enforced repatriation, which is
dangerously close to the British National Party, which is dangerously
close to all-out fascism.

There was uproar in the media, and UKIP quickly tried to extin-
guish the flames by blaming the Tories for the outcry.

A spokesman said:

UKIP and Mark have always been completely clear on this.
Do not believe the desperate last throw of the dice from the
Conservative Party. There is no intention whatsoever to back-
date future border controls to penalise those already here.
Mark simply made the absolutely common-sense point that
there will be a period after future border control arrangements
have been agreed before they come into effect.

That was not exactly what he said and, when he took to *ITV News
Meridian* later the next day, he managed to tie himself up in knots
again: 'We would allow people from the EU who are already here to
have a work permit which would allow them to stay.'

But, later in the same interview, he said: 'We're planning to allow
people to stay who are already in the country.'

If UKIP would let people stay who are already here, why would

they need a work permit based on 'an Australian-style points system'? It seemed that what Reckless was saying was if you're an EU
migrant already here, you can only stay if you have a work permit.
When challenged, he claimed everyone could stay.

Farage tried to help matters by saying Reckless was suffering from
'confusion'. The UKIP leader said:

> We have never suggested since 2004 that anybody who has
> come here legally and in good faith should be subject to
> retrospective legislation ... that would be unfair, un-British
> and wrong.
>
> Let me make this clear: during our divorce negotiations,
> even if the European Union was to behave badly, and was
> to say people living in Spain would be threatened with not
> being there, we would maintain the line that we believe in
> the rule of law, we believe in British justice, we believe any-
> body who has come to Britain legally has the right to remain.

Reckless's fuzzy thinking on what to do with EU migrants already
living in the UK may have caused UKIP some bad headlines, but it
didn't make a dent in the opinion polls – heading into election day,
the party was still favourite to win its second by-election.

Come Thursday 20 November, the day of the by-election, and all
Labour had to do was keep quiet. Just keep its collective head down,
and the by-election would have been about Cameron losing another
seat to UKIP.

Obviously as the main opposition party, Labour had to show it
was trying to win the seat, but the story wasn't about them; it was
about UKIP and Cameron. Ed Miliband's party was never going to
win – despite possessing an excellent candidate in Naushabah Khan –
so the party just had to stay out of the way of UKIP's People's Army
attacking Fort Tory.

But they didn't, and so instead of the next day's headlines being about another glorious victory for Nigel Farage, they were about a three-word tweet from Labour's shadow Attorney General, Emily Thornberry.

Like all loyal Labour folk, Thornberry had ventured down to Rochester to help local activists knock on doors and persuade supporters to come out and vote. I too had ventured down to Rochester, not to canvass of course, but to report on the election count. At about 3 p.m. I checked into my hotel in Gillingham, located next to the leisure centre where the count would begin that evening. Anticipating a long night ahead, I planned on having an afternoon nap before the count.

When I checked into my room, I discovered a large jacket and set of keys on the bed. There was also a muddy footprint on the blanket, and the window, which looked out onto a flat roof, was open. Had someone broken into my room before I checked in? Maybe my rivals at the *Daily Mail* were trying to bug my room, and they had fled just before I came through the door. I tried to call down to reception but the phone wasn't working.

I went down and told one of the hotel staff I thought my room had been broken into. I didn't mention my suspicions about the bugging, as she might have been in on it.

'Sorry, mate,' said a gruff voice behind me. 'I was doing some work on the roof and using your room to get onto it.'

We went upstairs to my room and he collected his things, plugged the phone back in (he didn't say why it was unplugged and for some reason I didn't want to ask) and left. I tried to shut the window but it was jammed open. The cold November air was blowing in and it was ruining my chance of getting some sleep. The maintenance man who had just left my room suddenly appeared on the roof, whistling to himself as he walked past my window.

'Excuse me,' I shouted over. 'My window is jammed open, do you think you could come in and fix it?'

He ambled over, looked me in the eye like the weak fool I am, and with his big, black boot kicked the window shut.

'Thank you!' I shouted through the glass.

If a speech bubble had appeared above his head at that moment with his thoughts about me in it, it would have shown just one word: 'Twat'.

At almost exactly the same time as the hotel's maintenance man was using his foot to shut my window, Emily Thornberry was putting her foot in her mouth.

While out canvassing, the Islington South & Finsbury MP came across a house displaying three St George's flags – one with a West Ham crest in the middle – and a white van in the drive. She took a photo of it and tweeted the picture with the words: 'Image from #Rochester'.

The Twittersphere went into meltdown.

In the minds of many, this was a perfect example of the metropolitan, north London elite sneering at the ordinary white-van man.

What was so noteworthy of someone flying St George's flags? Why did it warrant a photo being taken and put online? Why use the words 'Image from #Rochester', as if this sort of display of patriotism was coming from some far-flung part of the country?

It perfectly summed up Farage's attacks on Labour – a party run by a snobby elite who not only don't understand ordinary people, but have an actual disdain for them.

It was perfect for UKIP, and it was perfect for those Tory-supporting sections of the media who didn't know how to play another UKIP victory. Instead of piling praise on UKIP, or attacking Cameron, they could now lambast Labour.

Within hours of the tweet, journalists were despatched to the address to find out if the person who lived in the house shared the indignation of those who had seen the picture.

The Sun's Emily Ashton was the first on scene, and by now Thornberry had made the situation worse by telling the *Mail* online: 'It was a house covered in British flags. I've never seen anything like it before. It had three huge flags covering the whole house. I thought it was remarkable. I've never seen a house completely covered in flags.'

Ashton kept house-owner Dan Ware, a 37-year-old cage-fighting car dealer, who didn't even know there was a by-election going on, talking long enough for a photographer from *The Sun* to rock up and grab some snaps.

Farage got in on the act through his official Twitter account, posting 'What is Labour's Emily Thornberry trying to imply about Rochester and Strood? I suspect she's let Miliband's mask slip.' By the end of the night, the Labour leader ordered Thornberry to resign, and, by the next morning, Dan Ware was outside her house demanding an apology.

The Sun's front page the next day was 'ONLY HERE FOR THE SNEERS', and Labour had successfully managed to deflect attention away from the Tories losing a second by-election to UKIP.

Thornberry's actions were the talk of the journalists at that evening's election count. We needed something to while away the hours, as it went on ever longer than the one in Clacton the month before.

The Rochester count was held in a leisure centre, with a temporary stage constructed for the TV crews, and below them were rows of tables for print and online journalists. The parties all had their own tables in a cordoned-off area, just in front of the stage where the declaration was to take place.

In a repeat of Clacton, Priti Patel was down for the Tories and Chris Bryant was representing Labour. The two sparred on TV and radio at regular intervals, with Paul Nuttall from UKIP making up the trio.

Also there was Tracey Crouch, the football-playing Tory MP from the nearby Chatham & Aylesford constituency. I'm not sure what her official job was supposed to be that night, but I can tell you that more than one journalist came away from that evening thinking she was one of the funniest, friendliest, most 'normal' MPs they had ever come across. Crouch's confidence and approachability was a complete contrast to Reckless, who always looks as if he's just walked into a room he shouldn't have, and is hoping no one noticed.

If Crouch was providing the light that night, the shade was very much coming from Britain First. The far-right anti-Islamic group was contesting its first Westminster election, with deputy leader Jayda

Fransen standing. The group had achieved a small degree of notoriety in the months before the by-election for invading mosques and ranting at Muslims. In the Rochester by-election campaign, Fransen decided to get more political, and invaded the Tory HQ in the town.

She ranted about a so-called 'mega mosque' being built in Gillingham – which is not even part of the Rochester & Strood constituency – while Tory press officer Richard Holden tried his best to get her out of the office. As she repeatedly claimed the Tories weren't standing up for locals who were opposed to the mosque (the opposition was mainly on the grounds of the loss of a pay-and-display car park near the train station, not religious concerns), a worried-looking Holden asked: 'Could you leave please?' Forty-four times.

The presence of Britain First in the campaign had caused a headache for UKIP. This anti-Muslim, xenophobic group had been urging people to back Farage's party, and even put the slogan 'UKIP at the ballot box, Britain First on the streets – a winning combination' on its campaign literature.

UKIP, already sensitive to charges of xenophobia, had to warn its campaigners not to be associated with the group after three of the party's activists posed for a picture with Fransen, which was then uploaded to the Britain First Facebook page.

At the election count, Fransen and her cohorts sat round a table in the hall, muttering to each other for most of the night. In their dark green fleeces, they looked less like a people's militia and more like employees at a National Trust gift shop.

That was perhaps the reason BBC political editor Nick Robinson agreed to pose for a picture with Fransen. After the inevitable Twitter backlash, Robinson said he thought Fransen was a worker at the count. He tweeted: 'Lesson of the day. Never agree to have selfie taken without first checking who's asking. Shame but my mistake.'

The candidates arrived at various points as the night went on – Kelly Tolhurst for the Tories first, then Mark Reckless later. The greatest fuss was saved, of course, for Farage, who arrived with his newly appointed chief of staff, Raheem Kassam, at about 2.45 a.m. Just as in Clacton, the photographers and camera crews waited behind an imaginary line until the last possible moment, then sprung forward as Farage appeared.

His walk down the corridor from the leisure centre reception to the hall itself was particularly precarious, as a horde of photographers, camera crews and journalists walked backwards in one indistinguishable blob while the leader marched onwards. One slip from anyone and they probably would have been trampled on and seriously injured.

I found myself caught up in this moving media monolith when I came out of the toilet just as the procession was passing. I managed to escape the mob mere moments before a particularly aggressive-looking hand rail in the middle of the corridor was due to make contact with me in an area that would have left my eyes severely watering.

Alas for everyone in hall, Farage's arrival did not signify we were near to getting a result. The counting was still going, thanks in part to a number of local elections that had also taken place that day.

My night was about to get worse to the tune of £1.65, thanks to the combined effort of Bloomberg's Rob Hutton, the leader of the Monster Raving Loony Party and a banana.

Hutton was responsible for the £1 of that figure after he invited me to take part in the sweepstake on what the UKIP majority would be. The 65p was wasted on a banana I bought in the café, only to return to the hall to see Howling Laud Hope giving out fruit for free to everyone in the room. At 3 a.m., those things matter and it put me in a bad mood.

My mood soon went from angry to confused when one of the independent candidates appeared dressed as Father Christmas while riding a motorised scooter decorated with fairy lights, talking very seriously about the threat of nuclear war. I thought the banana I had eaten might have gone bad and I was hallucinating, but I was assured by equally bewildered colleagues that this was actually happening.

An hour later, and still no result, but I noticed Farage and Reckless engaged in deep conversation near the exit doors. I sidled over to listen in, on the premise of looking for a bin for my half-eaten banana.

Farage was telling Reckless that after the results were announced he would slip away as this was 'your night'. I had never thought of Farage slipping away anywhere, but even in my tired state I realised this meant the declaration was imminent.

As Hugo Fenwick, the returning officer and High Sheriff of Kent, took to the stage, hacks crouched over laptops and tablets, desperate to be the first to tweet out the result. The fact that the only people still awake who would care about the result were in the room with us, and therefore unlikely to get the news from Twitter, didn't matter. It was like a version of the Fastest Finger First round on *Who Wants to Be a Millionaire?* – except truly and utterly pointless.

The candidates lined up on the stage like they were waiting for a bus, Reckless standing nearest the returning officer, trying to hide a grin. The Father Christmas candidate must have been bending someone's ear about how nuclear waste had turned one of his reindeer's noses red as he was nowhere to be seen until the results started to be read out. He suddenly shuffled past the bottom of the stage and positioned himself at the end of the line.

Despite wearing a full Father Christmas costume, he wasn't the most ridiculous character on the platform. That honour didn't even go the Official Monster Raving Loony Party candidate Hairy Knorm Davidson. Britain First's Jayda Fransen, who won just fifty-six votes despite her claim to 'speak for the people', celebrated her measly total by shouting 'no more mosques' with a big smile on her face.

Tory candidate Kelly Tolhurst also had a smile on her face, but hers seemed to be painted on and remained entirely fixed in position as the returning officer announced she had won 13,947 votes, 2,920 fewer than Reckless. Ukippers, including Farage, cheered as Reckless approached the microphone to deliver his victory speech. In Clacton, Carswell used his address to paint a vision of a new and inclusive UKIP. Would Reckless do the same?

I'll be honest, if you had asked me after his speech what he had said, I don't think I could have told you. I completely zoned out. It was gone 4.15 a.m., and Reckless, in his monotone, trotting voice, just faded into the horizon.

I knew he was there, and I knew he was speaking, but I just couldn't get a mental handle on it. I'm pretty sure he did all the usual stuff like thanking the police and other candidates, but then he veered off and talked about the Chartists and Gladstonian economics, and my brain just said 'no'.

I think there was a dig at journalists in there as well, and maybe something about how UKIP was tolerant of all races no matter what anybody says. I've watched it back on YouTube a few times since to try to take notes, but I can't take anything in. His speeches are like Terry Pratchett's description of Death in the Discworld novels – my brain just cannot accept what is happening.

As Reckless was speaking, Farage was edging out the door. Of course he was.

With the result declared, laptops were snapped shut, chairs were pushed under tables and coats were thrown on. In an instant, the press pack had escaped from the artificial light of the leisure centre hall and into the natural darkness of its car park.

Despite the collective fatigue, we all wanted a drink, and managed to find out the location of the UKIP victory party. It was at the Tap 'n' Tin in Chatham, a short drive from the leisure centre, and we decided that, even though we had been told we wouldn't be allowed in, if we all turned up, UKIP would welcome us into the party with open arms.

I'm not really sure why we thought this, but thought this we did.

So, at almost 5 a.m. on Friday 21 November, Elizabeth Rigby from the *Financial Times*, Christopher Hope from the *Daily Telegraph*, Rowena Mason from *The Guardian*, William James from Reuters and I tried to gatecrash a UKIP party.

The bouncers were having none of it. We weren't on the list so we weren't coming in. We pleaded and begged, and pleaded some more, but to no avail. I was a student again, trying to get into Ocean nightclub in Nottingham on a Friday night when it was already full.

Except I wasn't trying to get into a cheesy club full of cheap drinks and drunk students, I was trying to get into a UKIP victory party. Had I gone up or down in the world?

Eventually Gawain Towler emerged and, in true Pontius Pilate style, washed his hands of us. Apparently the Kippers wanted to have a good time and let their hair down, and with us inside they wouldn't be able to.

'I wouldn't let you lot at them for all the tea in China,' were his words.

He was right not to, of course, but, alas for poor Towler, someone else in UKIP had already let in a journalist.

Somehow Richard Gaisford from *Good Morning Britain* was in the building, and happily tweeting out pictures of Farage queuing up for a pint at the bar.

I know the precise moment Towler found out about this as, while we were waiting for the taxi to take us back to our respective hotels, he stormed out of the Tap'n' Tin, swore loudly, and then with a giant swing of his right arm sent an empty lager can that had been perched on a handrail flying down the street.

He then stormed off into the night.

I felt a bit sorry for him. Once upon time he would have known every person in that party, but now journalists of all people were getting let in without his permission, or even knowledge.

A few hours' sleep and I was back in Rochester high street.

As with Carswell in Clacton, the order of the day was to get an interview with the glorious victor. A Ukipper told me it wasn't possible, but before I could go all 'Oh, hiding from the press already, is he? Well that lasted long, didn't it?' the Kipper said Reckless was already in Parliament. He had got on a train first thing that morning to take part in an NHS debate in the Commons.

It was hard to argue with that, so I swallowed down my self-righteous indignation and asked if Farage was about. 'Yes,' the Ukipper told me, and said if I waited outside the party HQ I could get a chat with him.

Predictably, all the other hacks were already there, all looking shattered. It was different for the Kippers, as they had adrenalin and a sense of achievement to keep them going. We just had permanently demanding news desks.

We waited in front of the HQ to be summoned in to see Farage. As with Clacton, chaos seemed to be reigning as we were told the interview would be 'soon', 'a while', 'definitely happening', 'maybe not happening', all at the same time.

Eventually, Towler opened the door and said we could all come in soon. Except Tamara Cohen from the *Daily Mail*. With that, he shut the door and went back inside. We were all perplexed, especially Tamara. What had she done to incur the wrath of Farage?

'The only thing I can think of is that I went to see his ex-wife the other day to see if she would be interviewed. She said "no", so I left. But I wasn't even the only one!' she said.

Towler stuck his head round the door to invite us in, minus Cohen.

Before he could get the words out, Rob Hutton said: 'Tell Nigel that if he wants to be a proper leader and a proper politician he needs to start acting like one. He can't pick and choose which journalists come into press conferences.'

Towler disappeared again.

This was becoming a worrying pattern. In Clacton, Hutton had been excluded from interviewing Douglas Carswell after his victory, without a reason being given.

Today, it was Cohen – again with no reason.

I know journalists are not held in particularly high regard, and the words 'moral high ground' are not associated with us by most members of the public, but there is an 'honour among thieves' aspect to the profession. We decided that unless Cohen was allowed in with us, none of us would interview Farage.

We were about to decamp to the Deaf Cat café when Towler opened the door again and invited us inside. Before he could say anything we marched in as one group with Cohen smuggled through in the middle of the pack – a Trojan Horse tactic. Within seconds we were all sat down in the back room of the HQ, and, after Farage finished his cigarette, he sat at the desk and the inquisition began.

The questions mainly focused on whether there would be another defector before the general election fewer than seven months away. Farage seemed confident and said: 'I would be very surprised if there weren't defections between now and the general election.' (Spoiler alert: there weren't. Whether Farage knew this at the time is immaterial. He knew just saying it would panic the Tories and Labour, and keep us journos writing and speculating – more coverage for UKIP.)

After more than ten minutes of questions about further defections, I asked about how the party would function with two representatives in the Commons. 'Are Carswell and Reckless now setting UKIP policy based on their votes in the House of Commons?' I asked.

Farage replied: 'I love this question. It's a wonderful Westminster question and it shows you why the country is in the mess that it's in…'

'Because of my question?' I asked. 'That's a lot of pressure, Nigel.'

'Absolutely! The political commentariat in this country think we have a House of Parliament that makes law. It doesn't! Nearly all of our laws are made somewhere else. MEPs vote on far more issues…'

'So why do you want to be in the House of Commons then?' I interrupted.

'Hang on,' Farage snapped back:

> MEPs vote on far more legislative issues as members of the European Union than any Member of Parliament does. The only big votes that really come up in the House of Commons that would, in a sense, point what UKIP's national policy is, would be on big issues like Syria, for argument's sake. But in terms of how we run our economic life, our business, our

energy policy, how we manage financial services, none of
that is decided in Westminster.

Of course, what I didn't quite grasp at the time, mainly due to lack of
sleep, was that Farage was asserting his authority over UKIP's new
parliamentary party. He was really saying: 'Reckless and Carswell
may be in the Commons, but I, Nigel Farage, am in the European
Parliament, which trumps it. I am still the boss. I set the policy. And
don't you forget it.'

Just before the press conference came to an end, Hutton got in
one last question: 'As UKIP isn't a racist party, how worried are you
that your candidate seemed to support repatriation, so it seemed that
UKIP supported repatriation?'

Farage replied: 'I didn't hear him say that, if you did, let me know
and we'll talk about it.'

Hutton came back: 'Well, we all did.'

'No, no, you didn't hear him say that,' said Farage:

> What he talked about was the complex question of transi-
> tional arrangements, so we leave the EU, we invoke Article 50,
> there's a two-year transition and that was picked up and
> blown out of all proportion.
>
> All I would say to you on that is ever since 2004, when
> this first became a big campaigning issue for us, in every sin-
> gle talk I've done on this subject, while I think it's madness
> to have an open door to ten former communist countries,
> many of whom have not made a proper transition to what
> we would call Western-style democracy, while I think that's
> madness, anybody [who] legally has come to this country in
> good faith has every right to be here.
>
> We have always said that, and maintained that, and I
> thought that the way Mark described that in his speech last
> night just puts that to bed.

No matter how hard Farage was trying to spin it, Hutton was right. Reckless had said: 'We'd have to have a transitional period, and I think we should probably allow people who are currently here to have a work permit at least for a fixed period.' By implication, when the work permit is up, they are no longer legally allowed to be in the country.

With the press conference over, we traipsed out of the HQ. Kippers were taking down signs, removing papers, even boxing up unsold UKIP mugs. Hutton tried to go back inside to see if he could buy one, but a Kipper stood in front of the door, arms folded, not letting him pass.

CHAPTER 9

THE MAN WHO WOULD BE CHAMP

AS NIGEL FARAGE FREQUENTLY points out, UKIP supporters are not just 'retired half colonels living on the edge of Salisbury Plain desperate for the re-introduction of the birch and only cheering up after the first pink gin of the day'.

Although, as he admits, the party does tend to do well with that demographic.

No, the People's Army is a broad church, and in its ranks it has many who rail against that stereotype. But there is one man in particular who is as far removed from being a retired half colonel as you can get.

A man who has been a member of the Liberal Democrats, the Conservatives, and UKIP spin-off Veritas, who stood for London Mayor as an independent and even formed his own short-lived political party.

A man who was England amateur boxing champion, ran a pub that was demolished after police raids, and, when he joined UKIP, almost immediately challenged Nigel Farage for the party's leadership.

By December 2014, he had stood in ten parliamentary, mayoral, council and party leadership elections in eleven years – losing them all.

He even auditioned for *The X-Factor* – unsuccessfully.

If there was an award for sheer determination, then UKIP's Winston McKenzie would beat even Eddie the Eagle.

I simply had to meet him.

I first became aware of McKenzie at UKIP's 'We're not racist!' conference in Westminster ahead of 2014's European elections. The Jamaican-born Commonwealth spokesman was one of the last speakers before Nigel Farage took to the stage, and won his own standing ovation by proclaiming: 'I'm black and I'm proud and I'll shout it out loud.'

McKenzie may have been one in a crowd of many Kippers that night, but he hit the headlines in his own right less than a fortnight later.

Just two days before polls opened in the European election, UKIP decided what it really needed to shore up support was a multi-racial 'Carnival of Colour' in Croydon, south London, where McKenzie was standing for the local council. He was tasked with arranging the event, which would highlight the party's inclusive nature and wide appeal.

The London Borough of Croydon is one of the most diverse regions in the country, with those classed as White British in the minority – 47.3 per cent of the 363,000 residents. Black Caribbeans are the second largest, at 8.6 per cent, with Indians the third largest – 6.8 per cent. According to the 2011 census, there are eighteen ethnic groups in Croydon. With this variety of races and backgrounds, a successful 'Carnival of Colour' would surely show just how inclusive UKIP was?

McKenzie booked a steel band to provide the entertainment, rounded up local activists to swamp the streets and arranged for Farage himself to address the predicted hordes of revellers dancing along to UKIP's Caribbean beat.

What could possibly go wrong?

Pretty much everything.

The steel band downed sticks when they learned who had organised the event, with the leader saying: 'To be seen here by many people [who] know us sets a different tone for our organisation and the young people I work with – I didn't know it was for UKIP.'

The expected hordes of pro-Ukippers didn't show up, but groups of anti-Ukippers did descend on the borough – successfully causing carnage and disrupting the gathering.

Farage, who was parked up round the corner waiting to make his big entrance, heard about the aggravation and cancelled his appearance at the last minute due to safety concerns ('He wouldn't feel safe and can you blame him?' McKenzie told reporters).

The day was a disaster for UKIP, making the leadership look as if they genuinely thought all concerns over their attitude towards race had disappeared since the gathering in Westminster less than a fortnight before. At the centre of the inevitable media scrum was Winston McKenzie, who managed to make a bad situation worse by telling a reporter from the local newspaper: 'Croydon at the moment is an absolute dump.'

Journalists had a field day – a UKIP candidate calling the area in which he is standing for election a 'dump' was without doubt a great story. Another UKIP gaffe to file away with the many others. What didn't get the same media coverage was the anti-UKIP 'Romanian' protesters who turned up to heckle the gathering. One woman brandished a sign reading: 'We are Romanians and we don't feel comfortable with racism.'

BBC producer Paul Lambert – known as 'Gobby' in media circles – asked a protester where in Romania she was from. It turned out she wasn't Romanian, nor had she even been to Romania.

Another protester, this time with a placard reading 'Nigel Farage Racist Scum', said it 'doesn't matter' whether the woman holding the sign saying she was Romanian was in fact Romanian. According to her, if Romanians are insulted, then we are all Romanians. She even told Channel 4 journalist Michael Crick that he was in fact a Romanian, to which he replied: 'No, I was born in Northampton.'

Whether the debacle of the carnival and the 'Croydon is a dump' line ultimately affected McKenzie's chances in the council election held just days later is hard to know. But what is certain is that he did not win any of the three seats up for grabs in the ward of South Norwood – instead coming in ninth and securing just 480 votes out of the 12,268 cast. As a man used to election disappointment, McKenzie quickly dusted himself off and put on a brave face for the TV crews at the Croydon count. In an interview with the BBC's David Dimbleby during the channel's coverage of the UK council elections, he was his usual animated self, proclaiming: 'The UKIP fox came along and feathers are rustling tonight, there are feathers everywhere.' He repeated the line on Sky News, telling Adam Boulton: 'What I can hear is UKIP, UKIP, UKIP and I understand the UKIP fox has struck yet again. He's struck and there are feathers everywhere.'

McKenzie clearly relished the media spotlight.

His next major appearance on national television was to defend the 'UKIP Calypso' song recorded by former Radio 1 DJ – and party supporter – Mike Read. The acoustic ditty featured Read singing in a faux-Jamaican accent, with lyrics eulogising Farage and painting a vision of the country under a UKIP government.

These included: 'Our leaders committed a cardinal sin / Open the borders let them all come in / Illegal immigrants in every town / Stand up and be counted Blair and Brown.'

And: 'With the EU we must be on our mettle / They want to change our lawnmowers and our kettles / Our hairdryers, smartphones and vacuum cleaners / But UKIP is wise to their misdemeanours.'

Read must have been pretty pleased with the chorus, repeating it six times throughout the song: 'Oh yes when we take charge / And the new Prime Minister is Farage / We can trade with the world again / When Nigel is at Number 10.'

The song received its live debut at UKIP's 2014 conference in Doncaster at an invite-only gala dinner, but it was only when it was released online for people to buy at the end of October that it caused a furore. Farage's official Twitter account endorsed the track, and, within minutes, newsrooms in Westminster were drowning in the sound of Mike Read and his cod-Caribbean accent as hacks digested the latest UKIP gaffe.

Despite its questionable musical merits, the tune clearly struck a chord with some people in Britain as, within three days of its release, it had reached No. 2 in the Amazon MP3 bestsellers list. According to the mid-week rundown, the song was at No. 21, meaning it was well on the way to being in the official top 40 when the chart ended that week. But, while the tune was lauded and applauded by lots of UKIP supporters, many felt it was outright racist. Labour's David Lammy, the black MP for Tottenham, said:

> If we needed any more evidence of the UKIP leadership being tone-deaf elitists then look no further. Their ruthless pursuit of power, using references to Bongo Bongo Land one day and cod-Caribbean accents the next, will be found out for what it is: a nasty creed of politics based on fear-mongering and resentment. UKIP's claim that they are not a racist party gets more and more incredible with every scandal.

Controversy around the song even reached BBC Two's flagship current affairs programme *Newsnight*, and, on 20 October 2014, a section of the programme was devoted to the question of whether the track was offensive.

Jamaican-born McKenzie was booked on the show to defend the song – something that the UKIP high command knew nothing about. *Newsnight* had approached McKenzie directly, completely cutting out UKIP's press office. The first anyone in the party heard about him appearing on the show was when *Newsnight* tweeted ten minutes before the start: 'We will be asking @TherealNihal & @Winston-McK whether this number from Mike Read's UKIP Calypso Song is offensive.'

The UKIP top brass frantically called and messaged each other to find out who had authorised McKenzie to be sent in to bat on the party's behalf. Once they realised no one had, and he was operating behind enemy lines without authorisation, they nervously sat down to watch the show, fully prepared for yet another media storm.

After telling presenter Evan Davis 'I've heard a lot about you' and shaking his hand, McKenzie leaned back in his chair and said:

> This guy [Mike Read] is good, man – he's almost as good as me! Now look, I'm hearing so much about this this evening – it's just crazy, I can't understand it. Ever since the beginning of time, the Beatles, Elvis, the Rolling Stones, they've taken off the black man's music. When I heard this song for the very first time I thought to myself, 'A white boy, singing calypso – fantastic.'

BBC Asian Network DJ Nihal was on the show to put forward the alternative view, and left viewers in no doubt of his thoughts when asked by the presenter what his initial reaction was to the tune.

'My initial reaction was it made my ears vomit,' he replied.

Nihal and McKenzie began trading verbal blows, but, after being interrupted one too many times by the DJ, the UKIP man told him: 'I'm an ex-boxer you know, don't get shirty with me.'

Davis tried to control proceedings, repeatedly appealing to McKenzie to stop interrupting his questions to Nihal.

Clearly, Davis had not come up against too many politicians like McKenzie before, and broke away from talking about the calypso to focus instead on the Ukipper's role within the party.

McKenzie gave a passionate recounting of his attempt to organise a Commonwealth trade fair in London, but it was his status as a black man in a supposedly 'racist' party that intrigued Davies.

'All the UKIP guys who I mix with, who I get on with, these guys are 100 per cent, they are down to earth,' said McKenzie.

After asking him why UKIP had aligned with a holocaust-denier in the European Parliament – 'I've not heard a single word about the story, I presume it's more lies from the PC brigade,' responded McKenzie – Davis brought the interview to a close.

To my mind, there were no obvious gaffes, and even McKenzie's jest that he wanted to punch Nihal was clearly a joke.

The next day it was McKenzie who received a beating – albeit a metaphorical one – from certain media outlets.

The *Huffington Post* website published an article headlined: 'Winston McKenzie defends the UKIP Calypso in the most bizarre *Newsnight* debate ever.' The article went on to say the interview was 'arguably the most utterly bizarre *Newsnight* segment in the show's history'. It added that Nihal 'did well not to walk away from the farcical argument' as McKenzie launched into 'a tenuous argument about how UKIP isn't racist'.

From what I could see, all McKenzie had done was stick to the party line, question why everyone was getting so overexcited about the incident and talk over his opponent on a political TV show – like every other politician basically.

His defence of Mike Read singing in a Caribbean accent had a logic to it – London-born Mick Jagger has made a career singing in an American accent. He could have also referenced Sting – a Geordie who sang early Police records with a Caribbean twang, or even Stockport band 10cc's 1978 hit 'Dreadlock Holiday', which espoused the wonders of a holiday in Jamaica. I'm not saying for a moment that I like the 'UKIP Calypso' song, but surely it was the lyrics more than the style of music that were offensive? I was struggling to see how singing a Jamaican style of music in a Jamaican accent was worthy of such outrage.

I was also perplexed at some of the criticism of McKenzie. At a time when politicians are criticised for all sounding the same, he came across to me as a genuine guy from south London – a little rough around the edges, sure, but was that a bad thing? Also, if a Jamaican-born immigrant to Britain did not find either the song nor his UKIP colleagues 'racist', why does his expression of that view make his argument 'tenuous'?

The unthinkable was happening, I was starting to feel sorry for someone in UKIP.

I needed to meet McKenzie to see for myself if he was the clumsy buffoon portrayed by the media, or the rough-and-ready normal bloke I was beginning to think he was. I emailed him asking if I could join him on the campaign trail to see him in action.

His PA Marianne Bowness replied: 'Hi Owen, Winston is certainly prepared to spend a full day with you. What would his fee be? A Sunday would be a good call, as a respectful amount of support for him comes from the black Churches. You are welcome to give me a ring a.s.a.p.'

I mulled over the email. His fee? I didn't expect to have to pay to spend time with McKenzie.

I called Bowness up, thanked her for the reply and asked which days would be best. I didn't mention any fee – maybe when she remembers I'm a journalist she'll realise it wouldn't be appropriate to ask for any money. But no, she was keen to know how much I would pay for a day with McKenzie.

Bowness was polite but firm, and I found myself stammering like a schoolboy as I said: 'I'll be honest, I, um, wasn't really expecting to, you know, pay anything. I just wanted to come down and see Winston on the campaign trail and then write something for the *Daily Express*,' I added in a whiney tone.

Bowness was not to be moved, and replied this was McKenzie's job, and one of the ways he made money, so he charges. I asked how much.

'Usually about £500,' was the reply.

FIVE HUNDRED POUNDS to spend the day with Winston McKenzie. This is a list of people I would spend £500 to spend the day with: Noel Gallagher, David Bowie, David Ginola and Jennifer Lawrence.

Not Winston McKenzie.

I told Bowness I couldn't afford it and left it at that. A few minutes later I had a call from McKenzie himself, assuring me it would be money well spent, and he would arrange a great day for me. After reiterating my enthusiasm to meet him, but my inability to raise the necessary £500, he relented, and lowered the fee by a couple of hundred pounds. Again, I said it wasn't possible. And that was that, or so I thought.

A couple of days later McKenzie called me up and asked if I had got any money I could put towards the day with him. Again, I said no, and told him I really didn't want anything special planned, just to accompany him on the campaign trail. 'It will be good publicity,' I said. Eventually, he agreed. No money was to change hands, but I did offer to buy him lunch.

And so it was that on Friday 5 December I travelled the relatively short journey from my flat in Mile End, east London, to South Norwood in Croydon to meet the man himself.

We arranged to meet outside a Wetherspoons pub on South Norwood high street.

The street was full of takeaways, independent shops and mini supermarkets. It was a cold morning and people were shuffling past wrapped up in scarfs and gloves, heads down, eyes on the pavement.

After waiting in the cold for a few minutes I saw McKenzie pacing towards me. He may not have boxed for thirty years but he still had the boxer's walk – precise, purposeful and with rolling shoulders.

He was wearing one of his trademark hats (this time a black trilby), a smart suit and a UKIP rosette. He was flanked by two men – both white and middle-aged. They weren't exactly hard-looking, but certainly not soft either. His outfit combined with his small entourage gave him the appearance of a low-level fight promoter.

McKenzie approached with a smile, shook my hand and told me the two men were fellow Ukippers from the Croydon branch. After the introductions, we set off along the high street for some campaigning. This mainly consisted of McKenzie taking me into the shops and cafés up and down the street and introducing me to the owners and workers.

There were three different reactions to McKenzie. The first, and most common, was: 'Who you standing for this time then, Winston? Yeah, I'll back you, mate.' The second was: 'I'll vote UKIP because I'm sick of these Eastern Europeans coming over here, taking our jobs/wages/benefits.' The third, and I have to say rarest, was: ' UKIP are racists, I'll never vote for them.'

McKenzie was on good form and seemed totally at ease engaging in pavement politics. He introduced me to a wide range of characters. Reaction 1 came from the Jamaican-born woman who ran her own clothes shop and from takeaway owners also from the Caribbean.

Reaction 2 came from: the white English glass shop owners who joked they had only hired a black member of staff so McKenzie had someone to talk to when he came in; the black woman who ran a hairdresser's on the high street; and a Lithuanian couple who owned a bric-a-brac shop near the train station. Like many others I spoke to that day, they were angry at the rise in immigrants from Eastern Europe: 'When we look around they hardly speak English. They turn up and want benefits,' they said.

Reaction 3 came from just one woman, who was working in a Caribbean takeaway shop on the high street. McKenzie looked uncomfortable as she dismissed Nigel Farage as a racist. He tried to remonstrate with her but, seeing she would not be convinced of UKIP's merits, we quietly left. After almost an hour going into shops, meeting people from a range of backgrounds and seeing McKenzie in action, nothing particularly remarkable or interesting or crazy or offensive had happened.

I felt disappointed. From what I had read and seen of Winston McKenzie, I was expecting a whirlwind experience. Perhaps that's what the £500 gets you.

After our trip through South Norwood, McKenzie and I left his two UKIP minders (perhaps they were there to make sure nothing remarkable, interesting, crazy or offensive would happen) and boarded a train to East Croydon to meet up with his assistant and get some lunch.

We nearly didn't get on to the platform as McKenzie couldn't work out if he had any money on his Oyster card, or how to top it up at the ticket machine – 'Can you help? Marianne normally does this for me,' he said. After taking the train one stop from Norwood Junction to East Croydon, we met Bowness in the lobby of the Croydon Park Hotel.

She was a white woman who appeared to be in her early fifties, with short, grey hair cut into a bob. Her cardigan and blouse combination gave the appearance of a head teacher from a Church of England primary school. She was well-spoken, but with a slight toughness to her accent that made me think that for all her middle-class appearance and mannerisms, she probably wasn't born anywhere near a silver spoon, or had certainly had to settle for just wooden ones at some point.

Bowness and McKenzie seemed an unlikely combination – she was an ex-mayoress of Croydon, who I would later learn had worked in Downing Street, while he was a first-generation immigrant who had fought his way out of the streets. But they seemed to work well together and certainly had a mutual respect for one another.

After a brief discussion in the hotel lobby, Bowness, McKenzie and I went through for lunch in the huge dining room. What with it being December, Christmas parties were in full swing. Long tables housed festive office get-togethers and groups of elderly people, all sitting with paper crowns on their heads as discarded crackers littered the floor. Christmas tunes were being piped through the speaker system, which together with the overly bright lights and increasingly loud background chatter, created a feeling of eating in an airport restaurant. It was a buffet meal, so people lined up with plates in hands, crowns on heads, to take big spoonfuls of the steaming vegetables presented in ceramic pots. We were shown to our table and left to fend for ourselves. After we too had queued and piled food on our plates, we sat down to talk.

The most obvious question to me was how had Bowness and McKenzie come to work together?

'I first met him about thirty years ago when I was mayoress of Croydon,' she said. Bowness's ex-husband had been mayor, and he had honoured the McKenzie family as Winston and two of his brothers, Duke and Clinton, were gaining prominence in the boxing world. She said:

> Croydon had never honoured a family before, but there [were] so many brothers all winning medals in boxing they decided they would honour the family, so it sticks in my mind. Then a few years ago Winston turned up in the shop I was working in and he was just opening a pub. I said: 'Let me run your opening...'

McKenzie interrupted: 'I walked into the shop and I saw this massive fat lady so I looked at it – really fat you know – and she had a little stick shuffling around the place.'

That was a hell of a way to talk about the person sitting next to you, but he carried on:

'She had this leg swollen out of all proportion, she was eighteen and a half stone and very, very depressed – her marriage had finished.' I looked over at Bowness, expecting her to be offended at the man employing her calling her 'it'.

But she was just eating her food, saying nothing, so McKenzie carried on: 'I thought to myself, alright, she might be overweight and looks obese, but I had never seen such an accomplished human being in terms of fiscal aspects of the business. I was amazed.'

At that moment, so was I, and still McKenzie kept talking:

> I stopped and I looked at her and I thought, if I had that woman working for me I would be really successful, do you know what I mean? But I thought to myself, how am I

going to get her into shape, with her blimmin' walking stick shuffling around? It was puzzling. I thought, if I get her into our gym – me and my brothers' – I'll soon knock her into shape. It started from there. I was taking her to meet various people I knew in business and they said, 'Where did you get her from? Bloody hell.' They said, 'Are you alright in the head?' I said, 'She's not my girlfriend, I wanted her brain.' They said, 'What are you going to do with her?' – so unkind they were. I got her down from eighteen and a half stone to 11st 4lb in no time.

Bowness suppressed a giggle as McKenzie was talking.

'Is this right?' I asked.

'Oh yes,' she replied.

'All these people who used to reject Marianne and not look at her and call her all these sly names, they're the same people today who can't do enough to help her,' added McKenzie.

To look at Bowness now you certainly wouldn't have thought she had ever been overweight, or needed a 'blimmin' walking stick' to help with her 'shuffling around'.

The relationship between the two became clear. McKenzie was the over-the-top cartoonish front man, full of confidence but lacking in organisational skills. Bowness was swept up in his charisma, and happy to coordinate and administer the Winston McKenzie brand. In other words, I was having dinner with the real-life version of Alan Partridge and his put-upon assistant Lynn.

As we ploughed through our plates of food, I decided to press McKenzie on his flirtations with all the political parties.

'I've never been Labour,' he shot back instantly, before telling me the bizarre story of how he was almost – in his mind, at least – a Lib Dem MP in 2003:

The Lib Dems, right, I got the huff with them because, had

they continued in the same vein with me, I would be an MP today. The Lib Dems were a great bunch. They had, like many of the political parties I have joined, a great perception of Winston McKenzie. I got on really well with them. I was due to become MP for Brent East – nailed on, and, as you know, Sarah Teather walked away with it. Now, I spoke to a Lib Dem MP, I can't remember his name – I think it was Simon Hughes – who interviewed me. They said, 'Is there anything in your background that might embarrass the party?' So I thought, 'I'm not going to lie, I'm going to be honest with these guys because if I do become an MP it's going to come out and bite me up the bum.' So I said to them, 'Look, we are going through a case with the police at the moment with my pub.' Because what happened was I came into the pub, me and my brothers, and we cleaned up all the drugs, got in all the heavies, got the gym going upstairs and then, unbeknown to me, I was being stitched up by the Metropolitan Police. They were devising – this is another story, this is – an entrapment process to try and catch me and my brothers selling drugs and things like that – exhibiting drugs in the pub. I said to the Lib Dems: 'There's a trial on at the moment and, to be honest with you, I nearly had a breakdown it was that bad. They are trying to accuse me of drugs and I've got nothing to do with all that.' They shut all the doors on me. They never answered the phone again. They called in Sarah Teather just before the election and, of course, she won. I was a bit gutted by that but I'm glad that things happen that way because what the Lib Dems are today I would be very embarrassed to be a part of.

Who would have thought that a minor incident such as the pub he owned getting raided by police and twenty-five of his punters arrested on drugs and firearms charges would scare off a political party from calling him back about contesting a by-election for them?

To be fair to McKenzie, twenty of the twenty-five arrested in the raid were released the next day without charge, and there was no suggestion whatsoever that he or his brothers were in any way involved with illegal activity.

But, even so, you can perhaps understand why the Lib Dems might have plumped for the far more wholesome Sarah Teather, already an Islington councillor and school governor, over a former boxer facing a potentially high-profile court case involving allegations of drugs and arms deals in his pub.

Not to be completely defeated, McKenzie contested the Brent East by-election as an independent. Result: seventh, with 119 votes.

After the Lib Dems, McKenzie joined Veritas, the party formed by ex-UKIP MEP Robert Kilroy-Silk after he left the party in 2005. McKenzie said:

> I tried to get away from Veritas until Kilroy-Silk turned up on my doorstep. I was shocked. Marianne happened to be down on that day so she opened the door and said, 'Winston.'
>
> I said, 'What?'
>
> 'Kilroy-Silk's at the door.'
>
> I said: 'Get out of here.'
>
> I went to the door and there he was, all perma-tanned and silver hair.
>
> I said, 'Mate, come in!'
>
> So I got him to sit around the dining table and we had a good talk and he said: 'Look, we want you to join us and represent the black community, because the fact is you lot have got no representation and what the likes of Diane Abbott are doing these days is nothing, but you'll make a real hit.'
>
> I thought about it and about two weeks later I said, 'Yeah alright, I'll take you up on that.'
>
> I went into Veritas and they did look after me. There was an

underlying element in some factions of racism – there was
– but these underlying elements is [*sic*] in every walk of life.

McKenzie stood for Veritas in Croydon North in the 2005 election.
Result: seventh, with 324 votes.

After the election he publicly blamed Kilroy-Silk for him losing his
£500 deposit – which election candidates only get back if they receive
at least 5 per cent of all votes cast. He told the *Croydon Guardian* he
had put 'a few thousand' into the campaign, and he was 'disgusted
and disillusioned with the party'.

When I asked him about the money, he seemed much more phil-
osophical than he had been just after the election defeat nine years
ago: 'I lost money, I lost a bit of money,' he said, 'but that's politics
for you – if the party don't back you, you have got back yourself.'

He quit Veritas, stood in the Croydon Council by-election as an
independent (Result: fourth, forty-seven votes), then re-joined the
party to take part in the leadership election triggered by Kilroy-Silk's
resignation (Result: third, 168 votes).

He then quit again.

With his dalliance with Veritas now definitely over, McKenzie
decided his route to political success was through the mainstream.
Forget all this messing about with the Lib Dems and Veritases of this
world in mere parliamentary elections, it was time for the big one:
Conservative candidate for the Mayor of London in 2008.

He told me:

> I met Dave [Cameron] and all that. The Tories – the members
> – are some of the most lovely people you could ever wish to
> meet and it was they who were propelling me to become the
> Tory mayoral candidate.
>
> They threw me in as a wild card and thought I would
> never get out of the net but I did and the Tories began to
> back me like billy-o.

Bowness, who so far had remained pretty quiet as McKenzie reeled off his political CV, jumped in:

> He was beginning to win the hustings as we went round the different London constituencies and they called him into the office. Before that, Nick Boles – who was expected to win – he could see one day that his staff came up to Winston and said: 'We're going to switch our allegiance to you.'

McKenzie interrupted:

> We were in New Cross – I couldn't believe it. We had done the hustings and they come up to me and said: 'We are going to switch our allegiance to you.' Nick said: 'It's all yours, well done, Winston.' Two weeks later he quit. I was becoming the number one.

In reality, Boles pulled out of the race because he was diagnosed with cancer.

McKenzie was, he claims, on course for a stunning victory.

But it seems the Tories weren't having it, and McKenzie told me he was then summoned in for a meeting by a senior figure at the top of the party to be told he hadn't made the shortlist. Such was the fear among senior Tories that McKenzie would win the hustings, 'the desperate calls to Boris became stronger', claimed the now UKIP man.

After thinking 'sod this', McKenzie quit the Conservative Party and stood as an independent in the Mayor of London election in 2008. Result: last out of ten candidates, with 5,389 votes.

'It gutted me because I liked the Tories, I liked the members, it really gutted me,' said McKenzie wistfully.

Rejected by the Lib Dems, failed by Veritas and ousted by the Tories, it seemed McKenzie was never going to achieve his ambition: 'I wanted to be Prime Minister – I still do.' In March 2009, McKenzie formed his own party, Unity, but it folded after just seven months due to lack of money.

Enter UKIP MEP Gerard Batten to the McKenzie story, who pulled the ex-boxer in from the 'wilderness'. Batten set up a meeting between McKenzie and Nigel Farage, and the ex-Lib Dem/Veritas/Conservative/Unity member took an instant liking to the UKIP leader.

McKenzie's eyes lit up as he recounted their first meeting:

> I met Nigel and I instantly thought, this guy – hang what UKIP stand for – this guy is trying to save British sovereignty. I don't care what they stand for, at the end of the day they are trying to save British sovereignty, so I'm backing him. He invited me into his office, I went up there.
>
> He said: 'Why do you want to join UKIP? You just want to use us, I know you just want to use us.'
>
> I said: 'Yeah, I want to use you, Nigel.'

I asked if he thought Farage minded being 'used', but McKenzie insisted the two have a 'pact'.

'We're using each other,' he replied with a grin:

> I'm using UKIP and UKIP are using me. My pal, he's my pal and I've got to call him my pal, Nigel Farage, he's the most fantastic thing that's happened to me in business. I look at politics as a business. This guy, whether he likes it or not, or whether he wants to hear it or not, is the most fantastic thing that's happened to me in business.
>
> Why? Because there are no airs and graces, no pretence, he tells it to me like it is and I give it to him like it is. We don't have a lot of laughs, we are very businesslike. I remember when he first met me and he was contemplating taking me into the party. He came downstairs big and bold, swaggering, opened the door, looked me up and down and I thought to

myself, 'What's his problem?' He said, 'Come in,' so I went in, went up the lift and he sat there and I thought, 'I'm going to knock this guy out in a minute, he's too flash.' I could see so much in him. You know when they say opposites clash, I could see so much in him, like the fighter instinct and his attitude that was in me.

Why all this flip-flopping between parties? I asked. Bowness, who clearly felt the need to protect her man/boss, was blunt with her response:

Winston is a black man. His parents were immigrants so he has been brought up in a culture unlike that in-born culture where I'm brought up in where you automatically take part in politics. I mean, in my youth there were a lot of people who went to the Young Conservatives – you took part, you felt like part of it. But with Winston, because his family are immigrants, they didn't necessarily take part in the local community, they were so busy working hard to try to get a foot on the ladder. So Winston along with – I think this is the problem with immigrants in general, whatever their persuasion – they are brought up in a culture where politics doesn't really reach them.

How can voters trust him to stay with UKIP? How can we possibly know McKenzie won't just walk away from the party if he doesn't get his way? McKenzie leaned forward and in hushed tones set out why he loved UKIP so much:

First and foremost, Owen, I think about this country that we live in. This is my home, England is my home and I'm dealing with someone [Farage] who is trying to maintain British sovereignty and so many more people should have it in their minds that they need to maintain, we need to maintain, British sovereignty and remain British, keep the British culture. Europeans wouldn't like it if we came to their country and we tried to change it and do anything with it, they wouldn't like it. So we, as a country, should maintain British culture and put our foot down. I'm not saying that we should be racist or arrogant or violent but we must maintain British culture. If you don't like the way we live here, go away, go and find a niche somewhere else, but please don't turn up and go on and on about racism. Black people came to this country in the early '50s, particularly the first wave of immigrants, and my God we worked. Our forefathers worked and toiled so hard that the likes of me could have opportunities and be what we are today and we just now as a society are turning our faces away from that and looking to Europe that offers us nothing.

McKenzie is clearly enamoured with Farage, and despite being ten years older than the UKIP leader, he refers to him as 'almost like a father figure'.

McKenzie stood under a UKIP banner in Tottenham, north London, in the 2010 general election. Result: sixth, with 466 votes.

Having been in the party for no more than a year, in September 2010 McKenzie decided he was the man to lead it forward, and stood in the leadership election against his new political hero Farage.

I asked McKenzie why he had stood against Farage, if he respected him so much? Bowness leapt to his defence: 'When Winston challenged him he had been out of the leadership for a while. He [Farage] had had his disastrous air crash.'

McKenzie was a lot more bullish: 'When Nigel ran the last leadership race, God, he had to pull his socks up, man, 'cos I was on his case. So he's a very clever man.'

He added:

I'd get on stage and I'd be challenging him and I'd have to say things like, 'Nigel, you are almost as good as me, man!' People would roar with laughter but he had to buck up. And he did. He slipped into gear during the leadership challenge, and they devised a strategy: 'Vote Nigel, Get Winston'. Immediately they brought that up among the members, the whole thing turned round – 'We're going to give Nigel another chance,' and it worked brilliantly because the guy's clever.

None of the Kippers that I have spoken to who were around in 2010 can remember that strategy. Maybe it was one of those 'unspoken pacts'.

Result: fourth, with 530 votes cast.

Alas, just like the Lib Dems in Brent East and the Tories in the London mayoral election, UKIP had again scuppered McKenzie's moment of glory.

McKenzie had another crack at standing for London Mayor in 2012, but didn't win the UKIP nomination after a ballot of party members.

Result: joint third with 7.4 per cent (the actual numbers of votes cast were never made public).

He did stand for the party in the London council elections that year in Croydon & Sutton. Result: fourth, with 10,757 votes.

Later in 2012, he was chosen as the UKIP candidate in the Croydon North by-election caused by the death of Labour MP Malcolm Wickes.

Result: third, with 1,400 votes.

With his love for UKIP laid out on the table, I asked if he had ever come across racism in the party.

He replied:

It's no use saying, 'Oh, well, this or that party are racist' – sorry, we all have racism in us, it might not be fervent or it may not be obvious, but whether you are white or you are black we all know our boundaries and we can only go so far. It's human nature. Anyone who says they haven't got a bit of racism is a liar. You make a judgement. I don't believe anyone who says, 'I'm not racist.' We have all got it in us whether you're black, white, whatever. If a white guy does something I will go home and say, 'Why did that stupid white guy do that?' and you can put that to racism if you like. I am not a blatant racist but I know by nature we all have a bit of racism in us. If you say you don't, you are lying.

So, according to McKenzie, you, I, and everyone we have ever known is a bit racist. I don't feel racist and I've never knowingly behaved in a racist way. But have I ever made a snap judgement of someone as soon as I've met them? Yes. Do I acknowledge the differences in cultures among groups of people that sometimes, but certainly not always, lie alongside people's race? Yes. But the key measure is: have I ever automatically thought anything negative about a person because of the colour of their skin? No, not at all.

But his view is very much based on the experiences of a black man growing up in south London, and not of this white man who grew up in leafy Hertfordshire. He probably knows what he's talking about when it comes to racism and how it manifests itself more than I do.

Our dinner plates were now empty and even McKenzie had managed to clear his plate despite spending most of the meal talking.

Bowness was constantly scolding him for talking too much – 'Eat, Winston, you must eat!' she exclaimed like a mother fretting over a child on more than one occasion.

McKenzie was clearly a strong personality, and I wondered how he and Farage interacted on a daily basis. Did the UKIP leader micro-manage his Commonwealth spokesman, or leave him to get on with it?

McKenzie replied:

He's level-headed. Sometimes I ring him up and he can hear

the anger in my voice, like when he wanted to move me from my position as culture, media and sport spokesman. I said: 'Guv'nor, you can't do that, you can't move me.' He knew I was angry but with his father-like attitude he said: 'Now, Winston, maturity in a politician is the ability to move when you're moved. I don't want any comebacks, I've got to move you.' I said: 'Alright, I'll chew on it, yeah, bye.' Then I text him back and said, 'Oh yeah, I get it.'

He added: 'I've never met personally such integrity in a politician.'

McKenzie admitted that he 'pesters Farage all day every day – he can't get rid of me', so I asked to see some of the texts between the two. McKenzie got his phone out and began scrolling through the messages.

He stopped at one and said: 'I wrote to Nigel "Morning Guv—" No, I can't say that, I'll get lambasted.'

'No, go on,' I said.

He smiled and said: 'All the gays will lambast me!'

In 2012, McKenzie provoked outrage in Britain's gay community after saying gay adoption would not be 'healthy' for a child.

He told the *Croydon Guardian*: 'To say to a child, "I am having you adopted by two men who kiss regularly but don't worry about it" – that is abuse. It is a violation of a child's human rights because that child has no opportunity to grow up under normal circumstances.'

Ben Summerskill, chief executive of LGBT rights pressure group Stonewall, accused McKenzie of having 'nineteenth-century views' that are 'not acceptable in the twenty-first century'.

McKenzie paused before reading out the messages:

I wrote to my guv'nor about the gays – you know what I mean. They done something. They done a thing the other day about World Aids Day and they dumped a load of horse manure outside my offices. You had two gays, piles of horse manure. Let me read to you what I said to Nigel. I said to the guv'nor: 'Good morning Guv. The bloody queers dumped a lot of horse manure outside my office on Monday morning to commemorate World Aids Day. It's on the internet under *Croydon Guardian*. Just shows what a load of crap they are. CHAMP.' I don't think the guv'nor got back to me on that one.

Before I left, I wanted McKenzie's take on the 'Carnival of Colour' that generated such farcical headlines for the party. 'Why on earth did you think it would be a good idea?' I asked.

He laughed and said: 'The steel band! I don't know where to begin on that.' He continued:

> I'm getting slated for it but Nigel's office called me and said, 'Organise this carnival, and can you get some people together and make it sound and feel really great, a carnival atmosphere.'
>
> I said: 'Yeah, I can do that.' And I done it and of course all the fascists got to hear about it and came down and caused a load of trouble. But Nigel's office was the one who asked me to organise that carnival and I did. It just turned into a bit of a farce because of those troublemakers, otherwise it would have been great if it wasn't for those. The steel band was a joke.

McKenzie broke out into a smile as he remembers the media scrum, which, thanks to Farage's absence, was centred on him.

'I had at any one time at least sixty, seventy, eighty, ninety, any number of microphones in my face, and boy, did I shine to it,' he laughed. 'I responded. I didn't give a monkey's about, "We're racist, we're xenophobic." Lovely! Bring it on, baby! And they did.'

Apparently, Farage's no-show was actually because McKenzie was loving the limelight so much: 'I was in constant contact with [UKIP's events manager] Lizzy Vaid and I said, "Please don't let Nigel turn up. I'm having a great time."'

Subsequent conversations with a source in UKIP HQ painted a very different picture, claiming that it was actually McKenzie who had suggested the Carnival of Colour.

We said our goodbyes and I left McKenzie and Bowness in the hotel dining room, having settled the bill as I promised I would.

McKenzie sums up everything and nothing about UKIP at the same time.

He has all the eccentricities, ego and lack of self-awareness of many of those involved in the party, and trots out the anti-EU, anti-mass immigration lines with the same pre-requisite passion of every other Kipper.

But he is a first-generation immigrant and, as such, is probably the reason UKIP were keen to put him front and centre as much as possible.

But the UKIP top brass recognised he was erratic. Why else would those at the top of the party have been worried about him going on *Newsnight* to defend the 'UKIP Calypso'?

His membership of five parties in fewer than ten years, and more often than not quitting when he didn't get his own way, was at odds with many Kippers' slow-and-steady-wins-the-race view.

Bowness may be right that it's taken a while for McKenzie to truly discover his political views, and which party represents those the best, but I'm not sure that really justifies seeking elected office on behalf of so many of them in such a short space of time.

Two weeks after our Christmas dinner together in Croydon, McKenzie hit the headlines again when he compared Farage to Jesus.

In an interview with Chat Politics, he said: 'Jesus was one man, we're his army. Farage is one man, and we're his army, and that's what it's all about. Everywhere he goes – it doesn't matter what he says or does – he gets away with it.'

He also claimed the Tories sacked him from the London Mayor race by text message, not after a meeting, as he told me.

A few days later, and the entire Lambeth & Croydon North branch of UKIP was disbanded after a number of members signed a letter of no confidence in McKenzie, the branch chairman. He remained the party's general election candidate for Croydon North, but lost his position as the party's Commonwealth spokesman in March 2015.

When I interviewed him about his demotion in favour of MEP Jim Carver, he compared it to the execution of Fredo Corleone in the classic film *The Godfather Part II*.

'The guv'nor said we have got this guy who is an MEP and he's got a lot of clout in foreign affairs. He said he would put the ball in my court, but you remember *The Godfather*? It was like going on the boat in the wilderness.'

Before I met McKenzie, I felt he was sneered at by some of the media for his working-class south London demeanour. I still do believe that, but he plays up to it – and he knows it. Winston McKenzie could provide a useful link to communities that feel neglected and unrepresented, but his constant moving from party to party makes him look like most others – an opportunistic politician.

I liked Winston McKenzie, but, like many others throughout the years, I wouldn't vote for him.

CHAPTER 10

HUNTING HIGH AND LOW

U KIP IS OFTEN ACCUSED of being little more than a one-man band, but not when it comes to embarrassing gaffes.

Indeed, Nigel Farage can be considered something of an amateur compared to the antics of his former Brussels flat-mate Godfrey Bloom.

He began scoring points in this particular league on his very first day as an MEP in 2004 when he said: 'No self-respecting small businessman with a brain in the right place would ever employ a lady of child-bearing age.'

He added: 'I quite simply feel that they don't clean behind the fridge. I represent Yorkshire women who always have dinner on the table when you get home.'

The comments led Labour MEP Glenys Kinnock to brand UKIP a 'Neanderthal' party, adding that it was 'absolutely terrifying' that Bloom could want to roll back women's rights.

After a few years of keeping his head down, Bloom decided he wanted a bit more notoriety and got himself ejected from the European Parliament in 2010 for shouting a Nazi slogan at a German MEP.

In 2013, he really hit his stride. First, he slammed foreign aid being sent to 'Bongo Bongo Land' – for which he initially refused

to apologise until his arm was twisted by UKIP's chairman Steve
Crowther. A few months later, he returned to his jokes about house-
work and blasted women who don't clean behind the fridge as 'sluts'
during the party's autumn conference. Then, after being confronted
with a copy of the conference programme that had only white faces
on the cover, Bloom struck Channel 4 reporter Michael Crick over
the head with it.

The whip was removed, he was deselected as an MEP candidate
for the following year's European elections, and, finally, in October
2014, he quit UKIP, claiming it was too 'politically correct'.

Bloom may no longer have been a member of the party, but his
'gaffes' left a permanent scar on UKIP in the mind of many. When
UKIP's immigration spokesman Steven Woolfe appeared on Sky
News on 4 March 2015 to discuss the party's migration policy, presenter Kay Burley closed the interview by saying, 'Quite a lot of the
girls here in the office – I think we've got four or five of them here
who are expecting babies at the moment – and they want to know
what you would do about maternity pay?' Woolfe replied: 'Well, I
think we've made it absolutely clear that maternity pay would stay
as it is. I've often found it surprising that people have suggested we
want to remove it – I've never seen that.'

More than ten years after Bloom's comments about pregnant women
and business, and they were still coming back to haunt the party.

Bloom had been close to Farage for many years. The pair had shared
a flat together in Brussels and in 2006 Farage defended Bloom's comments to a now defunct Belgian magazine called *Up Front*:

> Dear old Godders! Godfrey's comment that 'no employer
> with a brain in the right place would employ a young, sin-
> gle, free woman' has been proved so right. With this lunacy,
> that if you have children you get three months' paid leave
> off work, or six months' paid leave off work – he absolutely
> got it spot on. His comments get to the absolute heart of the

problem of the EU. Social policy against employment policy … that's why there are over 20 million unemployed in the EU.

Farage had defended him then but, after the 2013 conference, he had had enough, and the friendship was over.

I wondered how Bloom must be feeling that, while Farage was lapping up the adoration of millions and preparing for an assault on the House of Commons, he was no longer on the front line leading the charge.

I dropped him an email asking for an interview in early January 2015. I had a week off between leaving the *Daily Express* and joining the *Daily Mirror*, and that seemed a good opportunity to travel up to Yorkshire to speak to the former UKIP MEP in his own backyard.

Bloom agreed to the chat, but first laid down some ground rules:

Occasionally I have had visits from journalists who have already written the piece and want a veneer of objectivity with a cursory interview. I may therefore insist you read my comprehensive piece on the UKIP bandwagon on the Libertarian Alliance blog, to which I have very little to add. Also you will find my CV on my recent book *A Dinosaur's Guide To Libertarianism*. Most of the rubbish on Wikipedia is tabloid regurgitation of misquotes or smears, some of which paid for my Bentley (Thank you, *Daily Mail*), but seem impossible to move off the site. Neither do I ever engage in tittle-tattle on individuals, but I am sure everyone knows that by now.

Should you feel you wish to come on those terms I would be happy to meet you and indeed offer some appropriate Yorkshire hospitality.

They sounded like reasonable conditions to me, but our interview plan hit a snag when Bloom said he may be attending a hunt meeting on the day we had arranged.

A hunt meeting. An actual red-jackets, blowing-the-bugle, Hooray-Henry hunt meeting.

Now *that* is where I wanted to interview Godfrey Bloom. So I started sucking up in my emails (don't judge me, you would have done the same):

Me: 'Thanks for your response. I absolutely understand your desire to lay down some ground rules! I will indeed take a read of the pieces you highlight. I can assure you no article has been pre-written and my piece will be drawn from our interview. Please do let me know when you have the hunt calendar and you are free. Or maybe if possible I could come on the hunt with you – I have never been and would love to see one up close!'

Bloom: 'You would be more than welcome. I will fix something up. Bear in mind it is a sport where a large whisky is de rigeur [*sic*] at 11 a.m.!'

Me: 'Excellent – finally a sport I can get behind!'

Bloom: 'Mrs B tells me we are not hunting until next weekend. I could take you to one of the local meets to enjoy the traditional pastoral scene. Snag is they meet at eleven so you would have to be on a sparrows fart train from The Smoke or come up the night before. Tuesday or Wednesday is fine, or indeed Thursday.'

We agreed on the Tuesday meeting.

Wrapped up in my scarf, gloves and duffel coat I waited at Selby train station for Bloom. He rocked up in his Jaguar and stepped out with a broad grin on his face. He was a lot shorter than I imagined, with a smaller frame. But, like Farage, he was in full Kipper uniform – corduroy trousers, shiny tie, moss-green jacket and a flat cap. He could have been on his way to a *Last of the Summer Wine* Appreciation Society meeting. But he wasn't, he was there to meet me.

We shook hands and I got into the flash car. He assured me that turning up to a hunt in such a vehicle wasn't the done thing, and he would probably get mocked by the others at the meet. We set off, talking about nothing in particular, and soon we were on winding roads across north Yorkshire. Bloom was keen to point out various landmarks and points of interest in his fiefdom.

After driving for about half an hour, Bloom seemed worried. The directions he had written down for the hunt meet weren't clear and, even after consulting a huge A–Z map, he wasn't sure where to go. We ploughed on in the bright, cold, Yorkshire sun until we came upon a gentlemen in a 4x4 who had parked on the opposite side of a country road we were heading down.

'We're looking for this morning's hunt,' Bloom shouted across after pulling up and winding down his window.

'So am I!' came the reply.

'I heard it was round this way,' said Bloom gesturing forward with his hand.

'Yes, I heard it was this way,' said the man, pointing back down the road we had just come from.

'OK, see you there then,' replied Bloom, and both cars went off in opposite directions.

Hunting for the hunt was proving a task in itself.

After driving for another five minutes, Bloom spotted something out of the corner of his eye on the left-hand side of the road. A horsebox. Like a hound with the scent of blood in his nostrils, his eyes narrowed as he brought the Jaguar to a halt in the middle of the road.

'I'm pretty sure that's it,' he said, reversing backwards at speed.

We pulled into a small, gravelly car park, full of 4x4s and other vehicles suitable for off-road driving. Bloom was right – his Jaguar was a bit flash.

Walking through the gaps in the horseboxes, we made our way to where the hunters were gathered behind a large barn. Riders in traditional hunting dress mixed with those in wax jackets and flat caps. Huge, magnificent horses were being led out of steel boxes and prepared for the day's activities.

Bloom was shaking hands with most of the fifty or so who turned out, and whenever anyone asked if he was riding with them today, he cheekily replied: 'No, I'm just here to add tone.'

More than a few asked Bloom if he had his hip flask with him – it clearly had some notoriety. I asked one rider about it and she just shook her head and said: 'I don't know what's in it, but it's lethal.'

Despite it being before 11 a.m., the drinking had begun, even without Bloom's legendary hip flask. Drams of whisky were being handed out in small plastic glasses from a makeshift kitchen set up in a steel container. As well as whisky and other spirits, there were plates of homemade sausage rolls and mince pies left over from Christmas being passed around. There was even a raffle, which had a prize of a large bottle of port.

Bloom was clearly in his element – despite being a boy from south London, he was evidently at home among the Yorkshire toffs.

He talked me through how the hunt was structured, who followed whom, which rider was in charge, how they knew which fields they could ride through.

He shared a joke with everyone present. Some recognised him, some weren't sure if they did, but he treated them all the same. In the world of hunting – where everyone is white, upper middle class at the very least and possesses the very stiffest of upper lips – Bloom thrived.

This was his world.

After fifteen minutes or so of mingling, a large pack of hounds rushed past us and into a field. Bloom proudly told me how the lineage of the dogs could be traced back hundreds and hundreds of years. Pure breeds, with good temperaments. You are safe with these dogs because you know their parents were safe. The same goes for the horses. And perhaps, in this world, the people.

After the embarrassing moment when I won the raffle – much to the delight of Bloom and many cries of 'beginner's luck!' from the others – the hunt was ready to start. The riders were aboard their stallions and mares, with the hounds sniffing around the horses' feet as they waited for the off.

Before the charge, the lead rider addressed the small crowd. She thanked everyone for turning out, reminded them of future hunt dates and told everyone to discount the calendar they had all just been sent as it had the wrong dates on it.

With the admin done, the hunt went off! Not to catch a fox, of course, but to chase a scent.

Bloom saw away his drink, turned to me with his hands clasped together and, with a broad grin, said: 'Lunch!'

We hopped back into his car and set off once again into the Yorkshire countryside. So far, the conversation had been about nothing much. I was happy to let Bloom talk about his upbringing in Lewisham, south London, his pride at being on the economist lecture circuit in Europe and America, and his love of rugby and hunting.

After finding a suitable pub – proper food, real ales – we sat down to discuss all things UKIP.

Relaxing into the pub's chair, Bloom looked just as at home as he had been driving his Jaguar along the Yorkshire roads and rubbing shoulders with toffs at the hunt meeting earlier that morning. He didn't strike me as a man who stressed about life. So why enter politics, in which stress is pretty much the only guarantee? I asked.

Before he answered that, he was keen to impress upon me his success in the business world before joining UKIP in 1994 ('It was the year after it was formed, but I reckon I'm entitled to call myself a founder member,' he said).

> I was head of fixed interest at an investment house. I had done quite well. I was winning some international prizes and running a very successful fund, but it was in the days when fixed interest wasn't fashionable. Equities were fashionable, so, though I was running a very successful fund, I was still 'behind the filing cabinets', regarded as something of a geek by the industry. But one of the projects I was put on was the common currency.

I had a big team, I had resources, I had a team of statisti-
cians who had got a first from Cambridge in stats and stuff
– it was awesome, the brain power. They were all infinitely
cleverer than me.

Supping on his ale and reclining back on the pub bench, he went
on: 'I looked at the common currency and realised it couldn't be, it
couldn't possibly work. You can't have the same interest rates and the
same currency across such a broad spectrum without a common fiscal policy. You just can't, it's like a concrete aeroplane – it won't fly.'

After making this judgement, Bloom said he became interested in
the political aspect of the single European currency project.

'I could see that this was doomed to failure and that it was a political currency, so you had to take a political view, and that sucked me
into UKIP,' he said. 'There was only one party at the time saying
"not under any circumstances". Everyone else was saying: "If the
time was right ... maybe we'll talk about it."'

Having found his self-confessed 'natural home', Bloom stood in the
1997 general election in the newly created Haltemprice & Howden
seat in the East Riding of Yorkshire.

'It was fun. I bought a double-decker bus, open top,' he said with
a smile on his face. 'I spoke to the punters and everything I said
everybody agreed with me. I thought I was a shoo-in.'

Come the night of the election, alas for Bloom, he did not defeat
Tory candidate – and future leadership challenger – David Davis.

'I got 800 votes!' he said with a grin. 'I thought when people agreed
with you then they were going to vote for you! Of course it doesn't
mean any such thing. It means they vote this way because they hate
that fucker.'

Actually, Bloom got slightly fewer than 800 votes – 301 to be
precise – and came behind the Referendum Party to finish fifth. There
is no footage of Bloom's defeat, as, at the same time as the results were
being announced in Haltemprice & Howden they were also being

read out in Enfield Southgate, delivering the most infamous result of that election: the defeat of Michael Portillo.

Bloom may have been denied a seat in the mother of parliaments, but in 2004 he won a place in its big brother in Brussels. Having picked up three seats in the European Parliament in 1999, UKIP saw its allocation quadruple to twelve five years later. Bloom was one of six MEPs from Yorkshire and the Humber – the only Ukipper alongside two Labour, two Tories and a Lib Dem.

It was his old friend Nigel Farage – who had been elected as an MEP in 1999 – who convinced Bloom to stand.

'It was Nigel that dragged me in,' he said. 'I would never have become a politician if it hadn't been for Nigel – he bullied me into it. I didn't realise it was going to lift so much of my money when he got me in.'

Money?

Bloom took a large gulp of his beer and nodded his head.

'In 2003, he persuaded me to stand as an MEP. We all went down to Birmingham to have this meeting and we all had to put £20,000 in the kitty!'

According to the Electoral Commission, since 2001 Bloom has pumped £72,608.03 into UKIP. But it was not Godfrey Bloom, nor even Nigel Farage, who was the poster boy of UKIP in 2004 – it was former TV host Robert Kilroy-Silk.

I asked Bloom what he thought of Kilroy-Silk. I couldn't imagine the libertarian economist who loved playing rugby, hunting and copious drinking would have got on too well with a former Labour MP who once claimed government should 'impose its values on society'.

Actually, Bloom had a lot of respect for Kilroy-Silk and appeared to lament his leaving of the party after just nine months as a member.

It's interesting because, up until 2004, you could still have a conversation in a Cambridge pub with a post-graduate who had never heard of UKIP, and we'd been around by that stage for over ten years and fighting seats. So Kilroy-Silk did an enormous amount of good because you couldn't pretend you hadn't heard of UKIP. For better or for worse, everybody had heard of bloody UKIP by the time of Kilroy-Silk, which is the power of television.

Kilroy-Silk joined in a blaze of publicity, and left the party in the same manner too. I wondered if Bloom thought the former Labour MP would have any regrets about quitting the party so quickly. Bloom replied:

> What a lost opportunity for him personally. All he had to do was wait for eighteen months and he would have been leader. He would have been leader unopposed; nobody wanted the bloody job of leading UKIP, he could have done it. As a TV personality he would have moved it forward a lot quicker. He would have moved it to where we are now, he would have got us there in a couple of years.

'Do you not think he was an egomaniac though, who would have made it all about him?' I asked.

'I don't think it's possible to be a leader of any political party without being an egomaniac,' was Bloom's response. 'I just don't believe that is possible, particularly in the case of UKIP.'

But Kilroy-Silk's antics didn't mean Bloom was completely overshadowed upon his election to the European Parliament. On his very first day in Strasbourg, Bloom took up a position on the Parliament's Women's Rights Committee and it was then he made his comments about businesses employing women of a 'child-bearing age'.

In his first autobiography, Farage dismissed these comments as a Bloom 'family joke … which did not play in the hypersensitive atmosphere of Strasbourg'.

Bloom had gone even further in a conversation with *The Guardian*, saying that maternity policy should be: 'If you want to have a baby, you hand in your resignation and free up a job for another young lady.'

To this day, Bloom is unrepentant over both the context and style of the comments.

'There was a huge leader in the *Sunday Times* by India Knight saying, "By gosh, Godfrey, you're right".' (He is spot on here – that was the article's headline. Knight also wrote: 'Bloom is at least partly right: you don't have to like it, but people do shy from employing women who look like they might shortly go off and have a baby.')

> All her friends and colleagues in the smart set had written to her and said, 'He's right, look at what he said, look at eve-rything he said, look at his speech, look at the transcript.' They all told her stories that they had been almost crucified by a woman who joined their companies as you don't have to say that you're pregnant at interview, you don't have to say when you're coming back from maternity leave.
>
> The whole thing is stacked against the small employer and that was all turned round and suddenly I was right – I was talking sense.

Bloom also recalled a female television producer who offered him her support after the MEP had been interviewed about the comments via satellite link by a woman journalist:

> She said, 'Mr Bloom, can I just say that that was fantastic. You won't know this but you completely destroyed her and, at the end, the producer her end was having to prompt her with questions and responses because she went to pieces. Let me tell you I'm 100 per cent in charge – do you see those three empty desks over there? They are all women on maternity leave. I've decided not to get married, not to have a family.

I do all their work and I don't get home until ten o'clock at
night. You're absolutely right on everything you said and
we're right behind you.'

Almost whispering to himself, he said: 'Misogynist, misogynist,
misogynist. No, it's not like that, it's not like that.'

After the maternity leave debacle, Bloom hit the headlines again
after he complained about foreign aid being sent to 'Bongo Bongo
Land' in 2013.

I asked if he regretted using the words, but he stood by the phrase,
saying the outrage at the use of the term was orchestrated by the
media: 'I said at the time that if you can get me the ambassador to
the Court of St James's for Bongo Bongo Land I will gladly apologise. It's bullshit – it's theatre, isn't it? They are trendy metropolitan
elite, slightly leftie – they need to be offended.' He added: 'Yeah,
you're offended. Why would I care if you're offended? I don't represent you, you don't live in Yorkshire, you work for a newspaper
in London. I don't give a shit.'

As evidence for this faux outrage, Mr Bloom said nobody raised
an eyebrow when the BBC political editor Nick Robinson used the
term 'Bongo Bongo Land' in his book *Live From Downing Street*.

I told him I didn't know Robinson had used it, to which he replied:
'You fuckers never do any homework, do you?' He continued:

> Nobody was ever going to talk about foreign aid until I used
> Bongo Bongo.
>
> I tried it, I wrote to papers, I spoke to guys like you and
> said, 'Can I do an op-ed?' or 'Can we talk about it?' Nobody
> was interested. As soon as I used that phrase the whole coun-
> try was talking about foreign aid and the whole country was
> on my side. And, incidentally, what was quite interesting, the
> *Daily Mail* – after saying 'this man's dreadful' – three days
> later there was a double-page spread of me and my wife with a

very friendly feature. The press suddenly went: 'We've really
misread this; we've misread our readers.'

'You don't think the media outrage perhaps echoes the views of some
of your constituents who might have found it offensive?' I asked.

> No, because if I took you to the Boot & Shoe or the Barnes
> Wallis or the rugby club or the cricket or even pubs where
> I drink around in Beverley, all that ever happens is people
> come up to me and say: 'Bloody saw you, bloody great, you
> don't let them grind you down, the bastards, you tell them.'
> So then the answer's no. Who am I supposed to represent?
> These people.

He then regaled me with the time he had been recognised by equally
supportive people on the train from London to Leeds.

'"Yeah, yeah, that was great, I thought you got that right, gin and
tonics all round," they said to me. By bloody Doncaster we were all
completely shit-faced.'

Still there was more: 'I was at a race day the other day and I was
at the station in Beverley, and a whole bunch of girls came up wanting selfies and pictures. Yeah it's good, if I hadn't had that it would
have been very different.'

'But if you were speaking for the man in the street,' I asked, 'and
you really don't think it's offensive, why did you promise Nigel Farage you would stop using the term "Bongo Bongo Land"?'

For the first time, Bloom got angry, not with the media, but with
his former colleagues:

> That's where the UKIP hierarchy lost the plot. They should
> have said: 'Never mind about that, Mr Paxman, never mind
> about that, Mr Humphrys, he's right, isn't he? Godfrey
> Bloom's bloody right – a billion pounds a month and we're

closing hospitals!' Not, 'Well, we've had a word with him about his language and perhaps he might have not...' As soon as you've done that you've lost.

Slipping into a rugby metaphor, he said: 'They dropped the pass, I beat three men and I created an overlap and I chucked out the pass and UKIP dropped it, didn't they, as they drop every pass everybody gives them.'

Our sandwiches had now arrived and, after another couple of pints had been brought over, I asked him if he felt he could have survived in the party after hitting Michael Crick with the UKIP conference programme.

'Yes, of course!' he said instantly:

All Nigel needed to do was stick by his colleagues and say, 'They tried to hound me this morning over my time at Dulwich College [Channel 4 had screened a programme the night before the 2013 conference claiming while the UKIP leader was a student at a private school he often sang Hitler Youth songs – which Farage denied], they hounded Godfrey on the streets and we know Godfrey is just a lad from the rugby club and he lashed out – yes, he will. But perhaps what journalists could learn from this is to treat politicians with a little bit more respect. A little bit more respect and it wouldn't have happened would it?'

Bloom paused, and before I could ask if he felt betrayed by his old friend, he said:

In all fairness to Nigel, he went to pieces, he went completely to pieces. He completely broke down. As I said, all he needed to do was to say, as he said in his speech, 'They are after us, they are going to go after high-profile people.' He said, 'We've

got to stick together' and then of course I was ambushed
by Crick and all the rest of it and the first thing he did was
burst into tears and give up. But he's a very emotional man.

'Why do you think he didn't stand by you?' I asked.

Bloom, having had a good lunch, a fair few beers and the attention
of a journalist for a whole morning, let rip into his former flatmate
and friend.

'Nigel had to get rid of all the alpha males – I mean you are
talking primeval. There are no alpha males left in UKIP.'

He added:

> It was clear, and Nigel and I had many arguments about this,
> I was uncomfortable with the presidential Nigel Farage Party,
> because my view was it isn't the Nigel Farage Party. UKIP
> was started by Alan Sked years ago and the reason we are
> where we are is because an awful lot of people have worked
> extremely hard. A lot of members have walked through the
> rain and the snow delivering leaflets. Nigel popped up a bit
> later, bless his cotton socks.
>
> He was also a founder member but it's extremely rude in
> my view to claim it's Nigel Farage's party. It isn't Nigel Far-
> age's party – well, it is now – but it wasn't then and I used to
> say, 'Look, Nigel, it isn't your party, it's our party,' for which
> Nigel was clearly not comfortable, and there were others like
> me who felt the same.
>
> So, in some way or another, you have to get rid of the
> alpha males, it's primeval. It doesn't matter whether you
> are dealing with a North American bison, wildebeest, lions,
> elephants – the first thing you do is get rid of anybody else
> who might shag somebody else in the herd, which is what
> he's done and that's perfectly legitimate politics. I'm not
> moaning about it.

In 2014's European elections, UKIP won three of the six seats up for grabs in the Yorkshire and the Humber region. Despite not being a candidate, Bloom believes he deserves a huge amount of credit for the result.

'Why would you get rid of somebody, why would you hound somebody out of the party who's got the biggest northern vote in the history of the party: 400,000 votes? Where did that come from?' he said.

Bloom clearly felt his non-politically correct, combative, straight-talking personality meant he was a hit with the UKIP grass roots, and, as a result, Farage saw him as a potential leadership threat:

> If you had seen me speak at the Exeter conference, for example – which is still on tape somewhere as some members are very keen on it – there's about ten minutes on the economy. It was a good speech and when I was taking the piss out of [George] Osborne, the roof came off, I mean the fucking roof came off. Whenever I walked up to speak at conference the roof came off.

And it's not just the men who have been victims of Farage's 'primeval' way of running the party, according to Bloom.

'There is only one female at the moment who is, arguably, or *was*, arguably, leadership material, and that was Janice Atkinson. He successfully, very successfully, destroyed her political career. He killed her over ting-tong.'

'Ting-tong' was the term used by Atkinson – UKIP MEP for southeast England – to describe a member of the party from Thailand in August 2014. The BBC recorded Atkinson using the words after she left on her microphone following filming with a news crew.

Farage was quick to issue an apology to party member Fa Munday and her husband Vincent and even visited the couple in their home.

Farage told them: 'Something has happened that was offensive, unpleasant, didn't need to happen and I thought the only thing that

I could possibly do was to come up personally and say "I'm sorry for causing offence.'"

He said Ms Atkinson would be 'spoken to' and 'reprimanded', because 'this is not the kind of behaviour that we want from anybody, at any level, in UKIP'.

Bloom believed Atkinson was harshly treated.

He said: 'That killed her leadership chances and I think he did it probably quite deliberately. He either panicked, which would be, with his track record, quite possible, or he deliberately destroyed her career.'

I asked how many others Farage has 'got rid of':

How long do you want the list to be? There must be over 100 people. Over the last two or three years over 100 people who have been loyal servants to the party who have just been … what was it Nigel said on that admittedly terrible programme? 'Dross, old dross, idiots, dross.' People who might have given significant amounts of money to the party and significant amounts of time of their lives – 'dross, idiots'.

He added:

I know the membership are fed up with it. I know there's a lot of people – the people on the Facebook pages and stuff, which doesn't get into necessarily the public domain – who are very disappointed about how quickly UKIP crumbles to press comment, because all the press will do is go on for the next man now they've smelt blood.

If they catch you on eighteen-month-old telephone conversations saying 'poofter', they know UKIP will sack you. Well, you couldn't throw a bigger bone to the press.

Bloom was clearly angry over the way the party had changed, and in his mind Farage was behind much of the purge. From his description, it seemed Farage was suddenly almost ashamed of all those people who he had previously relied on. It was like the gawky nerd at school, who, over the summer holidays, has a growth spurt, gets a new haircut and suddenly the cool kids want him in their gang. Goodbye losers like Bloom, hello cool kids like Carswell.

'Exactly,' agreed Bloom. 'It's a bit like your working-class chap put through a posh public school and now he's embarrassed because his dad turns up with the van to pick [him] up at the end of term.'

> But it's not just Farage's leadership style that irked Bloom; it was the policy direction UKIP was taking – specifically its focus on restricting immigration: UKIP's now moved off from Euroscepticism to immigration, so we're now only talking about immigration. We're not talking about the economy, and, of course, as an economist I would suggest our real problem is our economy, and when it comes to immigration – again you see Nigel and I don't agree – we disagreed on so much policy.
>
> Immigration is about welfare reform and education reform. It isn't about a zero-sum numbers, it isn't about keeping people out.
>
> It's a question of changing our educational system, it's about welfare reform. None of this does the modern leadership in UKIP want to talk about.

Bloom said these arguments over policy had been going on between the pair for two years before he had the whip removed in 2013.

He claimed Farage was getting away with a policy black hole because of the poor level of political journalism in the UK. Journalists are too busy searching for gaffes and disputes to actually investigate what the party is – or isn't – proposing.

In many ways, I agreed with Bloom, so I asked what questions he thinks we should be putting to Farage.

What is their view on welfare reform?

Well it depends what day you ask Nigel the question. One might ask Nigel what does he think about the central bank – who should set interest rates? Should it be politicians and the central bank or should the market set interest rates?

Now, Nigel's on record as saying it must be the central bank. Nigel believes libertarianism is being able to smoke in the pub. I don't believe that. I think libertarian goes a little bit further personally.

A question to ask the UKIP leadership is: would you have bailed out the banks? They won't know because you won't find anybody since I left who can discuss banking.

Nigel doesn't know – he hasn't a clue. Nigel hasn't a clue about economics – he's good on fishing and cricket.

I started to laugh, and asked if there was anything else Farage was good at:

He was a very good golfer. He played down to something like four but he hasn't played since, and I said to Nigel you should.

'Oh, I don't have time,' he said.

'The President of the United States has time to play golf, who the hell do you think you are? You're the leader of UKIP for Christ's sake – you're telling me you can't have a holiday?'

He's a workaholic. He's a tremendously hard worker.

I asked what he thought of UKIP's shift from eccentric outsiders to mainstream players.

He said:

I would have been quite happy if we had stayed as a pressure group because I think even Kilroy-Silk would have taken the pragmatic view of: look, don't let's worry about whether you believe in flat tax or whether you believe in the NHS or welfare reform, don't let's bother about that. Let's get ourselves out of the EU first and misgovern ourselves later.

I would have gone with that, I still would go with that. It was only when we decided to become a political party with all the baggage that entails, therefore we need some policies and therefore we need some ethos, you suddenly find then, under the spotlight, that you don't share other people's opinions on anything else other than leaving the European Union.

Nigel has no political conviction at all, other than leaving the European Union – none. He just doesn't.

He added: ' UKIP should have stayed with Euroscepticism. We have a jolly good head of sales in Farage but soon as you start moving outside that phenomena you are then moving into what do you think about the NHS, flat tax, banking reform.'

In fact, Bloom believed UKIP's attempt to become a full-blown party with a range of policies is actually harming the Eurosceptic cause:

There's nothing wrong with being populist but the thing that worries me is that we are not moving forward along the main front. At the moment, in 2017, the Eurosceptics, I think, are going to lose the referendum.

The question is, as I said before, what is the end game? What is the mission statement of UKIP? Is it to get us out of the European Union? There's going to be a referendum in 2017, how are we doing? At the moment we are not doing very well.

How are we doing getting councillors elected in wherever the south-east equivalent of Bongo Bongo Land is – Little Dingly, Little Snodbury-under-the-Wold or wherever. We've

got two new councillors in those sort of places – tremendous,
let's all jump up and down and pat each other on the back –
but it isn't anything to do with the mission statement.

I wasn't convinced by this. Bloom was putting up a good front
of wishing for the good old days when it was just about getting out of
the EU, but I got the sense he would like to have been involved in the
here and now as UKIP prepares for its great assault on Westminster.

As he reflected on his previous role as UKIP's defence spokesman,
and as a former major in the Royal Logistics Corp, Bloom clearly
felt he brought great expertise to the post. 'What a card UKIP has in
me. Sorry to blow my own toot,' he said.

Toot blown, food eaten and beer drunk, my time with Bloom was
at an end.

He gave me a lift back to Selby train station, and we parted with
a handshake. It had been a bizarre day. For a man who travelled the
globe giving lectures on libertarian economics and had mixed with
many nationalities in Brussels for ten years, Bloom lived in a very
small world. In his mind, he could say whatever he liked as long as
those in the rugby club agreed with him. And perhaps that's how
Farage used to be – or at least pretended to be.

I could imagine Bloom and Farage together in the flat they shared in
Brussels, working their way through bottle after bottle of wine every
night, setting the world to rights with language and views perhaps
more associated with the nineteenth century than the twenty-first.

The difference is Farage is better at applying a 21st-century filter when he steps out the front door. Bloom has no filter. He felt no
shame at shouting the Nazi slogan 'Ein Volk, ein Reich, ein Führer'
(One people, one empire, one leader) to a German MEP in a parliamentary debate. No shame in using the term 'Bongo Bongo Land'
despite being well aware of its negative connotations. No shame in
calling a journalist 'racist' for pointing out the lack of non-white faces
on a UKIP conference brochure.

It was clear that for Bloom, UKIP was just another rugby club, another hunt meet, another opportunity to eat, drink and be merry with like-minded people.

In some ways, I did feel sorry for him, because the club he had been part of for so long suddenly changed the rules of membership. And not only did his drinking pal Farage support the changes, he was the one actually enforcing them.

Of all the phrases used to describe Bloom, the most apt is the one he used in his 2014 book on economics: 'A Dinosaur's Guide to Libertarianism'.

CHAPTER 11

JANICE ATKINSON – MY PART IN HER DOWNFALL

MARGATE – FRIDAY 27 FEBRUARY & SATURDAY 28 FEBRUARY 2015

TWO PINTS OF LAGER and a plate of sandwiches.

That was my contribution to the scandal that brought down UKIP MEP Janice Atkinson. A lunch she had organised at UKIP's spring conference in Kent on 27 February 2015 – which I was at – proved to be her undoing, thanks to some creative expenses-claiming by her chief of staff.

But before I go into all that...

The year 2014 had been the most successful in UKIP history: the party had won the European elections, poached two Tory MPs, been victorious in the subsequent by-elections, and seen membership rise beyond 40,000. Could they carry the momentum on into 2015, and make a significant breakthrough in May's general election?

If UKIP did, it would finally buck the trend of success at

European elections followed by failure at the following Westminster vote.

In the 1999 European elections, UKIP won three MEPs, with its 700,000 votes giving it a 7 per cent share. The next general election in 2001, UKIP won no MPs, with its 390,000 votes giving it a 1.5 per cent share.

In the 2004 European elections, UKIP won twelve MEPs, with its 2.7 million votes giving it 16.1 per cent share. In the 2005 general election, UKIP won no MPs, with its 606,000 votes giving it a 2.2 per cent share.

In the 2009 European elections, UKIP won thirteen MEPs, with its 2.5 million votes giving it a 16.6 per cent share. In the 2010 general election, UKIP won no MPs, with its 919,471 votes giving it a 3.1 per cent share.

If these patterns and ratios continued, then UKIP would need 109 per cent of the vote in the 2084 European elections to get a 10 per cent share for the first time in the following general election.

I'm no maths whizz, but I'm pretty sure it's impossible to get 109 per cent of the vote. Unless you are victorious in North Korea. Or Tower Hamlets.

UKIP needed a good start to 2015 to break the Euros: good/Westminster: bad election trend. Yet for all Nigel Farage's talk of new recruits in the aftermath of the Rochester victory, there seemed to be no more parliamentary defectors on the horizon. In fact, the only serious defection saw someone leave UKIP.

Amjad Bashir, the MEP for Yorkshire and the Humber and the party's communities spokesman, announced he was joining the Conservatives on 24 January, following a meeting with David Cameron the previous day. He claimed UKIP had become a 'party of ruthless self-interest', was 'pretty amateur' and had a 'ridiculous' lack of policies.

But word of his defection leaked to the party and, before Bashir could quit, he was suspended for what a UKIP spokesman described as 'extremely serious' financial and employment issues.

The resulting mud-slinging between Bashir, UKIP and the Tories did no one any favours, and what should have been a serious coup for Cameron looked messy. Farage appeared on *The Andrew Marr Show* the day after the defection/suspension was announced, and said he had become 'increasingly alarmed' by Bashir's behaviour, and others in the party had been 'begging' him to axe the MEP four months earlier.

Bashir cried sour grapes on the part of UKIP, but used slightly more colourful language on his official Twitter account when he took a swipe at Douglas Carswell's media officer Michael Heaver and Westminster gossip website Guido Fawkes, tweeting: 'only vermin, like you, abuse hospitality food & drink then piss and shit in the same plate.'

He then disappeared from public view, leading Guido Fawkes to hold a 'Free Amjad Bashir' protest outside Conservative Central Headquarters a week later. By the time of the general election, Bashir had been largely forgotten about by UKIP and the Tories.

Then UKIP hit back with a defection of its own, but this time from Labour, not the Tories.

Harriet Yeo, a former chairman of Labour's national executive committee, announced on 17 February she would now be voting for UKIP in the election as Ed Miliband was not committing to an EU referendum. Despite UKIP pushing it as a serious coup, after the fireworks of Carswell and Mark Reckless, this latest defection was barely a sparkler.

The fact that just a day before her big announcement she had been deselected by Labour as a candidate in the 2015 local elections undermined her motives. Also, she wasn't even joining UKIP, just vowing to vote for them. If that was the best they had, Labour and Tory chiefs could sleep easier at night.

Farage himself had all but disappeared from view at the turn of the year. He sparked minor interest when he revealed he was undertaking 'dry January' (having no alcohol for the whole month) but he was notably absent from most of the airwaves at the start of the year. The UKIP leader was actually on manoeuvres in South Thanet, the constituency in which he was standing in the 2015 general election.

Farage was hoping it would be second time lucky for him in the

Kent constituency, having come fourth in the seat in 2005 with 2,079 votes – 14,581 behind the Labour victor Stephen Ladyman. Laura Sandys won the seat for the Tories in the 2010 general election, but she announced in 2014 she would not be seeking re-election in the following year's vote.

Farage won the UKIP nomination for South Thanet in August 2014, and, in January and early February 2015, focused almost purely on campaigning in the constituency. The charm offensive involved numerous town hall meetings and door-to-door canvassing expeditions. The party knew the media focus on the seat running up to polling day would be intense, so decided to begin its wooing of the voters without hordes of cameras and journalists at every turn. Farage's campaign was being organised by the trusted Chris Bruni-Lowe, the data and campaigns expert who helped mastermind the party's success in Clacton and Rochester.

While his presence in South Thanet was going under the radar, Farage's absence from the national airwaves had not gone unnoticed by those in Westminster. At least one person from Conservative HQ started putting round that Farage was ill, and that was why he had gone quiet.

It was a pretty nasty tactic to employ, especially as Farage had already beaten cancer once in his life and survived two near-fatal accidents as well. With the UKIP leader and the rest of his team keeping a low profile, it was left to two TV programmes to keep the party in people's minds.

The first was a 'mockumentary' imagining life under a UKIP government.

Screened on Channel 4 on 18 February, *UKIP: The First 100 Days* was farcical. Intended to satirise the party and its leadership, it inadvertently satirised the trendy-liberal critics of UKIP instead.

All UKIP voters were deemed to be either racists or homophobes – or both. Apparently, the UK's immediate withdrawal from the EU would lead to an instant rise in unemployment, and the stock market would crash. Within months of Farage as Prime Minister, there would be hundreds of migration squads on the prowl, ransacking Indian restaurants for illegal immigrants. As someone close to the top of the party said to me the next day: 'The funniest thing about that was the idea UKIP could ever be that organised!'

The programme culminated with riots on the streets as anti-fascist groups clashed with UKIP supporters.

More than 5,200 viewers complained to media watchdog Ofcom about the show, with Channel 4 receiving a further 1,300 complaints.

While *UKIP: The First 100 Days* was more embarrassing for Channel 4 than Farage, the second television programme focused on the party to be broadcast that week was harmful to the leader. Screened six days after *UKIP: The First 100 Days*, the BBC Two documentary *Meet the Ukippers* focused on the party's activists in South Thanet.

The programme had already achieved a degree of notoriety long before it was screened. Camera crews caught on tape the moment a news team from the BBC overhead UKIP MEP Janice Atkinson describe a Thai supporter as 'a ting-tong from somewhere'. After a grovelling apology from Farage to the woman and her husband, both of whom were UKIP members, Atkinson survived the scandal.

But the moment that really made the documentary essential viewing was not some overheard muttering when someone didn't realise the mic was still on. It was the moment UKIP councillor Rozanne Duncan decided to reveal her dislike of 'negroes' during a conversation in front of the cameras.

Sitting in the house of South Thanet branch's press officer Liz Langton Way, Duncan began by saying she needed to watch her tongue because 'I can be very outspoken' as she filed her nails. Mrs Langton Way warned her not to 'come up with emotive comments', before adding: 'It's just a question of thinking first.'

Duncan, who seemed to be paying more attention to her nail-filing than the advice she was getting, went on to claim she is not a racist, but...

> The only people I do have problems with are negroes. And I don't know why. I don't know whether there is something in my psyche or whether it's karma from a previous life or

whether something happened to me as a very, very young person and I've drawn a veil over it – because that sometimes happens, doesn't it? But I really do have a problem with people with negroid features, I really do.

A friend of mine said: 'What would you do if I invited you to dinner and I put you next to…?'

I said, 'I wouldn't be there, as simple as that, I wouldn't be there.'

Mrs Langton Way looked on, aghast, and told Duncan her views were 'ridiculous'. But she still went on, giving descriptions of the features of 'negroes' she found objectionable.

After her racist rant, Duncan declared she had dinner in the oven and had to be going, leaving Mrs Langton Way and her husband confused, bemused and not at all amused.

Throwing her head in her hands, Mrs Langton Way said, 'I just sat there thinking … yes, OK, and you're a councillor already!'

The next morning, despair had given way to fury for Mrs Langton Way.

'She has been told time and time again to keep her bloody mouth shut and I thought that by now the message would have got through.' A dejected Mrs Langton Way added: 'I have to say that listening to somebody saying all that last night made me think: do I really want to be involved with these people? Because that was not what I was interested in.'

Duncan's comments were reported to UKIP's high command, and she was immediately suspended. The programme aired two months after the incident, and even though Duncan had since been expelled from the party, it was no less embarrassing for UKIP when the footage was screened.

The end of the documentary showed Mrs Langton Way and her husband, who was due to stand as a local councillor, quitting the party. The excuse was that Mr Langton Way was due to have operations on his knees and caring for him would take up most of her time. As the pair toasted their resignations while preparing a roast dinner, Mr Langton Way quipped: 'Thank God that's over.'

As the footage faded to black, it wouldn't have been a complete surprise if the following words came up on the screen: 'Since shooting this documentary, Mr and Mrs Langton Way walked out into the sea and never returned.'

All in all, hardly a great start to the year for the People's Army.

Against this backdrop, the party got together for its spring conference in Margate, Kent – coincidentally located in the South Thanet constituency in which Farage was standing – on Friday 27 February.

Billed as a chance for party members to get together ahead of the general election, it was essentially a 'get Nigel elected' conference – something that a senior party figure admitted to the BBC.

The venue was the Winter Gardens, a theatre and dining hall complex right on the beach. Gone was the flashiness of Doncaster Racecourse or the establishment feel of the Methodist Central Hall in Westminster. The seaside concert venue, complete with faded posters advertising shows from a by-gone era, was practically a bunker, positioned well below street level.

Perfect for the UKIP psyche.

The foot soldiers of the People's Army had clearly been learning how the media operated, and applied last-minute 'gaffe checks' to the venue. This involved removing anything that could lead to an embarrassing photograph, including a poster advertising a 'Circus of Horrors' – what fun there would be if Farage was snapped next to that.

The speeches were taking place in the main theatre, and we, the press, had been given our own area to report from – a balcony to the right-hand side of the stage.

As well as giving us a clear view of the speakers, it also gave the audience seated below a good look at us. Whenever a Kipper made a remark about the hostility of the press, hundreds of pairs of eyes darted in our direction, buried among scowling faces.

Directly opposite us was the balcony reserved for senior Kippers

and their staff. The People's Army generals sat above their foot soldiers, glancing down on their recruits located in a sort of no-man's land
between their balcony and the one occupied by the evil journalists.

On the Friday morning, I boarded the train to Margate from east
London, feeling a twinge of apprehension about visiting a UKIP
event, which I had not felt for a while. The reason for that was I was
no longer working for the People's Army paper of choice, the *Daily
Express*, but rather for one of its chief antagonists, the *Daily Mirror*.

I joined the *Mirror* in January 2015 as its first online political
reporter. A few people remarked it must have been weird moving
from a right-wing paper to a left-wing outlet, but it wasn't. Instead
of being paid to be sympathetic to Farage, I was now being paid to
be sympathetic to Ed Miliband. Same game, different team.

I wondered how Farage and other Ukippers would react to me.
Was I now on some sort of blacklist? When the Purple Revolution
came, and the People's Army swept to power, would I be one of the
first against the wall, shouting through tears about all the articles I
had written praising Farage while at the *Express* as a UKIP judge lists
my heretical stories from the *Mirror*?

Adding to my worried mind, I had forgotten to book a room for
the night in the Kent seaside town. I spent much of the train journey from east London to Margate ringing round all the B&Bs and
hotels in the area.

No luck.

Haunted by my memory of missing the Reckless announcement
at last autumn's conference, I was determined to be at every second
of this event.

But with nowhere to stay, it may be I would have to come back
that night, and potentially miss something amazing.

Maybe Farage would get wasted and go skinny dipping off Margate beach at two in the morning.

If so, I wanted to be there to see him in all his naked glory. (I know
what you're thinking: 'What sort of twisted mind would think such

things?!' I'll tell you: the kind of twisted mind who wants a goddamn front-page story!)

After an hour of trying, one B&B owner said she had just checked with a gentlemen whether he was staying again that night, and he had said no. The room was mine.

I arrived at the venue just before 9.30 a.m., ready to see Mark Reckless take to the stage to a standing ovation from the hundreds of UKIP activists in the hall. I was determined to listen to one of Reckless's speech and actually take in what he was saying. I refused to be beaten. I gazed out over the Kippers as they stood to applause, and strained my vision across to the opposite balcony, trying to see if Farage was in situ.

He wasn't, as, while his foot soldiers had been preparing the conference in Kent, Farage had been over in Maryland, America, addressing the Conservative Political Action Conference (CPAC).

The CPAC is an annual rallying cry for the American right, and is particularly popular with college-aged Republicans. Down to speak at the 2015 conference were political heavyweights including Jeb Bush, Newt Gingrich, Rand Paul, Rick Santorum, Donald Trump and the infamous Sarah Palin. UKIP was a fascinating beast to the American right, particularly the Tea Party movement of Republicans. American politics is even more of a duopoly than Britain's, and many across the pond still think of the UK Parliament as being just about the Conservatives and Labour.

The notion that a separate party, located to the right of the Conservatives, may start to win power in the UK is an intriguing prospect to the Tea Party. (If UKIP can do it, why not us?) But first it needs to be proven that it can work. Farage knew this, and he also knew that many in the Tea Party wanted to break away and form their own independent group.

So it was that, as Ukippers were finalising the preparations in Margate for the spring conference, Farage was in America, addressing an audience of fewer than 250 in a venue with room for thousands.

He was introduced by the editor of the conservative Breitbart news website Alexander Marlow, who tried his best to whip up the small crowd into some sort of frenzy. Marlow claimed that in the UK there was 'a revolt against the political establishments and the global elites and that revolt is being led by a party called UKIP, and a man you'll soon meet called Nigel Farage'.

He added that Farage's main issue was immigration, and that the UKIP leader was 'the only UK politician who has told the truth about the Islamic threat'. Farage addressed the small crowd for about twenty minutes, talking up his People's Army and the Purple Revolution, and won enthusiastic applause from those watching.

'Nigel Farage takes CPAC by storm ... or not. UKIP leader gives speech to nearly empty room' was the headline on *The Independent*'s website, while the *Telegraph*'s went with: 'UKIP's Nigel Farage fails to make a mark at CPAC 2015'.

His appearance at CPAC was put down to the influence of Raheem Kassam, a former reporter for Breitbart's London division. A known lover of American politics, Kassam was appointed Farage's chief advisor in late October 2014, although he had been informally working for the UKIP leader for a few weeks before the announcement.

The appointment of an unknown twenty-something was met with bemusement by many in Westminster, but *The Spectator* magazine's gossip columnist 'Steerpike' let everyone know what to expect from Kassam.

'Kassam is a wildly self-important figure who flits about on the internet right. Mr Kassam is famed for his inflated sense of self-importance.'

The article continued: 'Kassam is a professional wind-up merchant, of sorts, too – and trained in the arts of vicious American-style attack politics – which we can now expect UKIP to adopt.'

It concluded: 'If UKIP is trying to be popular, they could hardly have picked a more unsuitable hire.'

I can honestly say Kassam did not wind up a single journalist at that conference – he wasn't there. He overslept and missed his flight back from the United States.

Farage may not have been at the conference that morning, but plenty of others were, including, to my surprise, UKIP's first goth member.

John Hengsuan was manning a stall in the small section of the venue dedicated to promoting merchandise and affiliated groups. The pencil-thin 24-year-old had long, dyed-black hair, brushed up to create the true bird-nest look – except one section of his head was completely shaved, making it seem like he had run out of money for the haircut halfway through.

He told me he was a big fan of Siouxsie and the Banshees and The Cure, and I mentally flicked through the bands' back catalogues to try to remember if they had any anti-EU songs. (The Cure's debut single was called 'Killing an Arab', but I'm not going to read any significance into that whatsoever.)

Hengsuan was standing to be a councillor in May's local elections in Gravesend, Kent, and said the Kippers he had met were more welcoming than people his own age.

He said: 'I think UKIP believes in the youth of Britain. My stepdad and my Polish uncles and cousins all say, "Young people in Britain are lazy." We're not, and UKIP knows that.'

I asked how his unusual hairstyle goes down with fellow party members more likely dressed in tweed and sensible shoes. Hengsuan said: 'They are really open and nice. On the streets it's the young people who are shouting that I'm "fucking weird".'

A goth at a UKIP conference. Next up, a Rastafarian at the Tories' and a gangsta rapper at the Greens'.

Back in the main hall, and the press were listening intently to the speeches. I made my way back up to the balcony and flicked through a bunch of flyers I had picked up. The big story of the day so far was that UKIP's manifesto was not going to be presented, despite a rumour it would be unveiled at the conference.

Other than that, it was all very dull, to be honest. There was none of the electricity in the air you usually get when hundreds of Kippers are in a room together. As one broadcast hack said to me: 'What if there are no gaffes? We're going to have to start covering them seriously from now on, aren't we?'

I decided to take my life in my hands and venture into the no-man's land below filled with UKIP members, mainly because I wanted a cup of coffee and the snacks bar was down on the floor. I joined the queue of Kippers, who were talking among themselves just yards away from the stage where the speeches were being given. Unfortunately, they were talking a little too loudly.

'Can the people queuing up please do so quietly!' came the order from the stage. The Kippers all looked sheepish, but couldn't resist making a joke about it.

'Oh, it's like being back at school! Am I going to get detention?' one male Kipper in his sixties said to his friend.

'SSSSSSSHHHHHH!' came a hiss from another Kipper sitting just yards away, trying to listen.

'Oh, you're in trouble now!' the man's friend said back.

Another Kipper came over. 'Please, gentlemen! People can't hear the speeches!' he implored. The two looked down at their feet like naughty schoolboys, and the queue was finally silent.

For about five seconds.

'No, I said one tea and two coffees, not two teas and one coffee!' an elderly woman at the front of the queue shouted over to the people serving behind the bar. The other Kippers in line took this as an opportunity to start talking again, leading to more shushing from the audience.

A split in the People's Army, in front of my very eyes. It was somehow appropriate that is was over queuing etiquette.

After the excitement of Queuegate, I retook my seat in the media balcony to watch UKIP's health spokesman Louise Bours give her speech on the NHS. They was no danger the people queuing for tea and coffee would drown her out.

As with her address in Doncaster last year, she spent most of her time just shouting.

She reached peak volume within two minutes, hitting a crescendo as she said: 'Money is pumped into NHS management with high executive salaries, repayments for the hastily signed PFI contracts and policies of uncontrolled mass immigration pile on the pressure AND PATIENT CARE SUFFERS!'

With no sense of irony or self-awareness, the MEP and health spokesman for UKIP attacked the other parties for using the NHS as a 'political punch bag' – or, as she said: 'A POLITICAL PUNCHBAG!'

The Spectator's Isabel Hardman generously tweeted that Ms Bours had 'excellent voice projection' as she used to work in theatre. To my ears, it sounded like someone who has had too many glasses of white wine in Wetherspoons shouting at an ex-partner they have seen across the pub. (Ooh, get me with my metropolitan liberal elite snobbery.)

After listening to a few more speeches – mass immigration: bad; being British: good – it was lunchtime and I knew just where to go.

Now at my third UKIP conference, I knew the best chance of free food – and a potential story – was at the UKIP women's event. Organised by Janice Atkinson, MEP for the south east, the lunch took place in a pub called The Hoy, a five-minute walk from the conference venue.

As with the UKIP women's event in Doncaster, Nigel Farage's wife Kirsten was in attendance, alongside numerous MEPs, candidates and even one of the party's two MPs – Reckless. In terms of UKIP, this was star-studded.

It wasn't just the Kippers who had made the pilgrimage to the pub. Rumours of a free lunch had spread to Westminster's finest, and Lucy Fisher from *The Times*, the *Daily Telegraph*'s sketch-writer Michael Deacon and Bloomberg's Robert Hutton also descended on the venue.

Fisher and myself were the first journos to find our way to the pub, and, after I had got myself a free pint of beer and a plate of food, we located Janice Atkinson sitting at the head of a table of other party members.

Atkinson – never a lover of the press – was in a particularly hostile mood and gave us a cold welcome. Without much provocation, she bemoaned the British media for always giving UKIP a hard time and ranted about the lack of integrity in journalism.

'A lack of integrity! What a horrible accusation!' I thought, as I drank my free beer and ate my free sandwiches.

Atkinson claimed nobody in the press gave UKIP a fair hearing. In my experience, when a politician calls for a 'fair hearing', what they are really asking for is 'no scrutiny'.

I pointed out that, as a former *Express* journalist, I had been giving UKIP a 'fair hearing' for quite a while.

She didn't seem convinced.

I asked for her view on the *Meet the Ukippers* documentary, which had aired less than a week earlier.

'Stitch-up!' was her response.

'What about it was a stitch-up? That councillor made those comments without any prompting from the filmmakers,' I replied, referring to Rozanne Duncan's racist rant.

'Stitch-up!' was her machine-gun-like reply. 'Anyway, for legal reasons, I can't talk about it.'

Fisher asked what UKIP thought the press should be covering, and Atkinson began listing reams of European Parliament legislation.

I hate to say it, but Atkinson did have a point about the lack of coverage of what goes on in Brussels, but it is difficult enough to persuade editors to run stories on UK politics, let alone the complexities of what goes on in the EU.

By now, my glass was empty and, seeing as it was a free bar, I thought it would be considered rude not to have another beer. The queue was three people deep, as thirsty Kippers took advantage of the opportunity to get a drink without having to pay.

Little did we know that with every pint of beer being pulled, glass of wine being poured and spirit being measured out we were unwittingly becoming part of a dastardly expenses plot.

With a second pint of lager in my hand, I plonked myself down for Atkinson's big speech to the gathered faithful (and sponging journalists). In her three-and-a-half-minute address, Atkinson reminded the audience she was 'voted number three across the whole country' by UKIP members for the MEP selection list.

She attacked 'demeaning' and 'patronising' all-women shortlists used by other parties to boost female representation and hit out at schools 'pushing girls down the traditional route' of 'nursery nurses, hairdressers, manicurists, the arts'.

'Yes, they are all important,' she said, 'We need them. I go to the hairdressers. But too many girls in this country are pushed down this route.'

Not like Atkinson, who nobly decided to go into politics (initially as a press officer under former Tory leader Michael Howard in 2005, before unsuccessfully standing for the Conservatives in 2010 and defecting to UKIP in 2011).

She told the audience that becoming an MEP was 'the hardest thing I've ever done'.

> I'm on the front line. I could have actually just taken my salary as an MEP, gone to Brussels once a week, get paid for going there, come back on Eurostar, keep my head below the parapet. But like others in UKIP, when we stood to become MEPs, the first question we're asked is: 'Why do you want to be a UKIP MEP?' And the answer is…?

The audience replied as one: 'To get out of Europe!'

'We don't want to be MEPs!' was the actual answer, according to Atkinson.

Before handing over to UKIP's deputy chairman Suzanne Evans, Atkinson took a swipe at Labour's then deputy leader Harriet Harman.

'She is the high-priestess, the Harmanista, the high-priestess of the Guardianistas, the feministas. That's not us. We're real woman, we've all done real jobs and we're standing for Parliament.'

Atkinson was clearly a person of principle, who saw herself as a trailblazer for women in the male-dominated world of politics.

The next day, in her actual conference speech, Atkinson went further, attacking the media for obsessing over female politicians' hair, shoes and cleavages. She also spoke out against intrusion into politicians' family lives – no doubt thinking of the moment just two months earlier when her ex-husband spoke to *Channel 4 News* about the amount of child support Atkinson owed him in relation to the pair's two sons.

The story was somewhat embarrassing for a politician who had in the past criticised 'feckless families' who had to rely on state support to take care of their children.

Atkinson also took aim at the waste of taxpayers' cash by the European Union, claiming 'a powerful lobby group called the European Women's Lobby' received the equivalent of £1.1 million in funding in 2011.

'It's European taxpayers' cash and that's partly British cash as well.'

Musing on her own job as an MEP, Ms Atkinson appealed for sympathy from the audience, saying: 'It's a hard life, believe me, sometimes.'

One wonders how much harder it would be if the European Parliament didn't pay a yearly salary of more than £78,000, plus expenses.

Atkinson left the UKIP stage to applause, but within weeks would be kicked out of the party.

For someone so clearly motivated by strong principles (such as families taking financial responsibility for their children, right?), Atkinson appeared to have taken the eye off the ball when it came to her own expenses.

Perhaps it was the pressure of the 'hard life' of an MEP that led to her chief of staff, Christine Hewitt, trying to persuade the management of The Hoy to provide a receipt for more than three times the actual cost of the UKIP women's lunch.

David Goulding, manager of the pub/restaurant, received an email asking him to overcharge for the event, which actually came in at £950.

He was asked to address the invoice to a European Parliament address – meaning European taxpayers would be picking up the inflated bill.

He was so angered by the suggestion, he contacted *The Sun* newspaper, who set up a hidden camera for when Hewitt was due to arrive to settle the account.

Hewitt allegedly told a member of staff: 'The idea is we overcharge them slightly because that's the way of repatriating [the money].'

The staff member said: '£3,150, is that alright? Yeah, if you're alright with that? Is that enough for you?'

Hewitt replied: 'Oh God, yeah, that's more than enough.'

The story broke on Thursday 19 March and Farage immediately stuck the boot in, telling the *Telegraph*: 'I am astonished, totally astonished. If what she has been suspended for is right I am astonished she could have done something quite so stupid. I am very, very shocked and surprised.'

Four days later, and Atkinson and Hewitt were both expelled from the party. The Folkestone & Hythe constituency that Atkinson had been fighting for was given to Harriet Yeo – ex-Labour replacing ex-Tory.

Another one bites the dust.

Of course, at the time, none of us knew our love of free booze and food would be exploited in such a cunning way, and I thought nothing more of the lunch after I left.

As always, I was still desperate for a story, and so I made my way back to the conference centre to see if anything had broken out.

Walking past the large dining hall next to the main theatre, I realised this would be the setting for the gala dinner later that night. At the corresponding event a year ago, a comedian told some pretty offensive jokes about Eastern Europeans, and at the gala dinner in Doncaster, Mike Read debuted his 'UKIP Calypso' tune.

Maybe this room would furnish me with a story.

I sat down at one of the round tables already set out for the evening's meal, got out my laptop and began flicking through my notes of the day so far.

Opposite me, two older gentleman, both in smart suits, were deep in conversation.

After one left, the remaining man looked at me and smiled. He was in his early to mid-sixties, with white hair swept back over his head. He had a broad grin and spoke with a confident and educated air.

'Filing copy?' he said, clearly realising I was a journalist.

'Yes, just typing some things up now,' I replied.

He told me he did a bit of writing, and that he was currently working on a book about Islam.

I asked him what about the religion exactly, and, boy, did he answer – giving the most bizarre and uncomfortable lecture I had ever had.

Topics included:

- The rise of Islam.

- How to survive the end of the world.

- How I could only live three days without water and during the apocalypse I would have to slit my neighbour's throat in a rush to a hydrant.

- How to create a small radio using wire and batteries to communicate with the Resistance.

All he was lacking was a tin-foil hat. The guy was clearly two pints of lager and a plate of sandwiches short of a free lunch.

What was even more remarkable than the venomous tide of Islamophobia spewing forth, was the fact he was telling it to someone he knew was a journalist.

I wanted to see just how far the rabbit hole went in this bloke's particular wonderland, and so asked him if he thought Islam was more destructive than fascism and the Nazis.

He replied: 'Beyond your wildest, wildest nightmares.'
He continued:

> People say to me, because I don't dress it up, do I hate Islam,
> for instance? Hate? Hate? That would be utterly impossible.
> Hate is something that is quite close to love, as you know.
> It's bound by passion, it's bound by emotion. I cannot begin
> to tell you ... I could not bring the words together – and I'm
> not often lost for words – the utter, bottomless, pitiless con-
> tempt that I feel. It's nothing to do with hate.

'Do you take in moderate Islam with that as well?' I replied.
'There is no such thing as moderate Islam,' the man said.
'I live in east London, and I live with thousands upon thousands
of Muslims, and I don't feel that I'm living in an extremist place,' I
said back.
He responded:

> If and when the crap were to hit the fan and all your moderate
> Islamic friends were there, as moderate people – I'm not saying
> they were not moderate people, [but] they adhere to an ideol-
> ogy which is called Islam and one of the major problems with
> things like Islam is anybody who wanted to – because multicul-
> turalism is a mindless, facile, asinine nonsense, if any Muslim
> wanted to leave it, because they wanted to, they couldn't. It's
> an absolute impossibility. The Koran says that you must never
> have any intercourse with a kafir. If you do, you are an apos-
> tate, and the punishment for apostates is death.

'But that's extremism. That's people who read the Koran and take it
literally,' I replied.
'No, it's not. If you are a Muslim, you follow the tenants of the
Koran.'

'You could say that if you are a Christian you should be stoning to death those who commit adultery – it says that in the Bible and not all Christians believe that.'

After talking about how Muslims, Christians and Jews all worship the same god, he said: 'A thousand years ago, Christianity and Islam were exactly the same. Murderers, misogynists, homophobic, neo-fascist. The only difference is we've moved forward 1,000 years.'

It was after this he began talking about the breakdown of civilisation, and how I would need a shotgun to defend myself as my fellow man regressed to scavengers following the collapse of law and order.

I was gobsmacked. This was the jackpot, surely? All I needed now was proof he was involved in the party in some way. He told me his name was Brendan, but wouldn't give me his surname. I asked if he was standing for UKIP, and he said no. He said he was just curious about the party, and everything he said was his personal opinion, and nothing to do with UKIP.

My head was spinning with Islamophobia, doomsday prophecies, and his wide, Cheshire Cat grin. I wanted to stay and find out more about him, but the afternoon speeches were in full swing in the conference hall and Farage was due to make his keynote address.

I reluctantly said goodbye and made my way back up to the press balcony. Farage was the big draw in the afternoon, but first up was economic spokesman Patrick O'Flynn. The last time he had addressed a UKIP conference he had put forward the 'Wag Tax', which was publicly slapped down by Farage just days later.

O'Flynn was taking no such chances this time and, instead of putting forward any new ideas, he used his supposed speech on economics to warn against gaffes in the run-up to the election.

He said: 'We have a responsibility, as a collective leadership of the party, to all those candidates in those key target seats. I certainly don't want to wake up on May 8th thinking something that I said made a difference and cost a few votes either way.'

Having been hung out to dry by Farage after the 'Wag Tax' debacle in Doncaster, O'Flynn had clearly decided he did not want any such public flogging after this conference and used the final five minutes of his speech to praise Farage to the heavens.

'Politics is indeed a team game but every single team also needs leadership, and we are so fortunate in our party to have the most inspirational leader of all in Nigel Farage.'

He went on:

> He's someone who stepped from the wreckage of a light aircraft five years or so ago and did not walk away from politics but walked back into the political fray and not many of us knew how much he suffered and the problems he needed to get over. That was a very courageous thing in itself to take back the leadership of the party knowing he could achieve so much for us.

O'Flynn praised his leader for taking on the political titan Nick Clegg in the TV debates before the European elections and masterminding the devastating defections of Carswell and Reckless. He referred to Farage as 'our inspiration'.

To misquote William Shakespeare, O'Flynn was essentially telling the conference: 'I come to praise Caesar, not to bury him.'

Farage took to the stage to predictable applause, and immediately confronted the rumours about his health:

> There's been a lot of speculation about where I've been. Why have I not been seen on the television all the time? Why have I not been out there like the others making an endless series of promises, which of course they never intend to keep? Well, I'll tell you where I've been, and in fact my absence from the Westminster scene has even led my opponents to spread some really quite malicious and unpleasant speculation about my health, and it's said I'm seriously ill and that's why I've not

been seen. I know this will disappoint my opponents but can
I please tell everybody now and make it clear that rumours
of my demise have been greatly exaggerated.

His joke was met with laughter by the audience, but many hacks sitting in the balcony couldn't understand why he had publicly responded to rumours that hardly anyone outside of the Westminster bubble had heard.

Indeed, even some of the journalists in the bubble hadn't picked up on that particular bit of gossip, and they seemed to be the ones most confused as to why Farage had spoken about them.

To me, it was obvious – whether the rumour, or even the rumour of the rumour, was true, it gave Farage another opportunity to paint his Westminster opponents as desperate cynics determined to use all tricks necessary to halt the People's Army and its Great Leader.

He used the rest of the speech to warn activists of future attacks from UKIP opponents in both the political and media spheres, and urged them to run a 'positive' campaign.

'Everything about our campaign is going to be positive. It's going to be positive because we believe in Britain,' he said.

Turning to the issue of immigration, Farage said:

What we as UKIP have got to do is inject a positive note
into this debate. We've made the arguments over the years
about wage compression. We've made the arguments about
the stress on the National Health Service A&E departments.
We've made the arguments about the lack of primary school
places. What we've now got to do is turn this round and get
people to back something that is positive.

Just three months after UKIP used an image of a distressed white woman on a poster in the South Yorkshire Police and Crime Commissioner by-election under the words: 'There are 1,400 reasons why you should not trust Labour again', Farage was calling for a positive campaign.

With Farage's speech over, I descended from my seat in the balcony and made my way down to the bar.

Hacks including Dan Hodges from the *Telegraph*, Giles Dilnot from the BBC and my *Mirror* colleague Jack Blanchard also joined me for a drink, and various Ukippers milled about.

The bar began to fill up with senior party members, including O'Flynn and migration spokesman Steven Woolfe, but Farage was nowhere to be seen.

The Kippers all seemed in a happy mood. The day had gone off without any clear gaffes, and the speeches had – unsurprisingly – been received well. Journalists and the Kippers were buying each other drinks, sharing jokes and jointly speculating on the general election result.

Into this scene emerged the People's Army's commander-in-chief himself flanked by his bodyguards, followed by a camera crew and in deep conversation with the *Telegraph*'s senior political correspondent Christopher Hope.

The procession moved towards the bar, whereby a bottle of champagne was popped open and poured into flutes.

Just an hour earlier, Farage had been warning the People's Army of the hostility of the press, saying 'we have very few friends in the media'. Now he was quaffing champagne with one of the leading political journalists in the country.

The pair were toasting the deal between the *Telegraph* and Farage to serialise the UKIP leader's latest autobiography *The Purple Revolution*, due for publication the following month. The rest of us hacks looked on in amusement as Hope – nicknamed Chopper by those in the Westminster village – necked down the bubbly alongside Farage.

Like moths to a flame, or flies to shit, we all began moving towards the celebrating duo, hoping perhaps to get our own chat with the man of the moment.

Farage began working the room with his usual charm. When it was my turn, he asked me how my career move was working out.

I told him that if his party was really serious about attracting the disaffected ex-Labour voters, he should talk to the *Mirror* a lot more. I had already asked his press office if I could have a sit-down interview with him during the election campaign, and get *Mirror* online readers to send in questions.

He seemed enthusiastic: 'Yes, I definitely want to do that, I really do,' he said.

Other journalists began swarming round us, and the conversation turned to his trip to America. I asked him if it was true that he had refused to be in a photograph with Sarah Palin, and if so, why?

'Fuck off! You work for the *Mirror*! I'm not telling you!' was his response, delivered with laughter but no doubt a reflection of his true views.

So much for wanting to engage with the *Mirror* audience.

The bar emptied as Ukippers prepared for their gala dinner, which would be in the same dining room where earlier that day Brendan had spelt out his apocalyptic view of the future of mankind. The media pack also went off gently into the night, and those of us who were staying for day two of the conference set forth to find a curry house.

After a good dinner, in which I discovered the normally prim and proper Isabel Hardman could drink pints of lager and chow down on spicy curry in a manner that would have made Rab C. Nesbitt proud, I found my guest house, conveniently located opposite the conference venue.

Unfortunately, the man whose room I was supposed to be taking had decided to stay another night, so the owner of the B&B had to make me up a bed in the only space available – the kitchen.

To be fair, she had done a good job with sheets covering the dishwasher and washing machine, and the hatch for passing food out had been sealed shut.

There was even a television.

DAY TWO

After a good night's sleep in the kitchen – taking me back to my university days – I descended once again into the UKIP bunker.

Douglas Carswell was the big draw of the morning, and used his speech to talk about the Westminster 'cartel'.

'Many MPs become MPs by working in the offices of MPs. They've already been a special advisor, they've worked for a think tank. They are already part of the club,' he said.

It's always good to hear someone speaking from experience. Carswell had been part of that club himself during his early days in the Tory Party. He stood against Tony Blair in Sedgefield in 2001, the ultimate act of self-flagellation for a wannabe politician, keen to show he would take one for the team. In 2005, he worked in the Tory policy unit, reporting to David Cameron, as the future Prime Minister pulled together the Conservative manifesto for that year's election.

Carswell used the vast majority of his thirteen-minute conference speech to talk about constitutional and parliamentary reform – hardly the most sexy of subjects and not one that the activists in the hall would be bringing up on the doorstep while out canvassing.

('Well, I hear your concerns that our plans to leave the EU may deter international investment in the UK, leading to a lack of confidence in the economy, a rise in the cost of exports, the devaluation of the pound, an increase in unemployment and ultimately another economic collapse far worse than what we suffered in 2008 … but we do plan to create a parliamentary committee to approve future ministerial appointments. So shall I put you down as a "maybe"?')

If Carswell's speech failed to stir the UKIP masses, the party's heritage and tourism spokesman William Cash – son of Tory backbencher Sir William Cash – got the People's Army whooping and cheering with his passionate address.

Mocking the Labour Party's 'Pink Bus' women's campaign, Cash said: 'I have launched my "Tourism on Tour" campaign, and will be touring the countryside and seaside resorts in my new campaign car – a V8 Jaguar Sovereign in dark purple!'

The audience lapped it up. What vehicle could be more UKIP than a purple Jaguar?

Cash went on to blast wind turbines as 'unwanted towering industrial structures [that] not only make a mockery of so-called localism, they are symbols of atheistic, social and EU oppression!'

This time the audience added cheers to its applause.

He then called for a VAT cut on restoring listed buildings to 'boost skilled British workers and craftsmen such as stone masons, thatchers and carpenters whose traditional skills are the lifeblood of local communities'.

Which local communities was he talking about? I wondered. Those in the eighteenth century, before the Industrial Revolution, maybe?

Do you know what provided the 'lifeblood' of the small village in Devon where I grew up?

Farming, a McVitie's factory, and the yearly folk festival.

He finished with a flourish, and his call to 'weaponise' Britain's heritage was met with a standing ovation.

Castles, Jaguars, thatched roofs and Britain's seaside towns – all things the People's Army loved to hear and cheer. This is what they were fighting for.

The next person to get a standing ovation at the conference called for UKIP to fight for something very different, and not exactly a traditional subject at a rally of the People's Army.

Former boxing promotor Kellie Maloney had been involved with UKIP since 2004, when, as Frank Maloney, she had been the party's candidate for London Mayor. During the campaign, Frank was heavily criticised after refusing to canvas in Camden because there were 'too many gays' in the borough.

He added:

I don't think they do a lot for society. I don't have a problem with gays, what I have a problem with is them openly flaunting their sexuality. I'm more for traditional family values and family life. I'm anti-same-sex marriages and I'm anti-same-sex families. I don't think it's right for children to be brought up that way. I don't think two men can bring up a child.

If you are homosexual, you are homosexual – just get on with your life and stop bitching about things.

James Davenport, then chairman of the Gay Conservative group, called for Frank to be axed, calling him a 'dangerous extremist'.

Eleven years on, and Frank was now Kellie, having undergone gender reassignment in 2014.

Two days before Mahoney took to the stage in Margate, the head of UKIP's LGBT wing Tom Booker quit the party, saying he was dissatisfied at the 'failure of the leadership to set a gay-friendly tone'.

Leaflets being passed out during the conference by UKIP Christian Soldiers claimed sex education in primary schools was 'a recruitment drive' by the LGBT community.

'As such, people cannot reproduce their own kind, they must recruit and this is best done among children in schools, the younger the better,' said the leaflet.

It was against this backdrop that Britain's most famous transgender person addressed the UKIP conference, with a tearful plea for understanding of the LGBT community. She first of all addressed the comments made during her London Mayor campaign:

I have learned to say sorry and apologise if I am wrong. I made a terrible mistake in 2004 when I made a derogatory remark about the gay community, and to them I apologise. I had to come to terms with myself and accept that I was a transsexual. It is something I hid and something I fought. I wanted to transition very quietly, but unfortunately my transition is probably one of the most public events of 2014.

Mahoney read out a poem written by two children for their trans-sexual parent who had committed suicide, earning a standing ovation from the audience.

It was a bizarre moment. The People's Army, derided as close-minded, intolerant and in many cases racist and homophobic, standing to applaud a transsexual person urging for greater tolerance for peo-ple in her situation. The audience seemed genuinely moved by her speech, and Farage took to the stage to say Kellie's presence at the conference showed UKIP was 'open to everyone'.

The conference ended on a high. Well, almost.

To signify the end of the event, the audience rose to its feet to sing 'God Save the Queen'. Really badly.

The version of the national anthem being piped through the PA system had an extra few bars before the 'SEND HER VIC-TOOOOOOOOOORIOUS' bit, which meant the People's Army were out of sync with the music. Yes, that's right, UKIP were fucking up the national anthem. Surely that's a hanging offence in their world?

Outside the Winter Gardens, a few hundred anti-UKIP protesters marched along the street, banging drums, blowing whistles, and sing-ing. The police were in attendance to stop any trouble, but the only chance of violence breaking out came from a mob of Britain First members who had also turned up – in their 'minds', to protect Farage and the People's Army. They stood wearing their National Trust-style fleeces, scowling at the protesters as they marched past.

I thought about going to speak to them.

But I had spent the night in a kitchen and wanted to get back home to my own bed. Reflecting on the conference on my train journey back, I realised how distant Farage had seemed. There appeared to be more bodyguards than ever before, even flanking him as he walked into the hall full of UKIP members. What's the worst that would hap-pen to him there? A flirtatious Ukipper would try to give him a kiss?

In that case, having seen some of the Kippers, maybe the body-guards were a good idea after all.

CHAPTER 12

UNLOCKING THE WAR CHEST

'FOLLOW THE MONEY' IS the mantra all good investigative journalists live by.

Unfortunately for you, dear reader, I am a lazy political journalist, and so my information on those who bankroll UKIP is limited. However, through the course of my time following Farage I found myself repeatedly coming into contact with some of those who financially back the party.

I worked for a newspaper owner who made millions through pornography; shared a taxi and had dinner with a gambler who was friends with Lord Lucan; and had been in the country retreat of an insurance company founder who invested in diamond mines.

These are three of the people who have largely bankrolled UKIP; these are the people Nigel Farage owes much of his success to.

Let's start with the porn channel owner…

RICHARD DESMOND

The chairman of Northern & Shell, which, at the time of writing, owns the *Daily Express*, the *Sunday Express*, the *Daily Star*, the *Star on Sunday*, and *OK!* magazine, Richard Desmond made his first donation to UKIP in December 2014.

The tycoon – whose company also owns Portland TV, which runs pornography channels such as Television X The Fantasy Channel – had previously given money to Labour, handing over £100,000 during Tony Blair's leadership of the party.

But despite getting on well with Ed Miliband, with whom he shares a background in the north London Jewish community, it was with UKIP that Desmond decided to part with his cash ahead of the 2015 general election.

He first wrote a cheque for £300,000 in December 2014, boosting the coffers of the party as it prepared to enter a decisive election year.

Desmond then handed over £1 million on 17 April 2015, fewer than three weeks before polling day.

What a wonderful, public-spirited gesture.

My first encounter with Desmond came during my first full week at the *Express* in May 2013.

I was beginning my stint as a web reporter when I received an email on my first Thursday afternoon in the office in Lower Thames Street, near London Bridge.

It simply read: '20 minute warning'.

Reporters around me suddenly burst forth into a flurry of activity. Bags were pushed under tables, desks were cleared and, for some reason, water bottles were placed on the floor.

'What's going on?' I asked.

'Every Thursday Richard Desmond has a meeting in that room,' said a colleague, gesturing to a conference room in the corner.

'And?'

'He doesn't like mess. He doesn't like water bottles on the desk.'

Twenty minutes later, Desmond walked past us and into the room.

Almost immediately, the pungent smell of cigars wafted out of the meeting, and indistinguishable raised voices could be heard. This happened every Thursday afternoon.

Sometimes you could hear the crockery tap-dancing on the table as fists slammed down on the wood. After half an hour or so, Desmond would walk out, sometimes stopping to chat to one of my bosses.

One time he made a colleague jump out of her skin when he silently appeared by her side as she was looking through the latest copy of *OK!* magazine and happened upon a page that featured a large photo of Desmond himself.

'He's a good-looking man,' said Desmond.

My poor colleague nearly screamed twice, once out of the shock of someone appearing at her side, and again out of the shock of it being Desmond.

I saw this play out every Thursday for two and a half months, until our entire department moved down a floor and away from the meeting room.

Desmond had a reputation for being ruthless for one simple reason – he *was* ruthless. In my time at the *Express* I saw people who had worked for him for many years tossed aside as if they were mere temps. I knew that if I wanted to keep my job, I had to keep my head down and stay off his radar.

It so nearly worked.

Other than making money and not giving his staff pay rises for seven years in a row, the other great passion of Desmond's is his charity work.

No, really.

In September 2011, Desmond launched the Health Lottery, with 20 per cent of revenue going to good causes. As part of his public relations drive, Desmond liked to visit some of the projects that benefited from the charity's hand-outs.

On Friday 2 May 2014 he travelled to a community resource centre in Hatfield, Hertfordshire, along with the local Tory MP Grant Shapps (he of the 'I never worked under my alias Michael Green when I was an MP, oh you have a recording of me doing that, oops' fame). For a reason which is still not entirely clear to me, I was told by my boss to go along with a film crew from the *Express* website and interview the pair.

But not just any interview; I had to try to speak to them while they were knitting – in keeping with one of the evening clubs run from the centre. I had no idea why I had been chosen, but I suspect my boss was trying to get rid of me.

I knew the interview would break the Owen Bennett Golden Rule of working for Richard Desmond: never let Richard Desmond know who you are. If he knows who you are, you are one step closer to being fired by him. Desmond was notorious for getting rid of people and, a few days before the interview, the head of my department had been effectively booted out the company, despite having worked for Desmond for more than ten years.

Without warning, he was placed on 'gardening leave' – a luxury I would not get if he didn't like the cut of my jib as I was still technically a freelancer.

I knew if I rubbed Desmond up the wrong way, or made him look stupid while he was knitting, I would be out. Luckily for me, he was in a good mood. Maybe it was because he was seeing the fruits of the Health Lottery labour on the ground. Maybe it was because the sun was shining. Or maybe it was because, just hours earlier, he had sold off Channel 5 for £450 million, having bought it for a rumoured £103.5 million just four years earlier.

I'm not a businessman, but I imagine making a profit of £346.5 million in four years would put a smile on your face (although not a cost-of-living pay rise in the wage packets of your staff).

With the cringe-worthy interview done and the video put on the website, I breathed a sigh of relief. But Owen Bennett's Golden Rule had been broken, and two months later I was again summoned to interview Desmond at a Health Lottery project.

This time it was a cooking class for children in Twickenham along-side Business Secretary Vince Cable. I interviewed Desmond just after he tossed some small pancakes, and if you look closely at my eyes in the video you can see the moment my self-respect and pride completely disappear from my soul. I didn't get into journalism to produce Richard Desmond propaganda films.

After the cooking video, I managed to avoid being sent out on any more Health Lottery visits. A combination of doctor's appointments, sick relatives and family funerals (I think my gran was buried about three times in total) meant I was bizarrely never available when the calls came.

In the autumn of 2014, another round of redundancies was announced at the *Express* and *Star* newspapers. Many people volun-teered to go, but the threat of compulsory redundancies hung over those who couldn't afford to just leave.

It was against this background that Desmond gave his first dona-tion to UKIP – £300,000. If you've got this far into the book, I hope it's because you like what I've been saying, or at least find it inter-esting – perhaps even both. So please bear with me while I launch a small defence of the *Daily Express* and its staff.

Yes, it is easy to mock the newspaper, with its repetitive front pages about the weather, the latest cure for arthritis and sensational immigration figures. But let me say this: firstly, it sells an awful lot of copies because people know what they are going to get. Yes, it is an anti-EU, anti-mass migration paper. But whether you, I, or any-one else don't like it, a lot of people hold those views, and they are legitimate views to hold. The paper does not try to be anything that it's not. It puts its editorial policy out there for everyone to see. No one is going to pick up the *Express* thinking it is anything other than an anti-EU, anti-mass migration paper. It is not changing anyone's mind. People buy the *Express* because they think that way. They don't think that way because they buy the *Express*. Of course, it may firm up those views, but those views are there to start with.

When it comes to the staff, the people working on the *Express* – the journalists, sub-editors, news editors, web editors, designers, photographers – were some of the kindest, friendliest, most generous people I have ever worked with, and in an industry that does not necessarily promote those qualities.

So, when Desmond decides to donate money to UKIP instead of giving the staff a cost-of-living pay rise for the first time in seven years, it stinks.

And when he gives UKIP £1 million more a few months later, well it really fucking stinks.

ARRON BANKS

The former Tory donor gave £1 million to UKIP because his ego was bruised. The clearly emotionally fragile multimillionaire was set to give the party £100,000 in October 2014, with the cheque presentation planned for the final day of the Tory Party conference.

A press note was sent out from UKIP headquarters, inviting journalists to travel to Banks's grandiose estate on the outskirts of Bristol. It was 1 October, and just four days since Mark Reckless had quit the Tories to join UKIP, meaning it was entirely possible another defector was set to be announced.

The majority of Westminster's political journalists were in Birmingham for the Tory conference, and the sudden call from UKIP to travel to Bristol was not taken well. It had been an incredibly busy few months for Britain's political journalists.

UKIP kicked off the tour with Douglas Carswell's defection announcement on 28 August, which led the press pack off to Clacton in Essex to get the lay of the land.

Then the polls started to tighten in the Scottish independence referendum campaign, with one published on Sunday 7 September

– eleven days before voting day – putting the Yes camp in the lead for the first time.

This panicked the main party leaders so much they cancelled that week's PMQs in the House of Commons and went up to Scotland to beg the country to stay part of the Union. The journalists who weren't despatched north of the border along with Messrs Cameron, Miliband and Clegg were sent to the Trades Union Congress in Liverpool, which ran from 7 to 10 September.

The Scottish referendum took place on 18 September, but the press barely had time to get its breath back before the Labour conference in Manchester started on 21 September.

That finished on the 24th, and on the 25th, journalists flew across the ocean to America, where David Cameron was giving a speech to the United Nations in New York.

The UKIP conference began in Doncaster on 26 September, the same day that Parliament was recalled to discuss military action against ISIS. On 27 September, Mark Reckless announced his defection to UKIP, and the very next day the Tories began their conference in Birmingham.

That was due to finish on 1 October, but journalists were then invited to accompany the Prime Minister on a trip to Afghanistan the next day.

The Liberal Democrat conference took place in Glasgow from 4–8 October, and on the 9th, voters went to the polls in the Clacton by-election.

As you can see, it was a busy time.

So, when an operational note went out inviting the press to Banks's home just outside Bristol, the general consensus was there'd better be a damn good reason for adding something else to a very packed diary.

We already knew that former Tory donor Arron Banks was going to give UKIP £100,000.

When the news was briefed out earlier that day, former Foreign Secretary William Hague told BBC Radio 5 live: 'I've never heard of him so we are not going to get too upset about that … It's certainly not going to overshadow the Prime Minister's speech today that someone we haven't heard of has gone to UKIP.'

But UKIP sources insisted it was worth our while making the trip, so, suitcases in tow, Laura Pitel from *The Times*, Emily Ashton from *The Sun*, Christopher Hope from the *Telegraph*, Rowena Mason from *The Guardian* and Dan Martin from the *Mail* journeyed from Birmingham to Bristol.

I was probably the only journalist not to be annoyed at going. Having been at the Trades Union Congress, and the Labour and UKIP conferences, I was stood down for the Tory get-together.

While everyone else was up in Birmingham, I was the only journalist still in the House of Commons, haunting the corridors like a ghost.

I jumped at the opportunity to cover some news, and got myself to Bristol as fast as I could. The press call was at Old Down Manor, a country park 15 miles north of Bristol. Banks bought the Grade II listed mansion in 2011 from musician Mike Oldfield. The house is situated in the 66-acre Old Down Country Park, and, since buying it, Banks rents it out as a wedding venue.

When I arrived at around 4 p.m., staff in the house were preparing for a fundraising dinner for a Belize children's hospital due to be held that evening. As works of art were moved about, and waiters prepared tables, journalists were kept in a room at the back of the house, which had doors that opened out into the grounds.

The view over Bristol and beyond from the garden was spectacular, and rows of camera and film crews pitched up in the afternoon sun to get a majestic shot of Nigel Farage emerging with Banks out of the house.

But who else, if anyone, would be with them?

We speculated that it might be another high-profile Tory, and pressed UKIP sources for more information. They were being tight-lipped, although, of course, there was always the possibility they just didn't know what was going on.

The staff who had been bringing us drinks closed all the doors – save for the ones that led us out into the garden. This ramped up the intrigue even more. Why had the doors been closed? What was being hidden? We were convinced another defector had turned up and was being prepped for a big reveal. Why else would Farage have dragged us all the way out here?

I asked for directions to the toilet, and a member of staff escorted me out of the room to ensure I wouldn't try to slip away.

Back in the journalist holding pen, Farage had joined us. He had a pint of ale in his hand and a smile on his face. He was of course giving nothing away, but was clearly enjoying the moment. The Westminster pack again dancing to his tune – on the same day that David Cameron was giving his keynote speech to the Tory Party conference.

After half an hour of speculation, we were instructed to go outside.

Patiently, we waited for the doors to the house to reopen and for the purpose of our visit to be finally revealed. Farage, Banks and UKIP chairman Steve Crowther emerged and descended the steps.

Cunning, I thought. Get the donor out first, let him announce the money, and then send out the defector. Banks stepped up to the microphones and said:

> I woke up this morning intending to donate £100,000 to UKIP. I understand Mr Hague called me a nobody, so in light of that, and in view of the fact that I'm a strong advocate of leaving the European Union, I've decided today to donate £1 million to the party and not the £100,000 we originally agreed.

Farage then gave his thoughts, listing all the insults from Tories towards UKIP over the years, starting with Michael Howard's claim the party was full of 'cranks' and 'gadflies' and finishing with Hague's latest jibe at Banks that morning.

'Mr Nobody has bitten back!' said Farage, while a grinning Banks standing next to him added he was 'hoping that Mr Hague will now know who I am'.

A million-pound donation is eyebrow-raising news, certainly. But surely that can't be the only reason UKIP has dragged the press across the country? I thought. Just to massage the ego of a man who is so fragile he increased his donation ten-fold because one of the most senior politicians in the land had never heard of him?

There must be a defector.

Maybe Farage was going to do a *Columbo* and, as the press pack was about to pack away, proclaim: 'Just one more thing … Lord Norman Tebbit, everybody!'

Now that would have been worth the journey for all those tired hacks.

But no, the angry multimillionaire was all for the day.

On the train back to London, those among us who had come straight from the Tory conference to Bristol expressed their frustration at the afternoon's events.

'They could have put that out in a press release,' said one.

Another got a phone call from their newsdesk. 'Apparently there's a picture doing the rounds of Banks posing with a gun.'

Then another call from another newsdesk. 'It turns out Banks hasn't just made money from insurance, he also invested in a diamond mine in South Africa!'

One of the journalists had been searching for information about him online, and said: 'Have you seen this about his wife? She's a Russian woman who arrived in Britain on a student visa in the late 1990s, and, after her short marriage to an older English guy broke down, she met with Lib Dem MP Mike Hancock for advice!'

Hancock, who had recently quit the Lib Dems after admitting he had 'crossed the line' with his behaviour towards a female constituent, had previously hit the headlines for having an affair with a Russian employee who was arrested under suspicion of being a spy. She was later cleared of the allegation.

In the space of ten minutes, our angry millionaire with a fragile ego had transformed into a gun-toting diamond-mine-owner with a Russian wife.

This all led to one obvious question: was Arron Banks a Bond villain?

According to the Electoral Commission, by the time of the general election, Banks had given £674, 253.70 of the £1 million he promised, either in his own name or through Rock Services Limited.

STUART WHEELER

With his white hair, hunched shoulders and hearing aid, octogenarian Stuart Wheeler blends in perfectly at UKIP events.

He could be just another old white man attracted by Farage's anti-EU, patriotic shtick, prepared to shake his walking stick in support of the People's Army. But, from 2011 to 2014, Wheeler was UKIP's fundraising cheerleader, whose job as treasurer was to convince rich people to donate to the still fledging political party.

The sort of people Wheeler was after were Eurosceptic multi-millionaires, happy to hand over large sums of cash and prepared to put up with the inevitable scrutiny of motives, finances and personal life by the media and political enemies.

There was one person who fitted the bill perfectly, but UKIP would need a time machine to get him – Stuart Wheeler himself, back in 2001. At the turn of the century, Wheeler handed over £5 million to the Tories – at the time, the largest single donation in British political history.

If only present-day Wheeler could travel back, wrestle that cheque from his sprightly 65-year-old hands and save it for UKIP's 2015 general election campaign. He may not have given the party £5 million, but since 2009 he had handed over £770,000 of his cash to the People's Army.

Wheeler stood down as UKIP treasurer at the stroke of 10 p.m. on the night of the European elections in May 2014, but was still an active member of the party when I met him for dinner in April 2015.

I asked him for an interview after bumping into him at a post-Budget briefing in Westminster the previous month.

It was the first time I had seen him since we had shared a taxi in Doncaster the previous September and, after a brief chat, I asked if he would be happy to talk to me about Farage and his involvement with UKIP.

A few weeks later and I was waiting outside his private members' club, the Army and Navy, on the edge of wealthy St James's Square. The doorman refused to let me into the building until Wheeler had turned up, so I was forced to wait outside.

Once Wheeler had welcomed me inside, we made our way upstairs to the restaurant, but, before we were shown to a table, the waitress insisted we smarten up.

I say 'we'; it was actually Wheeler who was falling foul of the dress code, as he wasn't wearing a tie. After a spare one was produced for him from a drawer, we were seated.

Now *that* is what I want from a snooty private members' club.

Forget Blacks's 'Oh, just go and sit upstairs and wait for the club member to show up. Of course you can wear a T-shirt!' faux inclusivity, the Army and Navy Club had rules so strict you could set your watch by them.

Before dinner and wine were ordered, Wheeler called for a pint of bitter – surely the most hearty aperitif you can get. I echoed the order (when in Rome and all that…) and we got talking.

First of all, I asked him about that £5 million he donated to the Tories when William Hague was in charge. Hague is now seen as a towering statesman, but in 2001 he was viewed as a childish Tory boy who looked stupid in a baseball cap.

When I asked him about the sheer size of the donation, he said: 'I was much richer in those days than I am now.'

'What was the reaction of the Tories when you told them they would be getting such a windfall?' I asked.

'When I went to see William Hague to tell him I wanted to give him this money, before he could open his mouth I said, "And if I'm offered an honour I would reject it!" I think in those days it was almost a given that if you gave a million you could get a peerage!' he joked. 'I thought I didn't want to be given a peerage; if I had found a cure for cancer then, yes, maybe, but not just for giving money to a political party.'

Wheeler only became involved in politics in 2000, after now-Tory peer Rodney Leach kept bending his ear over the growing influence of the European Union.

Seeing the millions of pounds Labour was hoovering up in donations ahead of the 2001 election, he upped his original donation of £15,000 to the Tories to £5 million.

> It had always been a puzzle to me that there are a few hundred people in this country who are so rich that something like £5 million, or £10 million, which is very likely to transform a political party, would certainly transform UKIP nevertheless, and although it wouldn't affect their way of life in any way at all, they don't do it. And when, to my surprise, I temporarily became able to do that, I did it.
>
> The result was automatically I got to know the top people in the Conservative Party and so on, it was quite fascinating for me.

The Tories lost the 2001 election to Labour in what has been dubbed the 'quiet landslide' – making a net gain of just one seat from its 1997 humiliation.

Wheeler invited Hague round for dinner after the defeat, but before long the Tories had a new leader, Iain Duncan Smith, who did not enjoy the same financial support from the previously generous benefactor.

Just £28,500 left Wheeler's pockets during Duncan Smith's short-lived reign as Tory leader ('I thought he was an extremely bad leader of the Conservative Party but I think he is extremely good at what he does now [Work and Pensions Secretary]') but he clearly approved of Michael Howard taking over in November 2013, handing over £504,000 to the party just weeks later.

Wheeler backed Eurosceptic Tory Dr Liam Fox in the 2005 leadership election, donating £3,000 to his campaign.

'So you weren't keen on David Cameron even before he became Tory leader?' I asked.

He shook his head, and said:

> Michael Green, who was head of Carlton at the time and a member of my bridge club, stopped me in the street as I happened to run into him during the Tory leadership campaign and said: 'You are going to back David Cameron, aren't you?' So I looked a bit doubtful and then, as if to really clinch the argument, he said: 'You know he can be a real shit when he wants to!' I told that to David and he was quite amused.

The donations to the Tories did not completely dry up though, and Wheeler still swelled the party coffers by £316,300 from after the 2005 general election to 2008.

I ask what it is about Cameron he didn't like. 'I don't think he is very honest. I think he'll say whatever he thinks, within reason, is likely to get him a vote in the immediate future,' came the reply.

As Cameron's leadership progressed, Wheeler became 'more and more disappointed' in his attitude to the EU.

'Finally I decided I would vote UKIP in the 2009 European elections and that I would give them some money [£100,000] and I said so in public, so I was then expelled by the Tories – quite reasonably, I think.'

'How did you come to hear about UKIP?' I asked.

I suppose once Rodney Leach had interested me in the EU, I naturally heard about UKIP and so on. Then Nigel Farage did a very good soft sell on me. He invited me to a dinner with him and other UKIP people and then when I was expelled from the Tories, he hadn't really suggested it beforehand but fairly soon after I was expelled he invited me to be the treasurer.

I hesitated for some time but then accepted.

As well as counting the money, Wheeler's job was to get more of it – mainly through 'wining and dining' wealthy businesspeople.

But the biggest obstacle for Wheeler wasn't finding Eurosceptic millionaires; it was convincing them to give cash to UKIP.

He said:

One or two are billionaires who could easily afford to give us some money, which would make all the difference in the world, but understandably they don't. They think business might suffer or, in one or two cases, they are chairman of the local Conservative Party or something, so they obviously can't be seen to do it. So that's a real, real bore.

Whoever is in power can either do things which are favourable to your position or not favourable to your position, and of course being seen to give money to UKIP, the party in power might be disinclined to do favourable things – that's the fear.

It's probably exaggerated, but I can see somebody saying, 'It may be exaggerated but I really can't afford to take the risk. Why should I?'

He added: 'That's a very big factor indeed.'

Before we talked about his views on Farage and other people in the party, I wanted to find out more about Wheeler. He was born, in secret, to a 42-year-old unmarried woman called Chrissy in 1935, and immediately put up for adoption. Alexander Wheeler, an American who inherited a banking fortune, and his English wife Betty Gibbons adopted Stuart just before his second birthday. Five years later, Alexander died of leukaemia.

Wheeler was educated at Eton and, after completing his National Service with the Welsh Guards, went on to read Law at Oxford University.

'I came from a rather ordinary background,' he said.

'My mother supported me through Oxford, my father died when I was seven; she didn't have a lot of money when he finished wasting it all. Not a particularly wealthy background.'

After stints as a barrister and in merchant banking, Wheeler established IG Index in 1974.

The company pioneered spread-betting, initially on the price of gold, then other shares and later on sports events.

I had read up on this many times, but still was unsure how it worked.

As I tucked into my wonderful pea risotto, Wheeler tried his best to explain it to me:

> The easiest way of understanding how it works is by thinking about how many runs, for example, England will get in the next cricket Test match. We – as in IG Index, of which I'm no longer concerned with – might think they'll get 270 perhaps. So we would quote 265–275. If you thought they were going to make a lot of runs you would 'buy' them at 275 and so we would say, 'How big a bet would you like?' And you would say, 'I would like £10 a run, please.' So now, if they get 276, you are right by one run and you get £10. If they get 375, you are right by 100 runs, so you make 100 times £10 – £1,000. In the same way, if you are wrong, you lose.
>
> So that's how spread-betting works, except that, in the case of a share price or the level of a stock exchange index, your bet is about what the situation will be at the closing day of the bet, which may be three months or four months ahead.

I was still unsure and, a few days after the dinner, I downloaded the IG Index app, which gives you £10,000 to play with (alas, not real money) to see if I had understood how it all works. I lost it all in the space of an hour.

Wheeler, however, made a success of the real thing, and when IG Index was floated in 2000, it earned him £90 million in shares.

Such was the success of the company that £100 invested when the business started in 1974 was worth between £12–15 million when it went public.

If that figure made me choke on my risotto, what Wheeler said next made me almost spit out my wine:

> I made the worst mistake of my life and sold my stake with the rest of the investors. If we hadn't sold, that £100 would have been worth about £200 million now.
>
> So I made this terrible blunder of selling. I made more money than I ever thought I would in my life, but I would now be worth something like a billion if I hadn't done it.

Turning £100 to £200 million in fewer than fifty years – that is one hell of an investment.

The success of IG Index made Wheeler a very wealthy man, and his love of gambling – bridge and poker are his two main games – brought him into contact with a range of colourful characters. One was Sir James Goldsmith, the founder of the Referendum Party. Goldsmith was essentially Farage before Farage, but it is doubtful the UKIP leader would have the nerve to take part in Wheeler and Goldsmith's coin-toss game.

Wheeler said:

> I knew him quite well. We had a deal that even though I didn't meet him all that often, when I did meet him, he would toss a coin and I would call 'heads' or 'tails'. The deal was

if I was wrong – now we're talking thirty-five years ago
when money was worth more than it now is – I would pay
him £1,000, which was a lot, and if I was right he would
pay me £1,100. I liked it because the odds were in my favour.
He liked it because he knew it mattered like hell to me and
liked to see me scrabbling on the ground for the coin.

Another friend of Wheeler's was Lord Lucan, the man behind one
of the most mysterious disappearances in modern British history.

A known gambler, Lucan's life started to go downhill after sepa-
rating from his wife in 1972. The man who was once considered for
the role of James Bond became obsessed with getting custody of his
three children as he struggled with gambling debts.

On 7 November 1974, the Lucan children's nanny Sandra Rivett
was bludgeoned to death in the family home in London, and his ex-
wife was also attacked. She claimed Lord Lucan was the assailant, but
he disappeared without a trace that night.

Wheeler had been at his gambling club with Lucan just days before
the murder:

> I knew him quite well, really quite well. He was always at the
> Claremont Club – the gambling club and casino. I saw him
> there a lot. He was a member of my bridge club, the Falkland
> Club, and two days before the incident, shall we call it, I was
> playing – even though my club's a bridge club – I was playing
> backgammon with somebody there and Lucan, John Lucan,
> was sitting behind me and sort of giving me friendly advice.
> There was not the slightest inkling as far as I was concerned
> of what was about to happen.

Wheeler believes Lucan fled the country on a cross-Channel ferry
after the murder, and most likely took his own life by jumping into
the sea.

I quite liked him, he was always very polite to me. I wasn't one of his very best friends but I knew him very well. It was a terrible tragedy really. He and his wife should never have got married, he was completely unsuitable. Here was a chap who was only interested in gambling and having dinner with his friends and gambling again afterwards. She, I think, was struck by the attraction of being married to an Earl who was very good-looking and so on, but it was a terrible marriage. It was a great mistake. It didn't suit either of them.

Goldsmith and Lucan may not be around to gamble any more, but Wheeler still loves a flutter. Every year he travels to Las Vegas to take part in the World Series of Poker competition – the game's equivalent of the World Cup.

It costs $10,000 to take part, and the winner walks away with $10 million. Wheeler said: 'It's so different to any other ten days in my life in the year. It's fascinating. The only year I didn't go for a long time was for my eldest daughter's thirtieth birthday, which unfortunately clashed with it.'

Ah yes, Wheeler's three daughters. As well as being a multi-millionaire gambler, who counted potentially murderous Lords and flamboyant billionaires as friends, he is also the father of a supermodel.

Jacquetta Wheeler shot to modelling fame in the 1990s, and was on the cover of French *Vogue* when she was seventeen years old. In 1999 she was named 'Model of the Millennium' by *The Face* magazine.

His eldest daughter Sarah worked in an auction house, while his youngest, Charlotte, once worked for Tory election guru Lynton Crosby.

My one foray into playing poker saw me lose £40 in about ten minutes, so I asked Wheeler for some advice.

'Self-discipline and read a bit about the game,' was his response. Sounds like a bit too much work for me.

With the main courses despatched, the bottle of red wine nearing its end and dessert on the way, I turned the conversation to UKIP.

'Even though you are no longer the treasurer, what is your relationship like with Farage?' I asked:

> For a time it was close. Nigel does tend to have quite frequently his new favourite person, and I'm not saying I was his new favourite person, but I was certainly very close to him for a bit – but less so now. I admire him. I see his faults very clearly, but I admire him. He gave up a career in commodity trading, which I think was providing him with a good income, and I think if he had stuck to it I think he would have been quite rich now. Now he's devastatingly poor, there's no doubt about that, and he's given it all up for UKIP, and he has just boundless energy.
>
> We tried to persuade him – 'You must take a holiday occasionally' and all that kind of thing – but he doesn't and I think at the moment he is feeling and looking rather exhausted. He's very good at fighting back. If he could be persuaded to take a whole weekend off, and probably even go away from home and away from anything it would probably be a very good idea, but he won't do it.

'What faults do you see?' I said, tucking into a wonderful chocolate fondant dessert.

Wheeler responded:

> He's not good at keeping everyone happy with each other and stopping people from feuding. He's not good at that, but on balance he's a huge asset to the party and to lose him would be a complete disaster. I hope it wouldn't be fatal, I hope it's not going to happen, but if it does happen I hope it won't be fatal.

'Do you think he would be any good in government?' I asked.

> I don't think Nigel wants – he has said he doesn't, in fact – to
> be a minister. I don't think he would be a very good min-
> ister at all. He's absolutely brilliant on television, radio and
> public meetings, but he's really no good at organising a party
> and, of course, if you're a minister you have very clever civil
> servants to back you up, but even so I don't think he would
> enjoy that kind of thing.

The election was just a month away, so I asked Wheeler who he thought should take over as party leader if Farage didn't win his seat.

'It would be very difficult to think who the new leader would be. Douglas Carswell is impressive and he's obviously honest and so forth, but I don't think he's going to rouse and get standing ovations and so forth,' was Wheeler's view. 'Obviously there's quite a case for saying it should be Douglas Carswell, but I think long-standing UKIP members and activists would say, "We don't want this chap who only started to support us six months ago." But I'm not quite sure who they would put forward,' he added.

Wheeler knew Carswell long before he defected to UKIP, and he was one of eight Tory MPs he took to dinner at various times while treasurer to talk to them about Farage and the party.

He has never revealed the other names, and has vowed to keep them secret.

Back to the leadership talk, and I suggest UKIP deputy leader Paul Nuttall might be a popular choice with some activists, but a working-class northerner might alienate the Tory base in the south-east of England.

'Personally I don't think he would alienate anybody,' replied Wheeler. 'He's obviously a nice and reasonable chap and he could do very well in the north, but even though he wouldn't alienate people in the south, he might not particularly appeal to them.'

UKIP deputy chairman Suzanne Evans was another name frequently produced when talking about Farage's successor, but, surprisingly for one so involved in the party, Wheeler had never met her.

I remembered what Godfrey Bloom had said to me in Yorkshire about Farage getting rid of all the 'alpha males' in UKIP to protect his position as leader.

'There's an element of that, and I think he's probably neurotic [and] paranoid about the danger of losing the leadership. There may be an element of if somebody's doing too well in UKIP he begins to be worried about that.'

Like Bloom, I was also interested to know what he thought UKIP's ultimate goal should be. Was it to win seats in the House of Commons and be a full political party, or was it to get Britain out of the EU? If the latter, is it not counter-productive to take votes away from the Tories, when David Cameron has promised an in/out EU referendum in 2017?

Wheeler said:

> It certainly is to get as many MPs as possible. I think we would say, and I would say, that getting as many MPs as possible is going to increase the chance of us getting out of the EU. We will have the MPs in Parliament and their views will become dramatically more public and I hope will sound more sensible. I don't think there's really much of a conflict. Also, we are attacking Labour like mad, particularly in the north.
>
> Any political party which is certainly doing far better than a few years ago, of course it's going to try and get as many seats as it can. The idea that one would stop trying to win seats for the kind of reasons you've mentioned, although it's put to me all the time, it is really ridiculous. Any small party which is doing much better than it ever did is going to try and do as well as it can.

'But what about the EU referendum?' I asked. 'You are so close to getting what you have campaigned for, and put millions of pounds towards – Britain out of the EU.'

'I don't think we're going to get a referendum because the Conservatives are not going to get an overall majority.'

This position struck me as odd. By his own admission, Wheeler had come into politics late in life – sixty-six years old – because of his opposition to Britain being in the EU. He had moved his money around to back the party or individual that would help deliver that goal.

Partly because of him and his work with UKIP, Cameron agreed to hold a referendum if the Tories got a majority after the 2015 general election. Surely, that is what he wanted?

I ask him if he would ever go back to the Tories if the leadership adopted a very Eurosceptic position.

'It would have to be somebody other than Cameron,' he replied.

> But, in any case, because I feel so strongly about the EU, it would have to be somebody who at the very least would guarantee an in/out referendum and I would hope he was going to campaign for coming out. If somebody said, 'I'm now the leader of the Conservatives and we're now going to have an in/out referendum and I believe we should come out,' then I would have to think, but I don't think that's going to happen.

Dessert devoured and the wine suitably diminished, coffees were ordered for myself and my new multimillionaire friend.

What does this eighty-year-old gambler, whose money, influence and contacts have helped push Euroscepticism to the front of the political agenda, plan to do next?

'I shall go home,' he said.

'No, I meant next with regards to your political career and UKIP.'

'I shall probably continue to support them, but less actively, I think. To some extent, I'm – and I don't know what the logic is and at the age of eighty it would be odd anyway – looking for a new project.'

A new project, eh? Was now the time to mention that independent record label I've always wanted to start but never had the funding for – 'Checkpoint Charlie'?

It seemed not.

'One of my very greatest interests is in torture…' he said.

I knew there was something not quite right about him. He wants to string people up who are in favour of the EU!

'… – stopping torture, not doing it, of course, and looking after those who have been tortured,' he added.

'Oh, yes, of course,' I replied.

> Insofar as I give money to charity, as opposed to political parties, 90 per cent of it goes to anti-torture charities. Amnesty, Human Rights Watch and two or three others. I feel very strongly about that, and obviously money is very important to them and to some extent I can still provide that, but whether I can do anything more, whether I can be useful in any other way at my age is rather doubtful.
>
> People have very often asked me why I'm so interested in torture and my two reactions are: one, it may be partly because I'm such a physical coward myself, but leaving that aside, I sort of feel how can anyone not be horrified by torture and therefore keen to do something about it.

What a quandary for all those right-on lefties. This man helps fund UKIP (boooo!), but also gives money to human rights and anti-torture charities (yay!).

He is an Oxford-educated Old Etonian (boooo!), but spent his first two years in an orphanage after being given up for adoption by his unmarried mother due to the social stigma of the time (if not quite 'yay!', it's certainly more of a hard-knock start to life than some left-ies – Anthony Wedgwood Benn, for example).

He gave millions to the Tories (boooo!), but thought it would be wrong to get a place in the House of Lords on that basis alone (yay!).

He paid for our dinner (yay for me!).

We said our goodbyes in the lobby of the club and went our separate ways – me to my one-bed flat in east London, he to his millionaire's penthouse in central London.

But despite our difference in lifestyle, finances, age, beliefs and priorities, I had thoroughly enjoyed my time with Stuart Wheeler.

A 'relic from a by-gone age' is not quite the right description, but he was certainly a throwback to a different time. Money for him seemed to be a plaything, but at least he looked like he was enjoying himself. What's the point otherwise?

For all the money Richard Desmond had made, he was still not accepted by 'the establishment', and it rankles with him. Arron Banks's ego seemed to be so fragile he gave £1 million to UKIP because William Hague had never heard of him.

Having only known Stuart Wheeler for a few hours, I of course only scratched the surface, but at least he seemed to have a bit of 'class' about him. Not upper-class toffness, just a little bit of decency. Manners, even.

Maybe I had just been seduced by the club and the dinner and hearing stories about colourful characters, but this comprehensive-schooled, non-Oxbridge-educated cynical journalist actually liked this multimillionaire former Tory donor, who happily gambles away every year more money than I can even earn.

Was I going soft on UKIP?

CHAPTER 13

THE EGO HAS LANDED

NIGEL FARAGE IS ADMIRED for many reasons. His dedication to Euroscepticism, his tireless work rate, and his refusal to bow to political correctness are just some of the traits the People's Army love him for.

But his fashion sense? Well, yes, if you are his chief advisor Raheem Kassam.

Even before Kassam joined UKIP, he strutted around in a tan-coloured, knee-length covert coat with a dark collar – the same garment worn by Farage. Perhaps that was what clinched the deal in the job interview in autumn 2014.

'Raheem, I like what you're saying, and I think we'll get on well, but I'm just not sure if you believe in me enough.'

'I'll stop you there, Nigel, and ask you to take a look at my coat. Seem familiar?'

'Raheem, old boy, welcome aboard.'

The pair first properly spoke at a mutual friend's birthday celebrations at the posh Roux at Parliament Square restaurant in July 2013.

Farage and Kassam had met a few times before thanks to a shared love of the Westminster pub scene, but it was at the Roux where they began discussing politics properly.

I met Kassam for the first time a few months later, when I was drinking with Alex Wickham from Guido Fawkes in the Marquis of Granby pub in Westminster in October of that year.

He came over to say hello to Wickham, whom he already knew, and after I was introduced as working for the *Daily Express*, he said: 'Great, do you want a job?'

He started going on about how he was having meetings with some American company who wanted to launch a media outlet in the UK, and it was all very top secret, but there would be loads of cash floating about.

It smelt like bullshit to me, and I politely turned down his job offer.

Annoyingly, Kassam had been telling the truth, and four months later the UK branch of the American right-wing news site Breitbart launched and he was its managing editor.

I had no regrets about not taking up Kassam's job offer, however, as I really didn't want to work for an organisation that was so right wing it made the *Daily Express* look like the *Morning Star*.

While I had found Kassam to be a bit of a chancer, Farage was finding him to be a charmer.

UKIP's party secretary Matthew Richardson advised Farage to regularly meet up with Kassam, who was one of his friends.

Speaking to me outside the Westminster Arms pub in spring 2015, Kassam said:

> So Nigel requested I got special treatment ahead of the Carswell defection, so I got a heads-up there would be a big announcement, make sure you're there, bring a camera.
>
> As I was walking there, Nigel came up to me and said, 'Ah, Raheem' – I didn't think he would remember my name – 'Ah, Raheem, I thought it was really important you were here today.' That was quite interesting. I think he saw Breitbart as a conduit.

After the Carswell defection, Kassam accompanied Farage and

Richardson on a trip to America to look at Democrat and Republican polling techniques at the beginning of September 2014.

In his book *The Purple Revolution*, Farage says he asked Kassam to organise this trip 'as he had good contacts across the pond on account of his previous employment at Breitbart'.

However, Kassam told me that it was on this trip that Farage offered him the job, not before.

He said:

> Matthew and I and Nigel went to New York and Washington and I was there just covering the trip for Breitbart. Matthew is kind of a gregarious character so he would get out and about and just leave me with Nigel. So we would end up spending vast amounts of time together. Obviously because I wasn't in the circle or anything he was guarded, but you know what he's like, you know what he's like with you and Chopper [Chris Hope, *Daily Telegraph*], he's not that hostile. We would go out drinking a lot and I remember we were outside a German beer garden in Manhattan and this black guy comes up to us in the street and goes: 'You're Nigel Farage! I love your You-Tube videos, man' and all this stuff, and then he goes: 'Here, you want some coke?' Nigel said: 'No, no, no, I can't do any of that.' Then the guy goes: 'OK, tell me your room number, I'm going to send my girl Luscious up to your room!' Nigel says: 'No, no, no, I'm OK without Luscious, thanks!'

Kassam said it was on that trip the pair really bonded, and I asked if he thought Farage was missing his previous close advisor Annabelle Fuller.

He replied: 'Big time, big time. I remember the time we shook hands on the deal was the last day of [the] UKIP conference in Doncaster. Once he offered me the job, he turned to Kirsten and he went: "I've got an Annabelle again!" She said: "Please don't say that."'

It was at that Doncaster conference that Kassam offered me a job at Breitbart a second time. I didn't realise at the time that it was effectively his job I was being offered.

His appointment to Farage's inner circle was met with surprise by most in Westminster. The vast majority of journalists had never heard of this man in his twenties, who had little experience of working in politics. But those who had heard of him thought he was too immature, he rubbed people up the wrong way and he was too brash.

I asked Kassam if he recognised that description of himself.

He replied:

> The whole 'professional wind-up' merchant thing that Harry [Cole – for *The Spectator*] wrote about me is absolutely true, without a shadow of a doubt. It's not for any trying, it's just sometimes I put my foot in it, because I'm proud, I've always struggled to apologise to people, which is perfect for UKIP really.

I saw Kassam putting his foot in it for myself on the day it was announced he had been given the job as Farage's new right-hand man. I was sitting outside the Westminster Arms with the former holder of that post – Annabelle Fuller (we were discussing some controversy in the European Parliament) – when Kassam walked around the corner and came over to say hello.

Fuller and Kassam locked eyes, like two cats sizing each other up before a scrap.

'Congratulations on the job,' I said. 'So what exactly will you be doing for Nigel?'

Kassam pointed at Fuller: 'Well, she knows better than me!'

I think he was trying to make a joke to diffuse an awkward situation, but it only made the atmosphere worse. Fuller took a long drag on her cigarette and deliberately stared into the distance until Kassam went on his way.

Meow.

Kassam's professional life before UKIP is as controversial as some of the decisions he made while working for Farage. Before joining the party, he was involved with Conservative Future, the youth wing of the Tory Party.

He said he went 'out to target seats, helping out – a delivery monkey really. There were some underhand tactics which I learned, which I was able to deploy, counter-tactics against the Tories in South Thanet because I knew how they think and I knew how they worked.'

After UKIP's breakthrough in the 2013 local elections, he moved away from the Tories and towards Farage.

'That's when it really started dawning on me in terms of, "What have I done working for a Cameron government?"' he said. 'Gay marriage upset me as well, because it wasn't in the [2010] manifesto.'

While working as campaigns director at the right-wing think tank the Henry Jackson Society, Kassam also became involved with the Commentator blog. The level of his involvement is disputed. In the *Evening Standard* in April 2013 he was described as the site's 'editor', but a post on the Commentator's website after he left later that year described him as a 'former, part-time freelancer.'

The other notoriety Kassam had in media circles involved his Wikipedia entry.

On 1 June 2012, Sunny Hundal, who ran the Liberal Conspiracy blog, posted an article questioning why Kassam had a page on the online encyclopaedia.

He wrote:

> Kassam has a highly detailed Wikipedia page, with more than forty references so far. In comparison, *Guardian* editor Alan Rusbridger has just eight.
>
> Not bad for a guy who runs a barely read political blog, huh? His Wikipedia page was created by username 'Artievand' in March 2011 with: 'Raheem Kassam is a notable political and media figure within the United Kingdom.' The user made more than ten further additions and edits to Kassam's page in

the following months. 'Artievand' also removed two items of criticism from the Henry Jackson Society page.

Raheem Kassam says 'Artievand' is not his alias. He admitted to editing inaccuracies, but declined to answer which account he used to do so.

Kassam's Wikipedia page has been deleted three times – June 2012, February 2014 and November 2014.

The site's moderators make various comments about the page, including: 'This is a vanity page'; 'He is not ... an important figure or is widely cited by peers or successors'; and 'If this wasn't written by Mr Kassam himself, it is an elaborate prank to implicate him.'

I asked Kassam whether he had been writing his own Wikipedia page, something that, in this day and age, is seen as one of the worst crimes you can commit:

> No. Categorically no. Honestly, I promise you. I admitted in the past that I edited an article because it said 'Raheem Kassam is a cunt' so I went in and edited that out. I've admitted that, I did not ever start my Wikipedia page, I did not ever delete my Wikipedia page, but once, about six months ago, I wrote to Wikipedia and said: 'Look, this article doesn't need to be up, I'm not a person of note, please take it down.'

Regardless of whether or not Kassam was important enough to be immortalised on Wikipedia, Farage clearly rated him. The pair became virtually inseparable in the run-up to the general election campaign, with Kassam helping on speech-writing, presentation and media relations.

On news clips, Kassam was always in shot next to Farage, in matching coats of course, and in one broadcast he was seen sitting on a sofa next to the UKIP leader, proudly displaying his Union Jack socks.

It was clear Kassam was going to play a huge part in Farage's election campaign.

PART 2

WAR

'Everything about our campaign is going to be positive.'

Nigel Farage, Margate, 27 February 2015

CHAPTER 14

SATURDAY 14 MARCH 2015 – SANDWICH

LATEST POLLS:

ICM/*Guardian*: Con 36; Lab 35; Lib Dem 8; UKIP 9

Populus: Con 34; Lab 34; Lib Dem 8; UKIP 14

Ashcroft: Con 31; Lab 29; Lib Dem 8; UKIP 15

READING ABOUT NIGEL FARAGE'S lemon-sized, rock-hard testicle certainly wakes you up, probably in the same way morning sickness must do for a pregnant woman.

The lurid details of Farage's testicular cancer, which he suffered when he was in his early twenties, were prominent in that morning's *Daily Telegraph*. The paper was serialising the latest of Farage's autobiographies, *The Purple Revolution*, and the first extract focused on his three near-death experiences – in graphic detail.

I was contemplating Farage's testicles (I'll stop going on about this soon, I promise) as I sat on the train from Stratford International in east London to Sandwich in Kent.

I had been invited to watch Farage address a public meeting in the town, which was located in the South Thanet constituency he was hoping to win in fifty-four days' time.

Also on the train was Rowena Mason from *The Guardian* – hardly a UKIP-supporting paper – and, as I was at the time working for the *Mirror*, we figured the party must be trying to reach out beyond the usual media outlets.

Although the so-called 'short campaign' of the election had yet to start – that would come when Parliament dissolved on Monday 30 March – all the parties were already in full electioneering mode.

Ten days earlier, on Wednesday 4 March, UKIP unveiled the immigration policy it would be taking into the general election. Bizarrely, the party managed to complicate what should have been a very simple announcement by axing its own migration cap of 50,000 new arrivals a year just five days after immigration spokesman Steven Woolfe talked it up at the spring conference in Margate.

The cap had been part of UKIP plans for at least six months, but was ditched just twenty-four hours before the party was due to announce its immigration policy for the election at a rally in Westminster.

The decision was taken by Farage's inner circle of advisors, including Raheem Kassam, Chris Bruni-Lowe and UKIP's deputy chairman Suzanne Evans, who effectively tore up Woolfe's work at the last minute.

The U-turn was made after figures released at the end of February showed net migration was running at 280,000 a year, meaning Tory leader David Cameron had spectacularly missed his own target of reducing the figure to below 100,000.

Farage's advisors decided they didn't want to tie the party to a cap it might not be able to meet if in government. But they missed one obvious detail from their plotting: UKIP were not going to be in government. Even the most optimistic Kipper accepted the party was not going to win the general election, and Farage had already ruled out a formal coalition in the event of a hung parliament.

Frankly, UKIP could have announced a 'one-in, one-out' immigration policy for all the actual difference it made. So, instead of Farage spending his big immigration announcement day talking about concerns over open borders, he was forced to defend a needless U-turn.

'I'm not putting on caps or targets, you need to have more flexibility than that,' he said. 'You cannot have anything in politics without people obsessing over caps and targets and I think people are bored of it.'

Speaking to the BBC, Farage added: 'I'm afraid the media's obsession with targets is almost as bad as the political class's obsession with targets, and these don't work.'

Such was the confusion over the policy, and why the cap had been dropped, that UKIP press officer Gawain Towler took to Twitter later that day to write: 'Sad day: I've just failed to organise a piss up in a brewery.'

He followed it up with: 'I am considering my position – not nearly close enough to the bar.'

Ten days on, and Farage was back focusing on his own fortunes.

Sandwich is a beautiful town, with welcoming tea rooms, traditional pubs and ramshackle streets.

Mason and I walked the few minutes from the train station to the market square, where we were due to meet Farage and his entourage.

For once in my life, I was early, so we sat and had a coffee in a small café off the square. I asked the owner what she thought of Farage standing in the area and the inevitable media circus that would accompany him. She didn't say much about Farage, but wasn't overly keen on comedian Al Murray contesting the seat in his guise as comedy character 'The Pub Landlord'.

Like many others I spoke to that day, there was a feeling that those in South Thanet were being laughed at by the comedian. We spied Farage walking through the square and into a pub. It wasn't even eleven in the morning, but off he went through the door.

A host of photographers was already positioned outside by the time we finished our coffee and made it over, but no press were being allowed in. It seemed the landlord had opened the pub early just for Farage and other Ukippers to meet and have breakfast before the day's campaigning began.

After about twenty minutes, Farage emerged, along with his new personal press officer Sarah White. The former BBC producer, who spent eight years working for the broadcaster, followed Paul 'Gobby' Lambert to UKIP, and would be masterminding all Farage's press relations until polling day – and maybe beyond.

'Morning, how are we all today?' asked Farage, cheerily.

'Well, Nigel, I was OK until I started reading about your testicles in the *Telegraph* this morning!' I replied with a smile.

Farage was not seeing the funny side.

'You know it really was rather frightening,' he said earnestly.

Fair point, perhaps I shouldn't have been making jokes about his almost fatal cancer.

We set off to a car park where a host of local Kippers were congregating. Raheem Kassam had joined us, as had election data mastermind Chris Bruni-Lowe. Camera crews from national and local broadcasters were also present, and Farage gave a series of interviews about the suggestion in his book, repeated in that morning's *Telegraph*, that those who can afford to take out private health insurance should do so.

After the interviews, Farage beckoned Kassam over and they both disappeared together behind the car park's public toilets in deep conversation. At least that's what I think they were doing.

We followed Farage as he and the People's Army foot soldiers descended on a residential street in the town to do some old-fashioned door-knocking. Of course, it would be embarrassing with all the camera crews and journalists present if Farage knocked on the door of someone who wanted an argument, so the People's Army foot soldiers were sent out on scouting missions first, finding residents who would give him a warm reception.

Farage turned on the charm for all he met, and even disappeared inside a few houses after being invited in. The response he was getting (from the people who had already been identified as UKIP supporters) was positive. He even managed to find one old couple who seemed to be more anti-European Union than he was.

'Crikey, I think they wanted to dig Ted Heath up just so they could bury him again!' he joked.

As fun as it was watching Farage only speak to people who agreed with him, I decided to leave him and the rest of his foot soldiers to it and head back into the town. The public meeting as was at 2 p.m., and myself and Mason had been promised a sit-down interview with Farage beforehand.

I had just over an hour to kill, and walked back into Sandwich with UKIP activist – and local council candidate – Ted Bennett (no relation to me, or to Green Party leader Natalie). He told me a story I'd heard numerous times from pensioners wearing the purple rosette of UKIP. He had had little interest in politics until UKIP came along, and was attracted by the party's strong border-control message.

The Red Cow pub seemed like a good option for lunch and, within minutes of ordering a sandwich (while I was in Sandwich! Oh, the laughter!), a few Ukippers came through the door also looking for refreshments. One was Trevor Shonk, a UKIP county councillor who was standing for Thanet District Council in May. I sat with him, Ted and another man who looked like the spitting image of Ron Atkinson.

If you don't know Ron Atkinson, he was the former football manager and pundit who lost his job as a commentator after describing Chelsea defender Marcel Desailly as a 'fucking lazy, thick nigger'. The Atkinson lookalike in the pub was equally forthright in his views, and even claimed UKIP would win hundreds of seats in the general election.

When his comments got a little tasty, Shonk and Bennett were quick to correct him and take him to task, well aware that a journalist was sitting in their midst.

As I left the pub, Shonk tapped me on the shoulder and gestured to the man.

'Look, I know he said a few dodgy things, but he's not a member of UKIP or anything, and we don't agree with it.'

Kippers were now ultra-sensitive to any comments that could be blown up into a media storm, and were getting in their retaliation first. I assured him it was all fine, which it was. The man hadn't said anything racist, homophobic, Islamaphobic or revealed any other kind of prejudice. Well, not really, and, as he had pointed out a number of times, he wasn't a party member.

I headed to the Phoenix Community Centre ten minutes' walk away from the Red Cow for a chat with Farage before the public meeting. Mason and I sat with the UKIP leader in a small room next to the main hall, with Kassam next to us keeping an ear on what was going on.

We went over the usual topics: immigration; the EU; how UKIP is a threat to Labour in the north of England.

Then Mason hit him with a couple of questions neither Farage nor myself were expecting, introducing them in a wonderful *Guardian* journalist way.

'Can I ask you a tangential question, completely off-topic, but a question I've always wanted to ask you: is Nigel Farage a feminist?'

Farage chuckled: 'I saw Nick Clegg was asked that and said yes. I think by definition I couldn't be. I'm not sure what the word means any more.'

'So that's a "no"?' replied Mason.

'What does the word mean?'

'Somebody who believes in equal opportunities for men and women.'

'Is that what a feminist is?'

'I think so, yeah.'

'OK, I'm not sure that's what a feminist would call herself now. I thought feminists were anti-men and thought we were awful people. Do I believe in equal opportunities? – yes.'

'So if that's what feminism means then you would be a feminist?'

There was a pause and we all started laughing as Farage said with a smile: 'I'm not playing this game!'

Mason's 'Farage is a feminist' headline, complete with an article of all the sexist things UKIP MEPs and candidates had ever said, had been thwarted.

As our 25-minute chat came to an end, Mason hit him with another question he was unlikely to be asked again this campaign: 'Is there a year you think Britain was at its best?'

He said: 'Depending what part of Britain you were in, '88 was pretty good. Because of tax relief on mortgages, suddenly incomes going up. It wasn't so good if you were in South Yorkshire, but if you were in London it was brilliant.'

He left the room and the public meeting with about seventy people began in the room next door.

Farage was on good form, making the usual jokes about locking the doors until everyone there had joined the party. He focused his speech on national and local issues, and earned nods of approval and applause from the residents.

Questions were taken from the floor, and Farage seemed so much happier in the unpredictable nature of a town hall debate than knocking on doors of people who had already been identified as UKIP sympathisers.

Next to the entrance, a pair of women who looked like they had been drafted in from the local Women's Institute manned a table selling UKIP merchandise, including the now traditional fruitcake and the infamous Herman Van Rompuy 'damp rag' tea towel. Farage later claimed the tea towel was one of the party's most valuable fundraising tactics, and UKIP had shifted more than 10,000 of them over the years.

Next to the merchandise table, another party member shook a collection bucket as people left the meeting, appealing for spare change.

The unpolished, raw and slightly amateurish nature of the meeting was a complete contrast to the spin, sophistication and sound bites of election events organised by the main parties.

It was refreshing, and hard not to be impressed by. It seemed the party was planning to win over small sections of the constituency at a time, using Farage's natural charisma, confidence and showmanship to persuade people to back him.

And just in case there wasn't enough pressure, Farage decided to raise the stakes even higher. In the final extract from *The Purple Revolution*, the *Telegraph* revealed Farage would quit as UKIP leader if he wasn't victorious in South Thanet.

'The consequences of me failing to secure a seat for myself in the Commons would be significant for both myself and the party,' he wrote:

> It is frankly just not credible for me to continue to lead the party without a Westminster seat. What credibility would UKIP have in the Commons if others had to enunciate party policy in Parliament and the party leader was only allowed in as a guest? Was I supposed to brief UKIP policy from the Westminster Arms?
>
> No – if I fail to win South Thanet, it is curtains for me. I will have to step down.

Many senior members of the party were not aware of Farage's 'all or nothing' strategy until they read about it in the *Telegraph*. Some of the more seasoned campaigners in UKIP thought it was a huge error.

'It was the wrong decision to make,' Douglas Carswell later told me. 'If you have a swing voter in Thanet, if it's all about a chance to assist or not assist a politician, does that make you more inclined to support them?'

Three days after our interview in Sandwich, I was invited to Farage's book launch party for *The Purple Revolution*. It was held in a swanky hotel bar in Westminster, with wine, beer and food all laid on for invitees to enjoy.

Journalists, UKIP members and even MPs were in attendance, but any conversations at the event were 'off the record', according to the press release. So while I can't tell you what was said, I can tell you that the man I met at the Margate conference who warned me about the rise of Islam was there. I can also tell you I learned his name was

Brendan O'Brien, and I saw him and Farage in deep conversation as the UKIP leader signed his copy of the book.

I wondered if Farage knew about O'Brien's view of the world, but, alas, did not get a chance to ask him.

I did manage to get him to sign my copy of *The Purple Revolution* though: 'To Owen, Up the Mirror! Nigel Farage'.

BATTLE FOR NO. 10 DEBATE – THURSDAY 26 MARCH 2015 – SKY NEWS, OSTERLEY, WEST LONDON

LATEST POLLS

Populus: Con 31; Lab 33; Lib Dem 9; UKIP 16

YouGov/*Sun*: Con 36; Lab 34; Lib Dem 7; UKIP 13

It was the biggest will-they-won't-they since Tim and Dawn in *The Office*.

At least that's how it felt for political journalists.

Would David Cameron, Ed Miliband, Nick Clegg, Nigel Farage and all the others debate each other on television during the election campaign? Miliband was keen, but Cameron was doing his best to scupper the proposals. Ofcom ruled UKIP should be treated as a major party in election coverage, which meant Farage had to be invited.

If Farage was there taking votes away from the Tories, then why wasn't the Green Party leader Natalie Bennett there to take votes away from Miliband? was Cameron's view. The broadcasters agreed, and invited Bennett. And Nicola Sturgeon from the Scottish National Party. And Leanne Wood from Plaid Cymru. But not any of the Northern Irish parties. That would be taking it too far.

With the stage now full, Cameron decided he didn't want to take part in any debate during the short campaign, which started on 30 March. And he didn't want to take Miliband on in a head-to-head. Eventually, after seemingly endless negotiations, the Prime Minister gave way on the first point, but not the second. No head-to-head, but he would take part in a seven-way debate on Thursday 2 April. Farage would get his moment to grill Cameron after all. If he could get a word in among everyone else on the stage, of course.

Before the seven-way clash, Miliband and Cameron subjected themselves to a grilling by Jeremy Paxman and a studio audience in a joint Channel 4/Sky News programme, *The Battle for Number 10*, on Thursday 26 March. The format was: Cameron v. Paxman; Cameron v. audience; Miliband v. audience; Miliband v. Paxman.

Lobby hacks made their way to Sky News studios in Osterley, west London, to watch the show from the spin room. For those of you who aren't familiar with a 'spin room', it is basically the wet dream of a sixteen-year-old William Hague.

Journalists watch politicians being interviewed by other journalists or members of the public on a big television, and then other politicians tell journalists what they have just seen and why what they have just seen shows that the politician from their party is so much better than the politician from the other party.

It's awful, but I was desperate to be there because I like feeling important.

Walking into the Sky building that night felt like stumbling upon a rehearsal for a Pink Floyd concert. Coloured laser beams swooped and danced across the buildings as the technicians prepared for the arrivals of the leaders. I was shown into the press room, which even an hour before broadcast was full of journalists frantically trying to log on to Sky's WiFi.

A colleague told me he had seen Farage's name on the guest list, so I rang Raheem Kassam to see if the UKIP leader was definitely going to come along.

'No, he's not,' was the reply.

I tweeted out that Farage wouldn't be joining us in the spin room for the debate, and ten minutes later he arrived.

'Thanks, mate!' I said when I saw Kassam. 'Why did you tell me he wasn't coming?!'

Kassam just laughed, finding it funny that I had just looked like an idiot.

'Well, I suppose I'd better tweet out that you were the one who either lied to me or didn't know where his own boss was going to be tonight,' I said.

Kassam stopped laughing. 'No, no, don't do that, you can't do that,' he said quickly.

I left it, thinking it would be good to keep that one in my back pocket for later.

Within a few minutes of his arrival, Farage may well have wished his aide's answer had been correct. After nipping out for a cigarette just before the show was due to start, he was collared by three young black adults who were part of Sky's 'Stand Up Be Counted' campaign to get youngsters interested in politics.

The three – two women and one man – wanted to quiz Farage on UKIP's attitude to race and immigration, and the first woman left the leader in no doubt of her concerns. Speaking to him in the lobby of Sky studios, she said:

> I just think that your party, every day we hear in the news that somebody has said a racist slur or homophobic slur and you keep saying, 'Oh, that's not what my party represents, it's a couple of people,' but it keeps happening every time so it can't just be a couple of people, it's what your party stands for.

She went on: 'Racism is not gone, it's alive and clear. I was born in Barnsley. We used to have our house egged on a daily basis—'

'Is this a question or a speech?' Farage interrupted.

'It's a question!' the young woman replied, clearly shocked at

Farage's comment. 'I'm telling you, I'm a voter, I think you should listen to what I've got to say. I think you need to stop your divisive politics. You need to stop going on about immigration because immigration did not crash the stock exchange and put this country into recession.'

'No, what it did was make everybody—' Farage tried to reply.

'No, in places like you used to work actually—' said the woman, cutting him off.

'Well, if we can't have a conversation,' said Farage, throwing a hand into the air.

The young woman let the UKIP leader speak.

> Today a Liberal Democrat candidate has stood down because of charges of underage sex. They also had the Cyril Smith affair. Do we think the Liberal Democrats are paedophiles? I don't think the Liberal Democrats are paedophiles even though they have had some fairly appalling cases and, by the looks of it, another one today, and you will find that people in all parties, in all walks of life, will say unpleasant things.
>
> What is a fact is as we ran up to those European elections last year, there were more people from the black and ethnic minorities voting UKIP in the European elections last year than voted for the other parties, which I think proves the point.
>
> Now you mentioned immigration and the impact on the economy. What is beyond doubt, and even confirmed by Mark Carney, the Governor of the Bank of England, is the reason that people in Britain from all ethnic minorities, if they are on low pay or even medium pay, the reason they are no better off than they were five or ten years ago is because we have pursued a wholly irresponsible immigration policy of allowing unlimited, unskilled labour into Britain, which has forced people's wages down. The debate about immigration has nothing to do with race at all. It does have a lot to do with numbers.

Another youngster quizzed him on clamping down on tax avoidance by large companies, and a third asked how UKIP would tackle the high unemployment rate among Britain's young black community.

As Farage gave his answer – uncontrolled migration is harming employment opportunities for the young in Britain was his view – the first young woman stepped in again.

'I'm sorry, migrants do not undercut wages, employers need to pay the employees the living wage. You cannot pit Eastern European people—'

'I have no doubt your economic skills are brilliant...' Farage interrupted, sarcastically.

'No, no, no, just listen—'

'I spent nine years running a company, I've employed people...'

'Did you pay them the living wage?'

'I did better than that.'

'If you say so.'

'I did better than that because most people who run small companies actually treat their staff like members of their family.'

It was the first time I had seen Farage be sarcastic and dismissive to a voter who was pressing him. The young woman was being a bit aggressive, and certainly wouldn't cut Farage any slack, but was her behaviour any different to when the UKIP leader accused the president of the European Council Herman Van Rompuy of having 'all the charisma of a damp rag and the appearance of a low-grade bank clerk'?

Before the row could continue, Kassam dragged Farage away and steered him into the spin room to watch *The Battle for Number 10* commence.

THURSDAY 2 APRIL 2015 – ITV LEADERS' DEBATES – SALFORD

LATEST POLLS

YouGov/*Sunday Times*: Con 34; Lab 33; Lib Dem 8; UKIP 13

YouGov/*Sun*: Con 37; Lab 35; Lib Dem 7; UKIP 12

A week later, and Farage was not in the spin room, but on the stage. The seven-way leaders' debate was hosted by ITV and being held in Salford, Greater Manchester. It would be the only opportunity of the campaign for Farage to take on Cameron, who for years he had mocked for both his refusal to hold an EU referendum and then has sudden conversion to the idea in January 2013.

Unfortunately for Farage, he would have to battle to get his voice heard alongside the Labour, Lib Dem, SNP, Plaid Cymru and Green Party leaders.

Farage used his opening address to claim the other six leaders on the stage may look different, 'but actually, on some of the big issues which affect this country, are very much the same'.

He focused on UKIP's desire to get Britain out of the European Union, and added: 'We also believe that open-door immigration has depressed the wages for ordinary people, made buying houses for youngsters very difficult, made it tough to get a GP appointment, and [has] not been good for this country.'

The first question was on reducing Britain's economic deficit, which Farage reminded the audience was now running at '£90 billion every year', before listing how UKIP would reduce costs (no more money to Brussels, cutting the foreign aid budget, scrapping HS2, revisiting funding for Scotland). Other than a few digs at the 'canny Scots' for negotiating a better deal than the Welsh when the Barnett formula was drawn up in 1978, Farage had been relatively unremarkable.

But his answer to the second question of the night ensured he would dominate the next day's headlines: 'How will your party ensure long-term funding of the NHS, while keeping it as a public service accessible to all?'

Farage was given the first opportunity to answer, and referenced his own experiences with the NHS thanks to his numerous scrapes and health problems.

But it was when the debate was opened up that Farage made his headline-grabbing move. After talking about the rise in health tourism, he said:

> OK, here's a fact, and I'm sure that others here will be mortified that I dare to talk about it. There are 7,000 diagnoses in this country every year for people who are HIV-positive, which is not a good place for any of them to be, I know. But 60 per cent of them are not British nationals.
>
> You can come into Britain from anywhere in the world and get diagnosed with HIV and get the retroviral drugs that cost up to £25,000 per year per patient. I know there are some horrible things happening in many parts of the world, but what we need to do is to put the National Health Service there for British people and families, who, in many cases, have paid into the system for decades.

There was noticeable change in the atmosphere in the studio. I was watching the debate in the *Daily Mirror* offices in Canary Wharf, and colleagues around me paused for a moment as they considered Farage attacking those with HIV.

Plaid Cymru's Leanne Wood took Farage to task, telling him: 'This kind of scaremongering rhetoric is dangerous ... it divides communities and it creates stigma to people who are ill and I think you ought to be ashamed of yourself.'

Her comments drew a round of applause from the audience.

I was less surprised than most that Farage had talked about HIV sufferers in relation to benefit tourism, after all, he had already made that point after Douglas Carswell's by-election victory in Clacton.

But his decision to focus on HIV sufferers in the debate caused a rift in UKIP.

The idea came about during a practice session ahead of the debate, attended by, among others, his close advisor Raheem Kassam, head of UKIP's press office Gawain Towler and head of the party's broadcast media relations Alexandra Phillips.

It was decided an example was needed to focus voters' minds on the cost of health tourism.

Multi-drug-resistant tuberculosis was flagged up as one example, but then the idea of HIV sufferers was raised by Farage.

One UKIP insider told me: 'We actually talked about it multiple times before. The thing with the HIV stuff is it is the most glaring example of people coming here just to take from the system.'

Since Farage's comments about the illness after Carswell's by-election victory in October, the UKIP office had received numerous letters and emails from British HIV sufferers supporting his views. So, when in the practice session Farage was asked what evidence he had for health tourism, it was at the forefront of his mind.

At least one of those in the room raised concerns over using HIV sufferers as an example, but they were overruled.

Douglas Carswell, who did not know Farage was planning to use the example in the debate, thought it was an 'awful' move that could seriously backfire.

The UKIP MP told me:

> There's a powerful point to be made about health tourism. But would you say the same about people with leukaemia? People with leukaemia are desperate people, deserving of compassion. Don't single someone out. Why make the case that way? Why invite people who want to think the worst of you to have an excuse to think badly of you? It was awful.

After the debate ended, Kassam briefed journalists that using HIV was part of a strategy of 'shock and awe, or, as some would call it, "shock and awful".'

It was that briefing that infuriated UKIP's economic spokesman Patrick O'Flynn. He later told me:

> I did support it [the HIV comments], I certainly do think that's a very important issue.
>
> What I don't support is presenting it as part of a 'shock and awful' strategy. I did see it as an issue that needed to be addressed. I seriously disagree that raising the issue is 'shock and awful'.

MONDAY 13 APRIL 2015 – CIRCUS TAVERN, THURROCK, ESSEX

LATEST POLLS:

TNS: Con 34; Lab 32; Lib Dem 9; UKIP 14

YouGov/*Sun*: Con 33; Lab 34; Lib Dem 8; UKIP 13

'Occupations always fail,' according to Tim Robbins's character in Steven Spielberg's 2005 version of *War of the Worlds*.

He was, of course, talking about an alien army rampaging across the globe, killing and harvesting humans along the way, not the rise of UKIP in Britain. But if the People's Army wanted to win constituencies across the country, they would need to learn the lessons of the aliens from that story.

It is all very well turning up somewhere, all guns blazing, hoping to break the will of the people with sheer non-stop activity, but no invading force can keep up that level of attack forever. The aliens tried that in *War of the Worlds*, and what happened? Exactly, they got a cold and died.

You see my point?

The victories in Clacton and Rochester in 2014 were occupations. UKIP turned up, having been invited in by the man in charge, and campaigned, canvassed and postered the hell out of the places. The plan in South Thanet was not too different, but involved the People's Army smuggling in its leader and using his profile, charisma and charm to rally people to their flag.

But all of these victories were occupations, not insurgencies. They did not come about because of a groundswell of people on the ground in these areas wanting change; they were led from the top, not the bottom.

If UKIP really wanted to show it was a lasting political force, it needed to win a seat in the election without the advantage of a sitting MP or its leader being the candidate. Thurrock in Essex was the place most likely to give the People's Army that victory.

The seat had been won by the Tories from Labour in 2010, with Conservative candidate Jackie Doyle-Price sneaking home by just ninety-two votes. Labour had held the seat since 1992, making it a constituency Ed Miliband desperately needed to win back for a chance of moving his two kitchens' worth of crockery and saucepans into Downing Street.

One of Miliband's closest advisors, former BBC journalist Polly Billington, was selected to fight the seat in the 2015 general election. All seemed to be going well for Miliband and Billington, and Labour won control of the local council in 2012. But, two years later, the party started going backwards in Thurrock. UKIP increased its number of local councillors from one to six in the 2014 local elections, meaning Labour lost control of the authority.

It was one of UKIP's great success stories of 2014, and Farage travelled to the Hoy & Helmet pub in South Benfleet, Essex, the day after the results were announced to lead the celebrations.

Attitudes on the ground in Thanet seemed to be shifting. A Lord Ashcroft opinion poll carried out in the seat a month before the local elections put Labour ahead of UKIP by eight percentage points. When Ashcroft surveyed the constituency again a month after the local elections, UKIP was in the lead by six points.

As well as having a solid party base to launch its election campaign from, the party also had a highly rated candidate – Tim Aker. The University of Nottingham graduate would not even be thirty come the day of the 2015 general election on 7 May, but had already tasted success by winning a seat in the European Parliament a year before.

A former head of UKIP's policy unit, he was originally responsible for drafting the party's 2015 general election manifesto. However, in January 2015 he was replaced by UKIP's deputy chairman Suzanne Evans amid rumours – strongly denied by both him and the party – that the manifesto was way behind schedule.

But it wasn't his policy-wonk status that was scoring him points with the Thurrock residents; it was the fact he was a local lad. Born and raised in the constituency, Aker played the 'local' card over and over again throughout the campaign – and it seemed to be working.

There was a sense of UKIP momentum in the air when I travelled to Thurrock on Monday 13 April to attend a public meeting that Farage was due to speak at. Based purely on the sheer number of purple UKIP signs on display in people's windows, gardens and balconies, the party seemed to have a strong ground operation. During a walkabout in the town centre of South Ockendon that afternoon, people leaned out of their flat windows and cheered on Farage. Young mothers pushing prams happily took plastic 'Vote UKIP' banners and the party leader got an enthusiastic reception from the local shop owners.

That evening's big rally was being held at the Circus Tavern, an entertainment venue just off the A13 in Purfleet. It usually played host to cabaret acts and comedians, and, from 1994 to 2007, the World Darts Championship was held there.

Above the Circus Tavern was a pole-dancing venue called Tenshi Gentlemen's Club. According to its website: 'Tenshi is Japanese for Angel, and that is what our ladies are … Angels.'

A darts venue underneath a lap-dancing club. Ladies and gentlemen, we are about to hit peak UKIP.

As the public queued to enter the 1,100-capacity venue, ITV's Julie Etchingham recorded her final piece to camera for a Farage documentary due to air the next week. The film caught the leader in a reflective mood, and even showed him in a church.

While Farage was preparing to deliver a sermon of his own to the hundreds in the Circus Tavern, Aker used the meeting to whip up enthusiasm for his campaign. The atmosphere in the hall was less political rally, more end-of-season get-together for pub teams in a Sunday football league.

Lager was flowing freely, tables of men and women – mainly in their thirties and forties – were laughing and joking, and the atmosphere was relaxed. I could even detect cigarette smoke wafting through the air inside the venue. I'm not a sociological expert, but it was pretty clear it was predominately working-class and lower-middle-class voters who had turned out for this political meeting.

First up to address the 700 or so gathered in the club was Labour defector Harriet Yeo. She earned a huge round of applause when she proclaimed: 'The Labour voters are the voters who want somebody to listen to them, and that's why they're voting UKIP and that's why they're listening to Nigel Farage. The media might not like the message, but the people do.'

There was yet more clapping and cheers as she hit out at Ed Miliband for not agreeing to a referendum on Europe: 'If you can be trusted to vote Labour into power, why can't you be trusted to vote either in or out of Europe?'

So far, so good. Yeo was rubbing the egos of the people in the room. The message was simple: no one listens to you, but we do because we think you are important.

But then things got a bit weird: 'For some of the men now you are going to squirm, but just think of this as money in your pockets. UKIP said the other day that they would do away with VAT on sanitary wear.'

A Mexican wave of nervous laughter immediately swept around the room, and several men began staring intensely at beer mats or their phones. Yeo explained how EU regulations meant VAT was levied on sanitary products, which was another reason to leave the organisation.

'For you men that might not find this too comfortable, just think, that's 5 per cent of that money which you could use on other things, like a night out, or even a pint or two,' she explained.

More laughter, and even a call of 'even a night in!' from one of the men, followed by a wolf whistle. Being a man, I admit I don't have a great knowledge of menstruation, but I don't think abolishing VAT on sanitary products will somehow stop a woman's period from happening, thus enabling 'a night in' of the kind this man had in mind.

I did enjoy the inference that if sanitary products were cheaper, the money saved would immediately be given back to 'the men' so they could have 'a pint or two'. That's how the world works of course: men give women money to buy their women stuff, and any money left over goes back to the men.

After Yeo's barnstorming performance, Aker took to the podium. Aker is a small, slight man, who looks like he would be more at home in a garden centre than at a political rally for a populist party. The few times I had spoken to him before that night he had come across as measured, thoughtful and quiet, with none of Farage's tub-thumping charisma. I was interested to see how his meek, understated style would play with the audience.

'Good evening!' he shouted into the microphone. 'Are we good?'

'Yes!' shouted back the audience.

'Are we gonna win?'

'Yes!'

'Now there's something wrong with that because Jackie

[Doyle-Price, Tory MP for Thurrock] didn't hear you in Purfleet. Are we gonna win?'

'YEEEEEESSSSS!' came the enthusiastic response from the audience.

'Now I think Polly [Billington, Labour candidate for Thurrock] in Islington heard you as well,' he replied to much laughter.

I was taken aback. This meek, mild-mannered man had transformed into a passionate, powerful, public speaker. He had the audience in the palm of his hand, and, in a blistering ten-minute speech, took down the Tory incumbent ('Shame on you for supporting the cuts to Grays walk-in centre') and Labour's Billington.

He talked up his local connections, name-checked towns in the constituency and tickled the crowd's nostalgia bone by reminiscing about days eating burgers at the market.

Before introducing Farage to the stage, he hammered home how confident he was that Thurrock would go purple on 7 May: 'The bookies have got us as favourites. Lord Ashcroft, God bless him, has got us in the lead. YouGov showed we are in the lead, and we can do it.'

He ended with the now familiar refrain: 'If you vote UKIP, you get UKIP.'

The crowd loved it. Applause, cheers, whistles. I had never seen a political rally with so much passion.

Farage picked up where Aker left off, getting a huge cheer as he said: 'It's great to be in Thurrock, it's great to be in Essex, a part of the world in which people tell it as it is.'

He then went through the usual Farage script:

'I had a job once...'

'Britain is run by college kids...'

'The lie of the Common Market referendum in 1975...'

'No one would have heard of European Council president Herman Van Rompuy if I hadn't been his PR man...'

The audience couldn't get enough, but what sent them into a

collective orgasm of agreement was when Farage said: 'I don't believe that those who went before us and sacrificed and gave so much in two world wars did so...'

Before he could finish his attack on the EU, the audience were on their feet. Hundreds of people cheering, banging tables, clapping and shouting as Farage invoked the memory of the two most devastating conflicts the world has ever known. I felt uneasy. This 'we won the war' rhetoric is dangerous, and has been used by many people over the years to stir up far-right nationalism.

I'm not saying that was Farage's intention, but it is a risky game to play in the feverish atmosphere of a nightclub where the lager had been flowing and hundreds were all too ready to get fired up. It all got too much for a man at a table to my right. All evening he had been getting more and more aggressive, and his heckling was getting louder and more frantic.

The people he was with were getting annoyed, with a woman shouting at him: 'All I can hear is you. Why don't you sit down and shut up?'

As Farage was talking, the UKIP leader's bodyguards moved closer to the heckler – who, far from disagreeing with what was being said, was enthusiastically agreeing with it, repeating it loudly and adding his own analysis.

'Damn straight!' was one of his favourite phrases.

As Farage's bouncers tried to get him to quieten down, he tried to reassure them he was no threat to the UKIP leader.

'I love him, mate,' he pleaded.

As Farage carried on talking, the man left to go to the toilet. I know this because he shouted loudly: 'I'm going to the toilet.'

He didn't return.

Farage's speech ended with cacophonous applause. A woman behind me tapped me on the shoulder and said: 'He's brilliant, isn't he?' with a big grin on her face.

He had certainly roused the crowd, but Farage didn't seem quite right to me that night. His delivery was more rushed than usual. Normally he savours every gag and applause, but he looked distracted, as if he just wanted the whole thing over and done with.

After the meeting had ended and he finished signing copies of his latest book, he and his bodyguards rushed back through the empty venue and out the back door. Normally, Farage would go for a post-match drink with his colleagues, and sometimes even the journalists who had made the trip. I watched him weave his way through the now deserted chairs and tables – the empty pint glasses and crisp packets the only testament to the packed meeting that had finished half an hour before.

WEDNESDAY 15 APRIL 2015 – MANIFESTO LAUNCH – THURROCK HOTEL, THURROCK

LATEST POLLS
YouGov/*Sun*: Con 34; Lab 35; Lib Dem 8; UKIP 13
Ipsos MORI/*Evening Standard*: Con 22; Lab 35; Lib Dem 7; UKIP 10

Nigel Farage once joked to me that, if he had his way, UKIP would launch its manifesto the day before the election.

The political take on that is it would give opponents just twenty-four hours to try to debunk it and see if the 'sums add up'. The cynical view is that it would give Farage even longer to make policies up on the hoof and not actually tow any sort of party line. Alas for Farage, the manifesto wasn't published on Wednesday 6 May, but Wednesday 15 April.

The setting was the Thurrock Hotel in south Essex, which rather wonderfully also plays host to *Fawlty Towers* experience dinners.

Spirits were high, but attendance wasn't.

There were barely fifty actual UKIP members in the audience, and neither of the party's MPs had turned up. There were, however, a large number of journalists and sketch-writers, partly to provide comprehensive coverage and in-depth analysis of the manifesto, and partly (as was customary) hoping for a UKIP gaffe.

Some were hoping the two would combine and the manifesto itself would be one big gaffe, just like the 2010 document. That manifesto, produced by then UKIP MEP David Campbell Bannerman under the leadership of Lord Pearson, advocated such policies as ensuring people dressed smartly at the theatre, making the London Underground Circle line a circle again, repainting trains in 'traditional' colours and introducing a dress code for taxi drivers. Farage later described the 486-page document as 'drivel'.

UKIP were determined not to give their opponents any more ammunition with this manifesto, or indeed at the launch. Deputy leader Paul Nuttall was first up, and, with the event taking place in Thurrock, he began by heaping praise on the 'excellent' Tim Aker – who had been writing the manifesto until January.

Farage was up next, and ran through the document's highlights: abolishing inheritance tax; scrapping HS2; cutting the foreign aid budget; taking those on minimum wage out of income tax; and, of course, the usual 'control immigration and get out of the EU' pledges. Unlike the other parties' manifestos, this one was fully costed and independently assessed by an economic think tank, Farage boasted.

As he was talking, copies of the manifesto were handed out to journalists, who began frantically skim-reading it for spelling errors or bizarre pledges buried in the small print.

The manifesto itself looked good and, at seventy-six pages, was more than six times shorter than the 2010 effort. Each section began with a picture of the relevant spokesman in various settings.

Economic spokesman Patrick O'Flynn looked like an android who had just been wheeled off a production line in a robot factory.

Education spokesman Paul Nuttall was pictured in front of a wall of books – although closer examination showed that the bookcase had been copied and pasted to make it longer to fit the page. Or maybe Nuttall just had two copies of a lot of books.

Peter Reeve, the party's local government spokesman, appeared mopping the floor in a public toilet while wearing a high-vis coat, making him look less like a politician and more like someone carrying out community service.

Overseas aid spokesman Nathan Gill introduced his section on cutting the aid budget with a picture of him cuddling a smiling black woman in what appeared to be Africa: 'Smile for the camera so I can use this picture to illustrate how we care about foreigners after all … as we cut the money we send abroad.'

After Farage finished the introduction, UKIP's deputy chairman and manifesto author Suzanne Evans stepped up to the podium and gave a performance as professional as the document itself.

UKIP was playing a blinder. The manifesto was well presented, coherent and costed by a think tank. The launch wasn't all about Farage, but showed off the talents of UKIP's front-bench team, in particular Evans.

The whole event was going so well that Nuttall felt confident enough to make a joke at the expense of Chief UKIP Wind-Up Merchant Michael Crick at the beginning of the question section of the event.

'I'll start with Channel 4 – Michael – because, as another party once said, after that, things can only get better,' he quipped.

Ukippers and journalists found themselves united in laughter, and Crick was unable to get his question out for a good thirty seconds while he too tried to suppress some chuckles.

'I've run out of questions,' Crick joked as the laughter died down, a remark that only led to more cheers and applause.

He eventually asked Farage if the Tories getting rid of David Cameron was a 'red line' for him doing a deal with the Conservatives after the election – a question Farage batted aside easily.

A question from the BBC allowed Farage to praise the 'first-class' manifesto, which he had 'read, absorbed, and understood', leading to another round of applause and much laughter.

'That's the second question, so one more question than was asked at the Lib Dem manifesto launch this morning,' joked Nuttall from the stage.

Next up was Christopher 'Chopper' Hope from the *Telegraph*.

'Nigel, you said you read the document fully. Are you happy that the only black face in the document is on the overseas aid page?'

Before the question was even finished, the room descended into boos and jeers. Not in a pantomime way, but angry, aggressive boos.

All eyes turned on Hope and, as the jeering continued, a black UKIP member sitting in front of the journalists got to his feet. Then another black man stood up. Then a British Arab. Then a British Indian. The audience began applauding, as did Farage, as UKIP members created their very own 'I'm Spartacus' moment.

It was actually the best response to the question, and it made a change that the UKIP members were coming to the defence of the leadership, instead of the other way round.

If it had ended there, it would have been fine, but the booing kept on coming.

Kippers began shouting at Hope: 'Shame on you! Shameful.' I was sitting behind him, and could feel all eyes on the media pack. It was intimidating.

Raheem Kassam was standing in the aisle, joining in the clapping and shouting 'shameful' along with other Kippers. What exactly was 'shameful'? A journalist asking a question about the racial diversity of a party that is often criticised by its opponents for the racist comments by some members?

It seemed the People's Army liked journalists being in the room when they were laughing along at Nuttall's jokes, but not when they were asking difficult questions. Hope managed to get in a second question, this time about whether Tories should vote tactically in marginal seats to benefit UKIP. Farage chose to answer his second one and not the first.

Moments later, Andy Bell from 5 *News* asked: 'Mr Farage, would you stop people with HIV entering Britain?'

The question was clearly a follow-up to Farage's outburst in the seven-way leaders' debate about health tourism, but some Kippers in the room still groaned, made shushing noises and one even spun round on his chair and said: 'Disgusting question.'

Again, why was this disgusting? This is a subject Farage had tried to make political gain out of, not the media. The UKIP leader replied by saying it was a 'very good question' and repeated his attack on health tourism: 'Do I stand by that? You bet your life I stand by that.'

The manifesto launch came to an end and Farage disappeared into a room for some one-on-one broadcast interviews. Kassam tapped me on the shoulder: 'Next event is at a veterans' centre in Sandwich if you want to come.'

I grabbed a lift with Rowena Mason from *The Guardian* – who accepted payment in the form of a Subway lunch in a traffic island next to a service station on the M2 – and arrived at the Future for Heroes centre a few hours later.

Farage arrived with his seemingly endless number of bodyguards, and began speaking to some of the homeless veterans who used the facility. He was in a good mood, buoyed by – as he saw it – the successful manifesto launch and the obvious quality of the document itself.

A keen military history buff, he took a great interest in the tales of the soldiers who were now homeless and, in many cases, addicted to alcohol or other substances. But while Farage was focusing on the plight of those who had fought for the UK, much of the media coverage was focusing again on UKIP's race issue. The booing of Hope had been picked up by the news outlets, and people on social media were gleefully using it as another example of the party's race problem.

You would think that Farage would be furious with Hope for distracting attention away from the manifesto, but he seemed to relish the confrontation. The UKIP leader was asked to appear on Iain Dale's LBC radio show that afternoon to discuss the manifesto launch and the booing of Hope.

He telephoned in to the studio from his black Land Rover parked just outside the centre, while us journalists – including Hope – crowded round a phone to listen to what someone no more than 10 feet away from us was saying. After a few minutes attacking the media's obsession over race, he emerged from the Land Rover.

Now it was Hope's turn, as he too rang in to the LBC studio to give his version of events.

I would have loved all those Kippers who had booed Hope earlier to have seen just how close the relationship was between their party leader and the 'shameful' journalists. It looked like both were acting out parts in a radio play, phoning in their lines while standing next to each other.

Farage needed the press, and we needed Farage.

While Hope was speaking to LBC, I asked Farage if he thought the reaction to Hope's question on black faces in the manifesto would dominate the news agenda in the same way that Godfrey Bloom hitting Michael Crick after a similar question dominated the 2013 conference.

'I hope so,' he said, with a laugh:

> I do hope so. You will always get things that happen round the edge that attract a bit of interest and excitement. But I thought it was a very interesting moment. This was a classic question that UKIP always gets asked with the inference that comes with it and the answer was there to see. I thought it was great.

By now Hope had joined us. 'You didn't answer though,' he said.

'I didn't need to, not everything needs words you know. Pictures sometimes speak more loudly,' Farage replied, referring to the black Kippers standing up to show the party's diversity.

Hope tried again with the question about the lack of black faces, but Farage interrupted:

> You may well have done us the biggest favour anybody has

yet by helping to overcome the perception that people like you have tried to instil in people that somehow UKIP is all late-middle-aged white men who are all half colonels living on Salisbury Plain, and actually UKIP is far more diverse than that…

'Please, please answer the question,' interrupted Hope. '"Is UKIP racist?" is the question to answer.'

'Absolutely not, and you saw that loud and clear this morning, but, as I say, the effect of what's happened is it's going to go berserk on social media and I think it will help to break down that misconception that some people have,' was Farage's reply.

He was then asked about the shouting down of Hope after his question, with a journalist from the Press Association saying: 'If activists stand up and shout down people they don't happen to like, that's a pretty unpleasant image to put to floating voters.'

'Well, you and I are going to disagree on that, I'm going to say it shows passion and conviction,' replied Farage.

Before he disappeared into his black Land Rover to be whisked away, I asked Farage if he was enjoying the campaign. The usual bounciness and energy seemed to be in short supply, something I had noticed two days before in Thurrock.

'Most of it's been pretty good. I've got the energy for it but, let's be honest, I'm a bit creaky and I've been smashed up a few times,' he said.

And with that, he was off.

Us journos made our way into nearby Sandwich to file copy in a pub with WiFi, and the general tone seemed to be that Farage was remarkably upbeat considering the headlines would be dominated not by the manifesto but by the booing of a journalist.

To me, it was obvious. All the time spent asking questions about UKIP's race problem was time spent not asking Farage about the minutiae of the manifesto. He knows how to answer the race question – he has been doing so for years and years.

But, if we were to press him on how abolishing inheritance tax would appeal to its working-class supporters, how UKIP would fund any of this if Britain voted to stay in the European Union, and why on earth there is a specific pledge on protecting classic cars but no mention of LGBT rights, would he have been so relaxed?

Christopher Hope, *Telegraph* sketch-writer Michael Deacon and I boarded a train from Sandwich back to London. Hope began looking through his Twitter feed, where he was getting a lot of abuse from UKIP supporters over his question. Deacon and I suggested he read them out on video for the *Telegraph* website the next day.

Set to some melancholy piano music, with his best puppy-eyed look, he did just that.

Here are some of the tweets that upset Hope (actually, they just made us all laugh):

'What an utter cockwomble. How low has the Telegraph sunk? To the level of the loony left? Sad'

'Why is the only black face from Google image search for Daily Telegraph journalists Barack Obama?'

'Racist twat. That was a disgusting comment to make. Only racists like you notice skin colour. You should apologise to UKIP.'

'Sack Chris Hope for his racist comment. Shocking racist newspaper.'

'Sheer and utter gutter journalism. How about asking about policy rather than race-baiting, you shoddy Tory stooge.'

'You seem a bit of a cunt by all accounts'

MONDAY 20 APRIL 2015 – CORN EXCHANGE, ROCHESTER

LATEST POLLS
TNS: Con 32; Lab 34; Lib Dem 9; UKIP 15
YouGov/*Sun*: Con 34; Lab 35; Lib Dem 7; UKIP 13

Nigel Farage's fight to win South Thanet was not the most important campaign for UKIP in the lead-up to the general election.

It was Mark Reckless's in Rochester & Strood. If UKIP could not get Reckless and Douglas Carswell in Clacton re-elected on 7 May, it could wave goodbye to any potential defectors in the next Parliament.

'Yes, we can get you through a by-election, but no, we can't get you through a general election' – that would be the message.

Carswell in Clacton was thought to be safe. He had a majority of more than 12,000 and a huge personal following. The constituency itself was deemed to be the most 'UKIP-friendly' seat in the country by the academics Matthew Goodwin and Rob Ford, who had co-authored an award-winning book on the party's rise.

But Reckless in Rochester? That would be a struggle.

He had won his by-election with a majority of 2,920 – a victory that could easily be overturned by the second-placed Tories.

The seat was ranked as number 271 in Goodwin and Ford's 'UKIP friendliness' rating, which perhaps explained why Reckless wasn't shouting about his association with the party. He did not turn up for the manifesto launch in Thurrock, less than an hour's drive from his constituency, and, unlike Carswell, there was no photo of him in the document.

On Monday 20 April, Farage visited the town to help shore up support for Reckless, and in the evening took part in yet another town hall debate. A week before, he had been addressing working-class voters in a former world darts venue underneath a strip club in Essex. Now, he was due to speak to a crowd of far more well-to-do people in the grand Corn Exchange building in the picturesque town of Rochester.

Before the meeting started, Farage was holding court in a tea room opposite the venue.

TV crews and print journalists crowded in to hear his views on the crisis in the Mediterranean, where hundreds of migrants fleeing from Libya and Eritrea were drowning as they attempted to sail to Europe. Farage's solution was to 'send the Royal Navy' to rescue drowning migrants, but, unsurprisingly, he was strongly opposed to being part of any EU-led operations.

With the international situation dealt with from a tea shop, it was time to recommence the wooing of voters in Rochester. There were about 300 people in the Corn Exchange, all waiting patiently, politely and quietly for the event to begin.

Farage deployed his usual tactics of waiting in the wings before taking to the stage – always a good way of getting an additional round of applause, of course – so it was left to a local UKIP councillor to get proceedings underway.

After a short introduction, up stepped my concentration span's nemesis: Mark Reckless.

The monotone voice, the stifled delivery, the lack of enthusiasm – I couldn't believe I had subjected myself to this again.

On and on he went – emotionless, unrelenting, unfeeling. Every now and then he would trail off and the audience would wait a second before applauding, unsure of whether he had finished making his point or just run out of batteries.

People around me were rubbing their eyes, and one woman sitting in the row behind was actually asleep. The brightness of the lights in the Corn Exchange was increased by a technician after about ten minutes of Reckless speaking, probably to keep people awake.

After twenty-five minutes – TWENTY-FIVE MINUTES – Reckless stopped talking and it was time for Farage to take to the stage. He entered to applause through the middle of the audience and bounded up to the podium.

The UKIP leader usually uses a lapel or head mic when he gives a speech, allowing him to pace around the stage like an evangelical preacher. But in the Corn Exchange he was stuck behind a podium, which didn't allow him the same freedom of movement (ironic that, when you consider what he is against).

Being a good half a foot shorter than Reckless, the microphone was at the wrong height, but, instead of adjusting it before he got to the stage, the sound engineers waited until he was speaking.

So, while Farage was trying to fire up the crowd with talk of how Rochester should be deemed a city and not a town, and how honourable Reckless was for calling a by-election after he defected, a small bald man in his late fifties wearing a tracksuit wiggled his microphone stand around.

It was a bit like that *Morecambe & Wise* sketch with Shirley Bassey when the set falls apart and the duo sneak on to replace her missing shoe with a boot as she valiantly keeps singing 'Smoke Gets in Your Eyes'.

After a couple of minutes of trying to ignore him, Farage eventually said: 'Yeah, I'm shorter than him, aren't I?' provoking much-needed laughter in the hall.

Farage won a round of applause as loud as the laughter when he talked about the 'Australian-style points system' for immigration controls, but other than that it was a relatively unremarkable event.

What more was there to say? UKIP had already talked itself to death in Rochester & Strood fewer than six months ago. Not much had changed since then. There was a new concrete promise to keep Britain's military spending at 2 per cent of GDP, as per the terms of the country's NATO membership, but other than that it was the same as before – anti-EU, control immigration, UK is run by an out-of-touch elite.

Farage didn't hang around after the meeting ended, and was bundled into his Land Rover by his security team almost as soon as he finished speaking. If you liked this sort of thing, then this was the sort of thing you liked. But if you didn't, was there anything to win you over?

TUESDAY 28 APRIL 2015 – HARTLEPOOL

LATEST POLLS

Ipsos MORI/*Evening Standard*: Con 35; Lab 30; Lib Dem 8; UKIP 10

ComRed/*Daily Mail*: Con 35; Lab 35; Lib Dem 7; UKIP 11

YouGov/*Sun*: Con 34; Lab 35; Lib Dem 9; UKIP 12

U KIP's press operation was never the slickest in the world but, in the good old days, the party was at least glad when a journalist turned up to an event, even if the resulting article focused more on gaffes than policy.

The first hints of UKIP's changing attitude towards the media came in the Clacton and Rochester by-elections, with specific journalists banned from the post-result celebratory press conferences. By the time of the general election campaign, the party had gone one step further.

Nigel Farage's press campaign, which was being run by ex-BBC producer Sarah White, was now selecting which papers, and which individuals, were invited to certain events.

And it was seriously pissing people off.

I had returned to the *Daily Express* by this stage of the campaign. My brief stint at the *Daily Mirror* online came to an end after I was offered a post-election job at the *Huffington Post*. It was an opportunity too good to turn down, and I handed in my notice. Originally, I was going to stay working for the *Mirror* until after the election, but when I was taken off front-line political reporting duty, I decided to leave early. This was the most exciting election campaign since 1997 and I did not want to miss out on it. I contacted my old boss at the *Daily Express* online, Geoff Marsh, and asked if I could work for him as an exclusive freelance correspondent for the rest of the election, focusing just on UKIP. He said yes. Did I ever mention what a brilliant boss, and man, Geoff Marsh is? And how any criticism I levelled at him in the chapter on UKIP's Doncaster conference was completely unjustified? Good, I'm glad that's clear.

I told UKIP I was back at the *Express* online and, seeing as the organisation's owner Richard Desmond had just handed over a cheque for £1 million to the party, I thought Farage's press operation would welcome me with open arms.

Alas, no. Time and again throughout the campaign I asked for operational notes about Farage's media activities. Sometimes I was ignored completely; sometimes I was told I would be kept informed, then hear nothing back; and many times I was told nothing was planned, only to discover something was happening and other journalists had been invited.

This was not an experience unique to me. Journalists from other papers were also getting patchy information.

I was lucky that, as a freelancer, albeit exclusively for the *Express* online, I didn't have a boss breathing down my neck, but other reporters had to explain to news editors why they weren't at a UKIP event when their rivals were.

An insider to Farage's press team later told me I wasn't being paranoid, and some journalists were deliberately left off briefing notes and not told about events.

The insider added: 'Don't forget, we had in the back of our mind that you were doing this book.'

But journalists are a loyal bunch, and operational notes were soon being covertly forwarded on to make sure most people knew what was happening.

Despite this, there were a couple of UKIP events I missed out on.

The first was Farage's visit to Grimsby on Tuesday 8 April. The UKIP leader was in the town as the constituency of Great Grimsby had been identified as a winnable seat for the party. It was also there that Farage agreed to meet reality TV star Joey Essex, a man who admitted he is unable to tell the time.

The 24-year-old was making a special election programme for ITV2 in which he met with leading politicians on his quest to understand what the hell was going on in the world. Farage and Essex went out on a fishing trawler into the North Sea for their interview, and the UKIP leader explained the significance of being in Grimsby:

> It's symbolic of what's gone wrong. If we came here forty years ago there were thousands of men working here and a massive trawler fleet; it was the biggest fishing port in the country.
>
> We joined the European Union and now have to share all our fish with all the other countries. And what we're saying is: 'Let's take our country and our territorial waters back; Let's get our fishing industry back.'

Essex responded with: 'Sick.'

After the boat trip, Farage was supposed to travel to a local pub, the Hope & Anchor, where the barman had produced an ale in honour of the UKIP leader: Fraageale. Journalists, UKIP activists and party supporters gathered at the pub, waiting for Farage to show up. A small number of vocal protesters were also present.

Farage didn't arrive, as he was instead having a fish-and-chip lunch with Essex. Apparently his security team had raised concerns about his safety because of the protesters.

A UKIP HQ insider later told me Farage should have been braver and not have let his supporters down. But a source close to Farage's team hit back, saying the whole trip, which had been organised by HQ and not his South Thanet team, was a mistake.

'The press office was an absolute disaster throughout the whole campaign and everybody knew it,' said the source, adding that Farage's name was spelt wrong on the beer, his security team were never given enough advanced warning of plans arranged by the central press office to check out if an area was safe, and precious time in Thanet was being wasted because of these trips.

The other campaign day I was gutted to miss out on was on St George's Day. It began with Farage holding court in a pub in Ramsgate, which was suitably decked out in England flags.

At a press conference that morning, St George's hats were given out to journalists to help fire up their inner patriotism. Good to see that £1 million donation from Desmond being put to good use. Who needs to give their staff a pay rise when you can give money for hats, eh?

Farage clearly enjoyed the day, and he invited journalists to accompany him on a canvassing session. After the hacks went home for the day, Farage and his cohorts went for a boozy dinner in an Italian restaurant, which ended with him standing on a chair singing 'New York, New York'.

Rowena Mason from *The Guardian* was the only journo who managed to get herself invited along to UKIP's dining plans that evening, and wrote:

> That performance came after several renditions of 'Hi Ho Silver Lining', with Farage hollering down the phone to whoever happened to be calling.
>
> A little unsteady on his feet, the UKIP leader then rounded off the night with 'The Wild Rover' outside on the pavement, as aides persuaded him that moving on to a nightclub or revisiting his teenage days of skinny-dipping were not sensible for a party leader two weeks before the most important election of his life.

I was pretty angry at missing out on good news stories, and so, when I was sent an operational note that Farage would be up in Hartlepool on Tuesday 28 April, I was determined to go along.

I hired a car and began my drive north – I think the nosebleed kicked in around Peterborough. I stayed at my sister's house in Selby, north Yorkshire, the night before I was due in Hartlepool to give myself time to acclimatise from leaving the liberal metropolitan elite atmosphere of London.

The next morning, I got up at some ridiculous hour to make it to the Grand Hotel in Hartlepool for 9.30 a.m. sharp, as per the request of the operational note. The plan was that Farage was going to do a round of media interviews before giving a speech at 11 a.m. Three hotel rooms had been booked by broadcasters, and myself, Christopher Hope from the *Telegraph* and John Stevens from the *Mail* sat in on the interviews.

Sarah White told the journalists they had just five minutes each with Farage, to ensure that everyone got time with the UKIP leader. The first interviews took place in Room 101 and were with BBC journalists. Appropriate really, from Farage's point of view.

First up was Danny Savage from BBC News, who asked about the strength of UKIP in Labour areas. Farage replied:

> Particularly here in the north of England, there is a big move from Labour to UKIP and I think it's interesting that we hear a lot of talk from the Tory Party about the threat of a Labour/SNP coalition. Well, some of those Labour voters are already beginning to shift their vote on the basis of that.

Interview length: five minutes.

Savage got up and BBC Radio 5 live's chief political correspondent John Pienaar sat down to grill Farage.

He pushed him on whether he wanted people who identify themselves as racist to vote for UKIP. Farage said no, and then went on the attack:

> Well, the biggest racism I have seen in British politics is happening north of the border with the SNP, where some of the anti-English hatred is reaching a truly astonishing level, and

I would think that, if the BBC is worried about racism, that
is where they ought to be looking.

Interview length: eight minutes.

A Press Association reporter jumped in before Farage left the room,
and got his view on the sending of government aid to Nepal after the
recent earthquake and reinvigorating the British fishing industry in
the North Sea.

Interview length: two minutes.

Farage was then whisked out of Room 101 and into another hotel
room, where this time a BBC news crew from the regional *Look
North* was set up for an interview.

Interview length: five minutes.

Another hotel room, another interview – this time with ITV.

Rohit Kachroo asked him about the latest economic figures, which
policies he would insist on if his party held the balance of power after
the election, and Labour politician Chuka Umunna's claim that UKIP
was infected with 'the virus of racism'.

Farage replied:

> Chuka Umunna is running scared, Labour is running scared.
> They've seen the polling figures that I just told you about.
> Umunna, actually, is the high priest of the metropolitan elite
> among the Labour Party. He has no understanding or com-
> prehension of the damage to people's lives that open-door
> immigration has done.

Kachroo followed up a few moments later by asking Farage where
the greatest racism was – UKIP or the SNP?

Farage replied:

> The SNP are openly racist. The anti-English hostility, the kind
> of language that is used towards and about English people is

totally extraordinary. If my supporters behaved in the way that some of those pro-independence supporters behaved in that referendum, you would have painted me out to be the worst person that had been seen for seventy years in British politics.

Interview length: nine and a half minutes.

'We're going to go in another room now, and this is the last of the interviews,' White announced.

'We're not! We're not!' said Farage. 'I've got to ring Chris [Bruni-Lowe – his campaign director in South Thanet].'

Farage left the room, and we were directed back to Room 101 to set up for our five minutes with the leader. People were getting annoyed: this was supposed to be all done by now. Each interviewer was only supposed to get five minutes, but ITV and the BBC had overrun, making it unlikely us print journalists would get much time with him.

While Farage was downstairs making his phone call, White was told by ITV producer Sandi Sidhu that the interview he had just done wasn't a 'pooled' clip and the channel would be keeping it for themselves. White was furious, as she had given them extra time on the basis they would share out the footage. An argument erupted between the pair in the hotel corridor in front of more than a dozen journalists, camera crews and producers.

'I asked for more time because you gave the BBC about half an hour!' yelled Sidhu.

'I gave the BBC about half an hour because they wouldn't shut up talking to him!' replied White at the same volume.

'Well, that's not my fault, is it?'

'You said to me this was pool, and that's why you negotiated more time.'

'I didn't negotiate more time because you said it was five minutes—'

'You said this is for pool—'

'Don't do this, Sarah, it's not true!'

The pair carried on rowing, with Sidhu accusing White of being a 'liar' and White insisting Sidhu had agreed for it to be pooled. It was two stressed, tired people letting out weeks of frustration in a shouting match.

I had little sympathy for either of them. White kept cutting me out of what was going on, and ITV's interview – if not pooled – had gone on for longer than any of the BBC's (although the BBC did get three goes at it – national news, national radio and local news).

More importantly, where was my interview? I had hired a car and driven all the way to Hartlepool for this, and all I was doing was sitting in on other journalists' interviews like a media voyeur. The only interesting moments so far were that row, Farage nicking my bottle of water when he was thirsty (subtle tactic to silence the press by dehydrating them?) and the fact the UKIP leader was wearing Union Jack socks.

That Pulitzer Prize was getting further and further away.

Why didn't he get up on a table and start singing like he did for Rowena Mason? Where was my St George's hat? Why didn't anything 'UKIP' happen when I was around?

Farage emerged up the stairs and into the corridor in the middle of White and Sidhu arguing, but instead of acknowledging what was happening, he merely popped his phone in his pocket and walked into Room 101 for the next set of interviews.

As time was running short, us print journalists didn't get the separate interviews we had been promised, so we just fired questions at him.

John Stevens from the *Mail* got his question out first, as he always did: 'You're going to Strasbourg tomorrow in the middle of the election campaign, that's quite a big gesture – what's your plan there?'

The European Parliament was set to debate the migrant crisis in the Mediterranean and, as leader of the Freedom and Direct Democracy group, Farage would be given plenty of time to express his views on the matter.

Farage replied: 'I think what's happening in Strasbourg tomorrow is actually far more significant than anything that has been said by any of the party leaders about immigration in this campaign. They utterly refuse to accept that we are no longer in charge of our own borders...'

He went on with his usual rant about Miliband/Cameron not understanding what's going on when it comes to immigration.

Other questions were about UKIP's growth in the north, how it's not racist to spot racial differences, and how Peter Mandelson, David Miliband and Tony Blair had all been 'parachuted in' to safe seats in the region in the past.

Seven minutes.

White brought it to an end. 'What can I do? He's making a speech in fifteen minutes,' she said as we protested at the short amount of time we had had with him.

But one local reporter hadn't quite finished with Farage yet, and, while White was shutting us down, he snuck in some brilliant questions:

> Can I put an ethical question to you? We're in Hartlepool, where Hartlepool fans like to end the season in fancy dress. This year they propose doing it dressed as Bob Marley. Kick Out – the anti-racism campaign – has urged them not to and urged the police to take action if anyone should black up. What advice would you give to Hartlepool fans considering taking part in that?

Now that is a question! Does Farage think it's wrong to 'black up'? I think we all know what he's going to say about this...

'That's an impossible question to ask me,' he said. 'I thought you were going to ask me about monkeys because of the historical tradition with jokes about that in this town.'

He wasn't biting! How disappointing! I bet if I weren't here he would go off on some rant about how people think blacking up is now a terrible crime and it all used to be a bit of a laugh. I bet if Rowena Mason from *The Guardian* were here he would start blacking up himself just to prove a point, and deliver the whole of his speech downstairs with a dreadlocks wig.

But good old Nigel didn't let me down…

> Apparently, blacking up, though it used to be something that was thought to be in jest, is one of the worst crimes that you can commit in modern Britain and therefore they better not do it. The idea that football fans should have fun and a laugh and enjoy themselves? No, no, no! We must all take life much more seriously in this brave new world.

Once again, Farage just had to go that one step further.

In the TV debates, he couldn't just talk about migrants with illnesses, he had to bring up the very specific disease of HIV. He couldn't just say the SNP were aggressive, but that they were 'openly racist'. He couldn't just bat away the blacking up issue by saying it's 'an impossible question', he had to say it was something 'thought to be in jest' and it was just 'fun and a laugh'.

After his chat with us print journalists, Farage made his way downstairs to address a meeting of about fifty people on why they should vote UKIP in the upcoming general election.

Before he took to the stage, I grabbed a cup of coffee with him and told him I was no longer working for the *Mirror*, but was back at the *Express*.

'Fucking hell, I would love to hear this story!' he said.

'Well, Nigel, they wouldn't let me get out and report during the election, and I wanted to keep following you around.'

'Oh,' he said.

'You know I'm writing this book about you, don't you?'

'Yes, I had heard,' he replied and turned away, preparing to take to the stage.

THURSDAY 30 APRIL 2015 – AYLESBURY TOWN CENTRE

LATEST POLLS

ComRes/*Independent on Sunday*: Con 33; Lab 33; Lib Dem 8; UKIP 13

Opinium/*Observer*: Con 35; Lab 34; Lib Dem 8; UKIP 13

Populus: Con 33; Lab 33; Lib Dem 9; UKIP 15

YouGov/*Sun*: Con 34; Lab 35; Lib Dem 8; UKIP 12

Panelbase: Con 32; Lab 34; Lib Dem 8; UKIP 17

The election was a week away. Nigel Farage had just seven days left to convince people to flock to the People's Army flag.

An opinion poll of South Thanet released on Wednesday 29 April – the day before I caught up with Farage in Aylesbury – put the UKIP leader behind his Tory rival by two points. Nationally, UKIP's support was averaging 13 per cent in the polls, a long way down from the high point of 25 per cent, which a Survation poll for the *Mail on Sunday* had put the party on in the wake of Douglas Carswell's by-election win in October 2014.

How would UKIP fight back against this polling squeeze? What plan did Farage have to win back support in South Thanet?

He decided to go to war with the BBC – over something really quite pointless.

On the TV quiz show *Have I Got News for You*, aired on Friday 24 April, *Sunday Times* columnist Camilla Long made a joke about the UKIP leader only going to South Thanet 'a few times'.

Long was defending an article she had written about Margate, in which she said: 'The Isle of Thanet is a small nodule of erupted spleen at the eastern edge of England – a little bit of throbbing gristle that, given enough anger, enough bile, enough precision dyspepsia, could suddenly, magnificently, detach itself entirely this election.'

Charming – but then, of course, a privately educated Oxford

graduate who is descended from aristocracy is perfectly entitled to turn up and sneer at the working class.

If only the people in Margate and Ramsgate had grasped the opportunity to learn from this wonderful woman when she visited the constituency! Clearly she has overcome much adversity in her life, and could provide exactly the right advice on how to escape ... how did she describe the area again? Oh yes, 'Chernobyl-like'.

It was a disgusting article, and even though I'm not from Margate it made me absolutely livid. How dare she! This was not 'journalism', this was sneering condescension. You want to know why people vote UKIP? Camilla Long is the reason people vote UKIP.

When asked about the article on *Have I Got News for You*, she defended it entirely, and said: 'I went there more than Nigel Farage. By the time I went there, he had only been there a few times.'

Some 'journalist'. You can criticise Farage for many things, but 'hardly visiting South Thanet' is not one of them. From January 2015 to polling day, he took part in twenty-four public meetings in the constituency, as well as numerous canvassing sessions. Yet, as angry as it made me, I didn't decide to call the police over it – that would be ridiculous, right?

Not to UKIP apparently.

Farage's former advisor Annabelle Fuller called him the morning after the show aired to tell him about the joke. A few days later, Raheem Kassam reported the BBC to the police, claiming the comments had broken the Representation of the People Act.

He said: 'Camilla Long made false statements about a candidate at this election. The BBC chose to air it. If this isn't a breach of Section 106 of the Representation of People Act then we don't know what is.'

The BBC pointed out it was a joke, and Kent Police said there was no evidence of any offence and no action would be taken.

The complaint very much came from Farage's team in South Thanet, with many in UKIP headquarters in London baffled by the decision. A Ukipper close to Farage defended the decision to contact the police: 'It was a real point of personal upset for him that he was putting in such hard graft in Thanet, on the streets, in the wind, in the rain, all hours of the day, and the BBC were allowing something like that to be broadcast.'

Was this the same Farage who had the following quote on the back of his *Fighting Bull* autobiography?: 'Freedom of speech and belief is not subject to approval by a transitory authority. It is absolute or it is nothing. Such was and remains my conviction. And oh, it has got me into some delicious trouble.'

It seemed it needed a new line: 'Unless it harms my image in the eyes of the electorate.'

Farage had already fired shots in the war against the BBC before the Camilla Long complaint, taking a swipe at the audience in the contenders' TV debate on Thursday 16 April.

The debate was being hosted by the BBC and was taking place in the Methodist Central Hall, the scene of UKIP's 2013 conference. Labour's Ed Miliband, the SNP's Nicola Sturgeon, the Greens' Natalie Bennett and Plaid Cymru leader Leanne Wood joined the UKIP leader for the programme.

About half an hour in, and during a discussion on housing, Farage said: 'There seems to be a total lack of comprehension on this panel, and indeed among this audience, which is a remarkable audience even by the left-wing standards of the BBC, this lot's pretty left-wing.'

The audience started booing, and moderator David Dimbleby said: 'Nigel, let me just say this is an audience that has been carefully chosen—'

'Not very carefully!' Farage interrupted.

'…not by the BBC, by an independent polling organisation to represent the balance between all parties.'

This was met by cheers and applause from the audience, and a look of bemusement from the journalists in the spin room at the time.

Unlike the HIV comments in the previous debate, this aggressive attack was not pre-planned. A source close to Farage told me later:

That was him off the cuff. It was a fantastic idea because it

opened up this attack on the BBC and, actually, do you know
what? If you're an average Brit who pays your licence fee,
or even doesn't pay your licence fee and gets chased for it,
you can always point to something about the BBC you don't
like. It's an easy target.

Two weeks later, and with the corporation reported to the police,
Farage again stuck the boot into the BBC – as he was on his way to
appear on one of the broadcaster's shows.

That night, Miliband, David Cameron and Nick Clegg were due to
take part in a special *Question Time* show from Leeds. Farage had not
been invited, but he was given his own show that would be broadcast an hour later. Like the other party leaders, he would be grilled
for thirty minutes by a studio audience.

On the way to Birmingham to appear on the show, Farage decided
to stop off in the town of Aylesbury in Buckinghamshire. It seemed
an odd choice. UKIP had four members on the county council, but
overturning the incumbent MP's 24,123-vote lead over the party from
the 2010 election was unlikely. But who was the incumbent MP? Well,
it just happened to be Europe minister David Lidington.

With my FOMO (fear of missing out) already at dangerously high
levels, I got myself to Aylesbury with plenty of time to spare before
Farage's arrival. He was due to go for a walkabout in the town centre, and I was hoping for one or more of the following to happen:

1. Some Ukippers approach him and unleash a torrent
    of racism that he is forced to either agree with out of
    politeness or apologise for.

2. He has a liquid breakfast and instead of making
    yet another speech about the 'unelected officials in
    Brussels', he continues his Frank Sinatra singalongs
    with a rousing rendition of 'Come Fly with Me'.

3. A shopper mistakes him for David Cameron, and won't accept he isn't the Tory leader. He then has to argue against Tory policy to someone who thinks he is a Tory, leading to that person calling him a hypocrite and liar.

4. He punches Robin Brant from the BBC, shouting 'report this!' as he beats the poor journalist to the floor.

5. He does a magic trick.

As you can see, I was open to many exciting possibilities. Farage arrived just after noon, and made his way through the fifty-strong crowd of passionate UKIP supporters and mildly interested shoppers to give a speech underneath a statue of John Hampden. (Of course, everyone knows who John Hampden is, right? Well, for those of you not familiar with English Civil War history, Hampden was one of five MPs who King Charles I tried to unconstitutionally arrest, which sparked the war. Hampden died six days after being wounded in the Battle of Chalgrove Field in 1643.)

Addressing the crowd, Farage said:

> It's no coincidence that we are beneath this statue of one of the great parliamentary reformers, somebody who thought that the British Parliament ought to have power and ought to be able to change the laws of the land. Something which stood for centuries until the current crop of politicians decided to give that power away to a bunch of unelected officials in Brussels, and we are the modern version of John Hampden. We are the People's Army, we want to reverse all of this and get back control of our country and control of our borders.
>
> You'll read a lot in the newspapers and you'll see a lot on the television that tells you there are really only two parties in England contesting this election. It's all presented as if it's

Labour versus the Conservatives and there isn't much else that's going to happen. Well, one of the reasons I'm here today in Aylesbury is this is one of the seats in which we could produce a really major shock early in the hours of the 8th of May.

How dull and, more to the point, who was saying it was just a Tory/Labour battle in the general election? Everyone knew it was going to be a coalition.

Farage's biggest cheer came when he said: 'UKIP is the only party that has clearly stated, and it's in our manifesto, we are completely and totally and utterly opposed to that enormous white elephant that is called HS2.'

The second section of the high-speed railway line was due to go through large parts of the constituency, and was opposed by many on cost, environmental and business grounds.

With his speech over, Farage descended from the statue's base and into the street. He was immediately engulfed by journalists, camera crews and photographers. No one from the public stood a chance. I've said it before and I'll say it again: these media scrums are ridiculous.

If everyone just stood back and let Farage walk round and meet people, it would be more likely that something interesting would happen (see suggestions 1, 3, 4 and possibly 5, listed above). Instead, as always, it was mainly journalists who got to speak to him.

The news about the complaint to the BBC had been made public that morning, and Farage was in the mood to deliver another punch (alas, metaphorically). He said:

> There was the Ofcom ruling that said there were four major parties [in England]. I've got no complaints about Channel 4, ITV, Channel 5, Sky, who have covered us as part of the election campaign. You know, the good bits, the bad bits and all the things that happen. But I genuinely feel that if you were to watch the evening news on the BBC you would think that UKIP were just a bit-part player.

He went on:

> We have this bizarre state of affairs where the BBC, an organ-
> isation we are all charged £145 a year to have the benefit
> of seeing, aren't regulated by Ofcom, have made their own
> minds up [about major party status] and frankly produce the
> *News at Ten* every night as if there were just two choices in
> England in this election.
>
> I think they are biased.

The media scrum continued, but I couldn't be bothered to be part of
it. It made its way up to the high street like an organic blob, sucking
in passers-by. I heard one of Farage's security men who was ahead of
the blob mention 'The Kingsbury' into his radio mic. He was referring to a pub about 50 yards away from the blob. I knew how Farage's
security guards operated, and that, as soon as the UKIP leader got
near the doors to the boozer, they would stop the press going in.

I quickly walked over there, being careful not to move so fast that
others would notice and all rush towards the pub, but quick enough
to make sure I beat his bodyguards to the door – it was basically the
speed with which you would walk towards a buffet table that only
had one slice of cake left on it, and you didn't want to look too greedy.

I got in and went up to the bar. There was a beer called St George's.
Perfect, I'll buy him that and have it ready on the bar for when he
walks in. Then he'll have to talk to me.

'Sorry, love, the St George's is off,' the barmaid said.

I could see Farage edging closer to the door, the media scrum surrounding him, blocking the sun from pouring in through the windows.
Punters in the pub noticed a sudden darkness and turned to see what
was happening, half out of curiosity, half out of fear that because they
had started drinking in a pub at 12.30 p.m., they may have lost all
track of time and it was now night.

The blob surged against the door.

'That's fine,' I said to the barmaid. 'I'll just have two pints of whatever ale you've got.'

Sod it, I'll tell him it's St George's, he won't know the difference.

But my best-laid plan was about to go awry, as, at the last second, Farage decided he didn't want to go to the pub, walked away from the doors and got into his waiting black Land Rover.

'There you go,' said the barmaid, presenting me with two pints of ale.

I handed over a tenner, realising I probably shouldn't neck two pints at 12.30 p.m., but that I probably would.

I did.

SATURDAY 2 MAY 2015 – RAMSGATE

LATEST POLLS

YouGov/*Sunday Times*: Con 34; Lab 33; Lib Dem 8; UKIP 13

Survation/*Mail on Sunday*: Con 31; Lab 34; Lib Dem 8; UKIP 17

Email sent from me at 5 p.m., Friday 1 May, to Sarah White: 'Hi Sarah, Hope you are well? Are there any media events I can come along to this weekend for *Daily Express* online? Cheers, Owen.'

Reply from White at 5.01 p.m.: 'Nout yet!'

Reply to White at 5.02 p.m.: 'Ok. If you could let me know if anything's arranged that would be great!'

Reply from White at 5.26 p.m.: 'Sure'

Text from colleague at 5.45 p.m.: 'Did you hear about this thing Farage is doing tomorrow in Ramsgate?'

Reply to colleague at 5.46 p.m.: 'No I fucking didn't! Do you have any more details?'

Reply from colleague at 5.48 p.m.: 'Yes I'll send you over the information I've got. I'm not going, but have fun.'

Cut out of the loop. Again. But at least I had found out about it before the event, not after, like usual. The itinerary was three public meetings in one day – the final ones of the campaign.

I assumed that very few journalists knew about the day's events, so was somewhat surprised when I pitched up outside the Red Arrows social club to discover camera crews, photographers and a journalist from *Time* magazine of all publications were already there.

If White was surprised to see me, she didn't show it.

'Hi, Owen!' she said cheerily, with a big grin.

I was waiting outside the club with Paul Francis, political editor for a collection of local newspapers. It was a cold morning and we were keen to get inside and warm up. Farage emerged from the club's doors and sparked up a cigarette. He was wearing his trademark coat, but not his trademark grin.

'How are you today, Nigel?' I asked.

'I'm a bit knackered, old boy,' he said, taking a drag on his cigarette.

I asked him about the *Have I Got News for You* situation, and whether it was a bit of an overreaction to a joke.

'I've got no problems with jokes, none at all, but what went on clearly breached the Representation of the People's Act,' he replied.

Francis began interviewing Farage, and the pair discussed the importance of the local elections running alongside the general election. The UKIP leader repeatedly hammered home what a good set of candidates the party had and how he hoped they would win the council.

While Francis and Farage were talking, news came through that the Duchess of Cambridge had given birth to the UK's newest princess, weighing 8lb 3oz. The UKIP leader greeted the news in a wonderfully Farage fashion: 'Imperial measurements! Thank you! Who wants that bloody metric system?'

He was obviously pleased by his gag and phoned up Raheem Kassam, who was notably absent, to tweet it out from his official account. Speaking to the cameras he added: 'I've sent the order out to every UKIP candidate in the country to raise a glass to the royal baby girl today.'

Having given his congratulations to the royal family, he disappeared
into the building to prepare for the public meeting. Public – unless
you were press, of course.

Journalists were not allowed in unless they were invited, and one
of Farage's bodyguards stood in the hall entrance with a 'you shall
not pass' look on his face.

Once again I was on the outside, but then something magical happened: White invited me in! I was ushered past Gandalf the bouncer,
whisked through the corridor and allowed to sit in the social club.
There was myself, Francis and Farage, and that was it.

The meeting itself was being held in a room separated from the
bar area we were in by a curtain. Around fifty residents and party
members were listening to UKIP council candidates talk about their
plans for the area. In the bar area, I was sitting typing up Farage's
comments about the royal baby to send to the *Express* online. Farage
was sitting a couple of tables away, by himself, flicking through the
party's manifesto. He had no one around him, and instantly seemed
restless. For a few minutes he had nothing to do, and he didn't seem
to like it. Farage put the manifesto on the table, turned his head to
the right and caught my eye. We started talking about the royal baby
and his campaigning plans for the day.

I asked him how his health was, as the week before he had admitted that 'in the earlier part of the campaign ... I wasn't feeling quite
as sharp and as fit as I should have been'. He said he was feeling much
better, and that the problems had come from neglecting to do the
physiotherapy needed to help deal with the ongoing back problems
caused by his plane crash in 2010.

After a few minutes chatting, he got up and went to the back of
the room to talk to White, leaving me to my work.

The meeting was still going on next door, and the relative silence
in the bar area was broken by sporadic outbreaks of applause, like
thunder heralding an oncoming storm.

I thought my invitation inside the building would be the only surprise occurrence that day, but, like defecting Tory MPs, another one came along straight after. Mrs Farage walked into the room with one of their young daughters. I had not seen Mrs Farage on the campaign trail at all, and I had never seen any of his children at UKIP events. Farage got up out of his seat, gave her a peck on the cheek and said: 'It's really good to see you.'

Five minutes later, and he was on stage addressing the crowd.

'I don't know how you're feeling about the general election campaign,' he said, 'but it's been going on for rather a long time, hasn't it? It's been endless.'

Farage then spent twenty minutes talking about how UKIP 'believes in Britain', the UK's relationship with the EU, and immigration. It was a speech he had delivered hundreds of times before. The crowd lapped it up, from the elderly people in the front row to a young couple with their small child sitting at the back of the room. Farage seemed to be in his element, and far from 'knackered'.

One meeting done, two to go. But first there was a small matter of raising a glass to toast the birth of Britain's newest Princess. The celebratory drink was taking place in the Wheatsheaf pub, a brief walk from the Red Arrows club. The pub was decked out in St George's flags and bunting, and one of the photographers present had bought an 'It's a Girl' balloon for Farage to pose with. A pint of bitter was brought for him and he flashed his famous grin as he posed with the ale and the balloon as the camera shutters clicked and the broadcast crews filmed.

Having missed that morning's public meeting, Raheem Kassam arrived at the pub in time for a lunchtime drink. He had with him a small pink box tied with a pink ribbon, which he placed on the bar. Farage had walked off to talk to some of the punters who were looking on with expressions of bemusement at the sudden media invasion and Kassam whispered something to one of the bar staff.

He beckoned Farage back and got all the film crews and photographers to gather round.

'There's a special surprise in there,' said Kassam.

Farage looked nervous and asked what it was.

'It's a surprise,' Kassam said again.

The media were all gathered round, and Farage knew he couldn't back away. He slowly undid the pink ribbon and tentatively opened the lid. What should be inside, but half a pint of ale.

He burst out laughing, and joked 'It's a new form of milk, perhaps' as he lifted it out the box.

Kassam thought it was hilarious, but there was a certain 'drink for me, monkey' vibe about the whole proceedings. Also, Farage had two more public meetings to get through – shouldn't Kassam have been trying to keep him off the beer, not buying him more?

Farage returned to talking to the pub's patrons and he was enjoying himself. There was only about fifteen people there who weren't either part of his entourage or with the media, so they all got a good chat with him. He signed Pyrex 'Vote UKIP' boards for everyone, posed for pictures and even gave one boy who was about seven years old some life advice: 'Follow your dreams and if you do that you can do anything you want.'

'Blimey, you're starting to sound like you should be an *X-Factor* judge!' I joked.

'Well, you've got to encourage children,' he said to me, earnestly. 'Of course, Nigel, of course.'

Kassam was busy arguing with someone from the BBC crew about claims the organisation was biased against UKIP, but his stature as an ombudsman of press fairness was rather undermined by the way Farage kept tugging on the back of his (matching) coat to tell him to go and get more Pyrex boards from the car.

With Kassam despatched for a bit of fetching and carrying work, Farage began talking to me and a few other journalists about his life outside politics.

He talked about how one of his sons was a City trader and was a better public speaker than he was: 'The day I leave the party he will join and then you'll see something.'

He talked about how the testicular cancer that nearly killed him when he was twenty-two years old spurred him on to have his first child at the age of twenty-four.

He talked about his love of fishing, particularly off the coast of Dungeness in Kent and in the waters surrounding Cornwall in the West Country: 'When I do it, I don't mess about. I do it seriously.'

He talked about his friends from the old days in the City, some of whom are now dead because of the lifestyle they used to lead, while others drink just mineral water these days because of too much drinking: 'Do you know what we used to call our lunches? PFL. Proper Fucking Lunch.'

It was one of the first times I had been able to chat with him about subjects other than politics. He seemed in a reflective, wistful mood. It was a side of him I had not seen before.

Farage and his crew left the pub and headed off for some lunch before the next public meeting in St Mark's Church.

I stayed in the pub and had some lunch and a second pint of beer. I think reporting on Farage was rubbing off on me. The second meeting went even better than the first from a UKIP point of view. The church hall was busier than the social club, and the applause was even greater when Farage touched on all his usual themes.

Fortunately, I had missed the beginning of the meeting when former Radio 1 DJ and calypso superstar Mike Read read out a special UKIP poem he had written.

Unfortunately for me, about seventy-five people from Ramsgate and, if I'm honest, the honour of every English-speaking person in the world, he repeated the poem at the day's third meeting in a hall in Ramsgate town centre.

The genius that is Douglas Adams, in his perfect creation *The Hitchhiker's Guide to the Galaxy*, described the bureaucratic alien race of Vogons as writing the third worst poetry in the universe.

The second worst, according to Adams, comes from the Azgoths of Kria.

During a reading by the Azgoths' poet master 'four of his audience members died of internal haemorrhaging, and the President of the Mid-Galactic Arts Nobbling Council survived by gnawing one of his own legs off'.

The worst poetry was authored by Paula Nancy Millstone Jennings of Greenbridge, Essex, and was destroyed along with Planet Earth at the beginning of the story. Well, move over Paula Nancy Millstone Jennings, your crown has been taken by Michael David Kenneth Read of Planet Read.

Before we got to the poetry, we were 'treated' to his take on the five-way challengers' debate, which, although it had taken place sixteen days earlier, already felt like light years ago.

Speaking quickly into a booming microphone that made it difficult to understand what he was saying, Read gave the audience his take on what had happened in the debate in the style of a horse-race commentary. Fun. That was his word to describe what was about to happen. Fun.

> Just five runners in this novice hurdle, none of the entrants having previously won at this distance. Cameron on Call Me Dave scratched before the off, leaving stablemate Clegg unable to declare on Middle Ground. Surprisingly no Northern Ireland representatives in the line-up as the handpicked crowd leaned heavily to the left to get a better view of the runners and riders. The going was good to soft, with a fair bit of mud being thrown up from all directions. At the first, Farage on Fanfare for the Common Man appeared to have his nose in front with Bennett on No Points System running wide to get the greenest track. Miliband on Rhetoric appeared to have been heavily trained – some might say slightly over-trained – while Sturgeon on No Right to Buy seemed determined at all costs to affect the quinquennial Westminster Stakes whatever it took. So keen she was to win she even threatened at one point to bring down the non-runner, Call Me Dave...'

And on and on he went. No one in the audience laughed, and when he reached the end of his little sketch no one applauded.

By now people were starting to talk among themselves, so Read decided to pull out his primary weapon – his poetry. Turning his genius to Ed Miliband's decision to be interviewed by Russell Brand for the self-confessed revolutionary's 'Trews' YouTube channel, Read recited this ditty:

> *His reasoning's unsound and Miliband's found*
> *Brand rants like a mule or an ass debates.*
> *He has more dosh than those he calls 'posh'*
> *For he's richer than those that he castigates.*
> *Is Miliband mad to go to Brand's pad?*
> *Where he sits on the sofa berating him.*
> *If he goes on like this he will get a Judas kiss*
> *Or the next thing you know he'll be dating him.*
> *Brand believes the solution is to talk revolution,*
> *What juvenile waffle, the silly man.*
> *He thinks Farage would be hopeless in charge –*
> *As would Clegg and Cameron and Miliband.*
> *He's hitting Red Ed with some facts that he's read*
> *That smacks of a weird personal odyssey.*
> *He's talking to Labour as if he were the Saviour,*
> *Yet he's all for a non-voting policy.*
> *Ed told Brand post-election there will be resurrection*
> *And the UK will no longer be Tory ... err.*
> *The lies that he'll feed yer like 'I'll break up the media'*
> *But without all that 'giddy euphoria'.*
>
> Written by Mike Read (aged 68 and 1/6th).

I have never been so pleased to see Nigel Farage take to the stage, and, judging by the applause from the audience, they were equally thrilled.

Farage began by revealing the arch-pro-European bogeyman Jean-Claude Juncker ('If he wasn't a euro-fanatic, [he's] the sort of chap I might quite like really,' he admitted) had put his arm around the UKIP leader's shoulders in Strasbourg earlier that week and said: 'I want to tell you, on a personal level, I wish you the very best of luck in South Thanet, because if you win, we'll never see you here again.'

He then launched into his usual town hall speech. It may have been the third time that day he had given the address to the people of Ramsgate, but it was the twenty-fourth time since January that he had spoken at a public meeting in the constituency.

Despite the rehashing of well-worn phrases, he was in good form and sounded like he was saying the words for the first time.

It struck me that he was less a politician, more a stand-up comedian when in front of an audience such as this. Farage knew when to pause for effect, when to deliver each joke, which ones worked with which crowd. Even when an elderly gentlemen sitting in the front row got up and walked slowly down the central aisle to leave the meeting, Farage made it part of his act. 'Goodbye, sir!'

'No, it's not against you, mate, it's nothing to do with you,' the gentlemen replied.

'In the European Parliament when I get up to speak, they walk out in droves! I'm pretty used to this kind of thing!' Farage quipped.

He went on, ramping up the passion and the volume. Farage was speaking without a microphone, but was louder and clearer than those who had gone before him. He ended the meeting with an appeal that had the audience on their feet:

> What can you do, if you want us to win on Thursday? What you can do is become our crusaders and become our messengers. Whether you become party members or not, you can go out and talk to your friends and talk to your family, and whether it's the golf club or whether it's the local pub, or wherever it is you go, please, please bore and bully into

submission everyone you know and let's make the Purple Revolution spread, let's make Thanet purple next Thursday. Thank you.

Applause, cheers and whistles bounced around the hall. Even though the election was still five days away, there was a sense that this was the end of the section of the campaign designed to win people over. The next five days would be spent making sure those who said they were going to back UKIP would turn out and vote.

Far from seeming 'knackered' as he had done that morning, Farage seemed energised, enthused and excited.

'I bet you're glad you don't have to do these meetings any more,' I said to him after he finished signing copies of his book and UKIP posters and banners.

'These are what I love the most,' he replied with his Cheshire Cat grin.

There are people who think Farage is addicted to alcohol, but based on what I had seen throughout the campaign, I would say he's addicted to applause. The day had gone spectacularly well from a UKIP point of view, and the positivity and the cheering could well reach beyond the three meetings and carry across South Thanet.

But while Farage had been inside the hall talking about how nasty the press had been to him and how UKIP would not sink to the 'gutter' with negative campaigning, a party candidate was outside telling an undercover reporter he wanted to shoot his Tory rival 'between the eyes'.

Robert Blay, who was standing in North East Hampshire, was one of the party volunteers helping at the meeting, and, wearing his high-vis UKIP-branded vest, he was caught on camera making some truly horrible comments.

When told by a *Daily Mirror* undercover reporter that his Tory opponent for the seat, Ranil Jayawardena, had been tipped to be the country's first British Asian Prime Minister, the 55-year-old said:

If he is, I will personally put a bullet between his eyes. If
this lad turns up to be our Prime Minister, I will personally put a bullet in him. That's how strong I feel about it. I
won't have this fucker as our Prime Minister. I absolutely
loathe him.

Blay also attacked Jayawardena's status as a second-generation
immigrant.

His family have only been here since the '70s. You are not
British enough to be in our Parliament. I've got 400 years
of ancestry where I live. He hasn't got that. I said to his dad
about two months ago – 'When did you come to Britain?'
He said, 'In the '70s.' I said, 'Why did you come?' He said,
'Things weren't very good politically in Sri Lanka and I came
here and I could train as an accountant.'

So he's come here and ponced off us, hasn't he, like all the
East Europeans are? That's what is happening. Continually.

Referring to a row he had had with an Eastern European while out
canvassing, Blay said: 'He's in my country. He's a fucking immigrant
and I'm not putting up with that shit, because that was abuse.'

The recording was made public three days later and Blay was immediately suspended by UKIP. Even heading in to the most important
election of the party's existence, the same accusations of racism and
xenophobia were plaguing UKIP's appeal.

WEDNESDAY 6 MAY 2015 – RAMSGATE

LATEST POLLS:

Ipsos MORI/*Evening Standard*: Con 36; Lab 35; Lib Dem 8; UKIP 11

Ashcroft: Con 33; Lab 33; Lib Dem 10; UKIP 11

YouGov/*Sun*: Con 34; Lab 34; Lib Dem 10; UKIP 12

Panelbase: Con 31; Lab 33; Lib Dem 8; UKIP 16

ICM/*Guardian*: Con 35; Lab 35; Lib Dem 9; UKIP 11

A gust of wind flew through Ramsgate town centre, looking to cause trouble. Unfortunately for UKIP Thanet Council candidate Trevor Shonk, it was at the precise moment he emerged from the party's headquarters with a giant placard, easily 5 ft high and just as wide, bearing a photo of Nigel Farage's face. Together with the metal pole it was attached to, the placard easily protruded above the crowd of journalists, camera crews and photographers who had come down for the last day of campaigning. As Shonk fully lifted it into the air, the gust of wind struck, knocking it sideways and downwards towards a crowd of journalists. Shonk managed to get the contraption under control at the last second, sparing the journos from being knocked flat by Farage's smiling face.

The real Farage had emerged from the office with his many bodyguards to begin a final walkabout in the town before the polls opened the next day. The media scrum was ever so slightly more relaxed than usual, meaning Farage could actually walk down the street, not just shuffle.

'Six weeks on, how much progress do you think you've made?' asked the BBC's Danny Savage as we began moving through the streets.

'I think we've done remarkably well,' replied Farage:

> We're firming in the polls, I think we're going to surprise

people with the votes we get. I really do think this problem of the 'shy Kipper' is true, as people just won't tell pollsters that they're going to vote UKIP, and I think tomorrow they are, and I think we're going to wake up on Friday morning and a lot of people will have voted for us.

Apparently, 'shy Kippers' were the reason for the fall in support in the opinion polls. I think I can speak for most journalists when I say that is a bizarre notion. Every UKIP supporter I've ever met has been the opposite of shy. Far from getting them to talk about the party, it's getting them to shut up about it that is the real trick.

As well as Danny Savage from the BBC, most of the familiar Farage followers were present: Christopher Hope from the *Telegraph*, John Stevens from the *Mail*, Rohit Kachroo from ITV.

Also trailing the pack was an anti-UKIP protester, Gary Perkins, a 37-year-old fine art lecturer at Central St Martins School of Art and Design in London. With his grey beanie hat and forlorn-looking greyhound dog, Perkins repeatedly heckled Farage as he walked through Ramsgate.

Eventually, Farage had had enough and, during a discussion with some builders in the town centre, he confronted Perkins, initially asking for one of the flyers the lecturer had been handing out.

Much to the amusement of the builders, Farage began reading from the leaflet, which he quipped was his 'alternative CV'.

'What have I done now?' he said as he started to look at it. 'Oh, I'm discriminatory, racist, sexist, and I was a banker ... well, that's not true.'

'No, you were a stockbroker,' said Perkins.

'No, I wasn't! You haven't even got your facts right, mate!'

Before he get shouted down, Perkins complained that he hadn't been allowed to attend the 'so-called public meetings' in Thanet throughout the campaign, and this was his chance to question Farage.

But, alas for poor old Perkins, he suffered what Green Party leader Natalie Bennett might class as a 'brain fade'.

After turning down invitations from Farage to meet the chairman of UKIP's LGBT wing and the first black mayor of Gloucester, who defected from Labour to UKIP, to refute the accusations of racism and homophobia, Perkins asked: 'Have you got the Bristol candidate with you today? Have you got Johnny Rockard with you today?'

Johnny Rockard, real name John Langley, was a UKIP council candidate in Bristol who was better known to a certain section of Britain as an ageing porn star.

The 59-year-old specialised in the 'girl-next-door' genre of pornography, and his alter ego caused much titillation when it was revealed earlier that month.

Farage responded to Perkins's question about the whereabouts of Rockard by saying: 'So, what's he done wrong?'

'He's a disgusting person.'

'Why?'

'He shouldn't be fielded for a political seat.'

'Why's that?'

'Why's that? Because he's a disgusting, kind of, err … err…'

Perkins was struggling to explain why Rockard was so 'disgusting', and his hesitation led to jeers from the builders and other UKIP supporters crowding around Farage.

'Do you think it's alright for a porn star to stand for election?' Perkins said when he got himself together.

'He's done nothing illegal,' Farage replied calmly. 'We in this party believe live and let live! Be happy everybody!'

And with that, and an almighty cheer from the builders, Farage left Perkins to continue spluttering about Johnny Rockard.

Poor old Perkins. He had waited four months for his big moment with Farage, and when it came to it, and with a crowd of people watching on, he just couldn't perform.

Not something you could ever accuse Johnny Rockard of, no doubt.

Farage seemed buoyed by the confrontation with the heckler, and had a smile on his face as he continued his walkabout. Even when his now familiar black Land Rover pulled up, usually the sign that Farage was going to make a quick getaway, Farage was having such a good time he dismissed it, instead walking down to Ramsgate harbour. Given that Farage was going to step down as UKIP leader if he didn't win his seat, he was no doubt lapping up what could be the dregs of media attention in his career.

Farage led the media pack over to a small café called Ship Shape, which overlooked the harbour. He disappeared inside to get a cup of tea, leaving the photographers outside sizing up a good shot for when he came out.

Farage's press team were happy to let their boss pose underneath the sea-blue sign with 'Ship Shape' written in large letters. The words were a wonderful contrast to how Farage himself had admitted he felt at the beginning of the campaign. Unfortunately for Farage's press team, they hadn't noticed a four-letter word that had been scratched into the wood of the door frame just below the sign: TWAT.

Farage emerged with his mug of tea and happily posed and grinned for the cameras, all the while with the word TWAT above his head.

The UKIP leader came over and spoke to me, Christopher Hope and John Stevens from the *Daily Mail*. I asked him whether he felt the Robert Blay story had set the party back at all, and Hope asked him if he thought UKIP attracted people who wanted to shoot others. But Stevens came out with the best question of the morning: 'Mr Farage, have you prayed about tomorrow's election?'

There was a moment's silence as all three of us were taken aback. Hope and I were thinking what a brilliant question it was. I'm not sure that's how Farage viewed it.

'That's a private matter,' he replied, after a pause. 'But tomorrow morning I will certainly be having a couple of moments of quiet thought.'

We all broke out into laughter, including Farage.

Stevens then decided to go into full wind-up mode, and started asking Farage how many gin and tonics he planned to have before tomorrow night's count: 'Would you be legal to drive yourself to the count, do you reckon?'

'Do you know what? At the New Year I gave up booze for the month, but I thought, longer term, what is my New Year's resolution? Something's gotta go. Is it drinking, or is it driving? So I've given up driving.'

Another journalist asked him if he had any regrets about the campaign.

'I wish I had started the campaign feeling a bit stronger than I was,' Farage replied:

> That was silly, and I should have got that dealt with more quickly, but no, I think we've fought a good campaign, we've produced a professional manifesto. We've tried like hell to have a serious national debate on the big issues, but we've not always been able to engage in those debates. I think UKIP's fought a good campaign. I think the party's matured a lot.

Farage gave a final wave to the photographers before saying: 'I think this has gone on quite a long time now, chaps, really' and walking towards his black Land Rover, which had appeared next us.

'Right, chaps, all jolly good fun,' he said, and just before he got in the car he threw one final line out to the eager press pack: 'If you believe any of it, you're silly, but never mind.'

We all laughed, but weren't sure what the 'it' he was referring to was. The campaign? Having no regrets? The party maturing? That it had all been 'jolly good fun'?

Hope, myself and Ben Quinn and John Crace, both from *The Guardian*, made our way back into the town centre to find a suitable café (WiFi, power points, a relaxed attitude to a group of journalists nursing a cup of coffee for an hour while they typed). The next item on the day's itinerary was Farage playing bingo late in the afternoon. He had cancelled the bingo photo op the day before, much to the disappointment of the photographers and broadcasters. Crace, *The Guardian*'s sketch-writer, was hanging around in Ramsgate for that very event, but, by lunchtime, it had been cancelled again. Farage later said that, as he had been complaining that coverage of the general election had been trivialised, he would have felt a hypocrite playing bingo for the cameras the night before the polls opened.

We didn't catch up with Farage and the rest of the People's Army until 7.30 p.m., when we rolled up to the final rally of the campaign in the coastal town of Broadstairs. Home to a beautiful sandy beach, Broadstairs is most famous as the location where Charles Dickens wrote *David Copperfield* from 1849 to 1850.

But it was as the birthplace of another man that made it a perfect venue for the final UKIP rally of the 2015 general election: Ted Heath.

The mere mention of the hated Heath name in a crowd of Kippers draws boos and hisses. He was the one who took Britain into the European Economic Community in January 1973, he was the one who started Britain down this road to European integration, he was the one who betrayed our country! Or so the UKIP mantra goes.

The rally was held in a venue called the Pavilion, which had a wonderful patio looking out over the beach. In the bar next to the patio, the press pack gathered, many relaxing with a beer as the fatigue caused by the gruelling election campaign finally washed over them like the waves falling on the sand outside.

As we were talking in the bar, Farage and his entourage appeared on the patio outside, the UKIP leader smoking one of his customary Rothmans cigarettes. We pulled the sliding glass door aside and joined him in the temperate but windy spring evening sun.

Farage appeared relaxed and happy, far more like the man I met in Hoddesdon in 2013 than the one I had seen during much of the general election campaign. That was until he saw John Stevens from the *Daily Mail*. Stevens had been with us that morning in Ramsgate, but disappeared after Farage had left. He had been working on a story about the best man speech Farage gave at his brother's wedding in 2001.

A video had emerged that showed Farage making a joke about the death of Stuart Lubbock in the swimming pool of Michael Barrymore's house earlier that year. Addressing a wedding crowd that included singer Rod Stewart, Farage said:

> As far as smokers here are concerned, there's good news and bad news for you. The bad news was we were not allowed to smoke until the coffee was served. But the good news for us who are smokers is that we are far better off here than if we had been at Michael Barrymore's house. Because there they removed all the ashtrays on the basis that now they chuck all the fags in the pool.

Stevens had contacted Farage for a response earlier that day, and the UKIP leader had replied with a very angry phone call. In Broadstairs that evening, Farage apologised for what he had said to Stevens, but added: 'I'll put the bastards out of business.'

It was unclear who the 'bastards' whom he was referring to were, but the article appeared in the paper the next day.

Farage didn't seem too affected by the story, and he carried on talking to us reporters in his man-having-fun-in-the-pub kind of way.

Inside the Pavilion, the Thanet regiment of the People's Army was gathering. Unlike the twenty-four other meetings Farage had addressed in the constituency since January, the majority of people were standing, with just a few chairs at the side for some of the more elderly foot soldiers. It had more of a pub gig atmosphere than political rally.

I recognised many of the faces from the campaign, most of whom I had seen at other public meetings or out at canvassing events. Also in the crowd were Liz and James Langton Way, the Kippers who had witnessed Rozanne Duncan's astonishing racist rant in the *Meet the Ukippers* documentary. Mr Langton Way was gripping onto a walking stick. The knee operation, which was the excuse the pair used to stop their official involvement in the party, had clearly taken place. Or maybe he was just keeping up the charade.

While the Kippers drank beer and wine, shared campaign stories and congratulated themselves for all their hard work, 'Nigel Farage – The Movie' was being projected onto a screen above the stage.

The ten-minute film, which was on a loop, showed clips of Farage throughout the years, including the infamous Herman Van Rompuy 'damp rag' speech, the launch of the 2015 general election campaign in Canvey Island in February, and what appeared to be a wedding party chanting 'there's only one Nigel Farage' at him in the grounds of a hotel.

It also showed Farage barracking Tony Blair at the European Council in 2005. But, alas, not Blair's reply: 'Let me tell you, sir, and your colleagues: you sit with our country's flag, you do not represent our country's interest. This is the year 2005, not 1945, we are not fighting each other any more, these are our partners and our colleagues and our future lies in Europe.'

After UKIP's Thanet Council candidates had taken to the stage to receive a round of applause from the foot soldiers, it was time for Farage himself. Entering the stage through the crowd, he lapped up the acclaim:

> Thank you for coming along to this, the twenty-fifth of our meetings in what has been an amazing campaign. Tomorrow, I guess, is the biggest day in my political career. It's a political career that began, as you saw from the video earlier, when I had very dark hair and when I was very shy… no, that's not true. Tomorrow is a very, very big day, and I've been very thoughtful today about that long journey that I've been on over twenty-one years, and I'm reminded of what Gandhi said: 'First they ignore you, then they laugh at you, then they attack you, and then you win.'

A huge cheer went up. Perhaps the first time Gandhi had ever been cheered in Broadstairs.

Farage continued, listing the various names UKIP supporters had been called in the 'they laugh at you' stage of Gandhi's timeline to success.

'We were called "cranks", "eccentrics", "gadflies"…'

'Fruitcakes!' shouted out an excited Kipper in the crowd.

'No, wait for it!' Farage shouted back. 'My particular favourite … FRUITCAKES!'

The whole crowd joined in, and descended into applause and laughter at the mention of their favourite insult.

'I've never seen so many weirdos in one room!' said Farage.

You may think that, Mr Farage, but I couldn't possibly comment.

Farage then went through the 'they attack you' stage, focusing on the criticism the party received in the run-up to the 2014 European elections.

Now the 'winning' part. The mere mention of Douglas Carswell and Mark Reckless drew passioned cries of 'yes!' from the crowd. He attacked the 'disgusting' behaviour of the anti-UKIP groups such as HOPE not hate and Stand Up To UKIP, which he claimed had 'peddled a whole series of lies that had frightened many parts of the community'.

Farage then slipped into his tried and tested attacks on the European Union and open-door immigration, and his advocacy of an 'Australian-style points system'.

He rounded up his speech by urging those in the room to 'tomorrow wear a UKIP rosette, wear a UKIP badge, wear a UKIP sticker all day. Talk to your friends, talk to your family, talk to your neighbours, bully them all into submission. Get them out there and voting UKIP.'

Farage went on, getting louder and more passionate, his rise in volume matching the raising of the political stakes he made when he vowed to step down as UKIP leader if he didn't win the seat:

> We are going to need volunteers and help from you in this room, to go out tomorrow afternoon, to go out tomorrow

evening, to knock on the doors of those who had said they'll vote for us. If necessary, to give them a lift to the polling station. If necessary, to put them over your shoulders to carry them down there. We need your help tomorrow. I need your help tomorrow. The fifty-six men and women standing for Thanet District Council need your help tomorrow. Are you with us?

'YES!' shouted the audience as one.

Farage then concluded what could very well be his final speech as UKIP leader: 'Bear in mind the historic geographical significance of where this battle will take place tomorrow. It is from this town of Broadstairs that came a man later to be known as Sir Edward Heath.'

The audience, like Pavlov's dogs, responded in the expected way by booing and hissing Heath's name.

It was Heath who on a lie took us into something which my mum and dad endorsed in a referendum which was then called the Common Market. So I would like to think that Broadstairs as a battleground tomorrow is a place where we can begin to right that wrong because we want to get back our country.

Let's also remember the historical significance of Ramsgate, and of Broadstairs too. It is from here, seventy-five years ago, that a complete, total and utter miracle happened that was called Dunkirk. It was this country over centuries built by men and women, after Magna Carta established perhaps the fairest relationship between the individual and the state. The men and women that went before us created the greatest country in the world.

And it was from these harbours that fishermen, and ordinary people with boats, went across and risked their lives to get back the British Army so that, in the end, we, and the rest of the Western world, should be free.

And it is since then that our career political class, who have no understanding or feeling for history or community or who we are as a nation and who we are as a people, and they have given it away and tomorrow, if you come and help us, we will make one massive stride forward towards getting back our country, getting back control of our borders, getting back our pride and self-respect in who we are as British people.

We can win tomorrow. Please help us do it. Thank you.

THE GENERAL ELECTION – MARGATE – 7–8 MAY 2015

EXIT POLL – BBC/ITV/SKY NEWS/GFK-NOP/IPSOS MORI

Conservatives – 316 seats

Labour – 239 seats

SNP – 58 seats

Lib Dems – 10 seats

Plaid Cymru – 4 seats

UKIP – 2 seats

Greens – 2 seats

'That can't be right, can it?' said Christopher Hope.

I was open-mouthed, which couldn't have been nice for those around me as I was eating fish and chips at the time.

'It must be wrong,' said Laura Pitel.

'What if it's not?' I replied.

'Then we all look like idiots and everything we've been saying for the past month or so is wrong,' surmised Hope, succinctly and accurately.

We continued our walk up Fort Hill in Margate towards the Winter Gardens. The election count was being held in the same venue that hosted UKIP's spring conference. We passed the Hoy pub, scene of Janice Atkinson's infamous lunch that cost her her career. We were all silent as we digested the exit poll and, in my case, fish and chips. All the polls leading up to today had shown Labour and the Tories neck and neck, which, when applied to the number of seats, should have given Ed Miliband a route into Downing Street, largely thanks to SNP support. But this was showing a Tory minority government was most likely on its way.

The UKIP prediction was also a shock: just two seats. Matthew Goodwin, the academic who co-authored the award-winning *Revolt on the Right* book, which looked into support for UKIP, claimed as recently as March that the party was 'likely to win six parliamentary constituencies. They have pretty much got three or four seats now in the bag unless there is a monumental mistake and a car crash before May 7.'

I had put my money where my mouth is and stuck £10 on UKIP getting three seats – Clacton, South Thanet and Thurrock. If the exit poll was right and my bet was wrong, then someone in UKIP owed me some money.

We consoled ourselves that we could be in a '1992' situation. On that election night, the exit poll predicted a hung parliament, when in fact Tory Prime Minister John Major was returned to power with a majority of twenty-one.

Regardless of whether the exit poll was right or wrong, we knew we had a long night ahead of us. The South Thanet declaration wasn't expected until 6 a.m., and we all tried to work out the best time to get some sleep through the course of night.

I had already had some sleep in my B&B opposite the venue. It was the same B&B that I stayed in at the spring conference, although this time I had got my act together and booked a bedroom, instead of leaving it too late and being left with a kitchen.

I went down the long path into the foyer of the Winter Gardens and, after my press credentials had been checked, I was allowed in. The press area was situated in the room where UKIP had held its gala dinner at the spring conference. It was also the room where Brendan had outlined his apocalyptic vision of an Islamic fundamentalist-controlled future. It felt good to be home.

Due to my ever-changing employment situation, I almost didn't get accredited for the count. Hundreds of journalists, photographers and film crews applied for passes, and space was limited. When I initially applied, I was working for the *Daily Mirror*, but I left the company before Thanet Council had decided who would be allowed in. I contacted the council worker who was administering the count, Katy Hooper, to tell her I was now working for the *Express* online.

'Will that be a problem?' I asked.

'Well, you've changed organisations and we've done the accreditations based on that,' she said.

I started to panic. I needed to be at the count. I had been following Farage for two years and if I missed what would either be his greatest triumph or the end of his career I would be gutted. And I started thinking about you, dear reader, who has followed me on this journey. What would you think if, having come this far with me, right at the end I let you down and had to write the last chapter from the perspective of someone watching it on television? I had missed Mark Reckless's defection, I had missed Farage with Joey Essex, I had missed him standing on a table singing 'New York, New York' and I would be damned if I was going to miss him finding out if he was either an MP or standing down as party leader!

I didn't quite say that to Hooper, but I think she detected the desperation in my voice. I re-sent my accreditation form and received the following email: 'Thanks for this. I have spoken to my manager and can't foresee this being a problem.'

Oh, happy hour! I was in!

I set myself up at a table, plonked down my supply of food for the night (sausage roll, Mars bar, banana) and went to investigate. There was just one television in the room, so most of the hacks were gathered round it watching the BBC coverage of the election. Representatives from the parties started to dribble into the room, and I grabbed a quick chat with someone from the Labour candidate Will Scobie's camp.

From what he had seen out at polling stations, he predicted Farage not only wouldn't win the seat, but might come third. Now that would be a shock. I didn't buy into it too much – of course a Labour supporter is going to say they've done well – but still tweeted out what I had been told: 'Labour source at South Thanet count reckons UKIP third, with Tory/Labour fighting it out for win.'

I put my phone in my pocket, went back to the desk I had set up on, checked a few things online and then checked my Twitter feed. Boom – 500 retweets and 100 favourites in the space of five minutes. A text message from a friend: 'Nick Robinson clearly follows you on Twitter.'

Apparently the BBC's political editor had read out my tweet, while referencing me as a 'local BBC reporter', which had sent my Twitter feed crazy. Fame at last.

Farage wasn't due to arrive at the count until an hour or so before the declaration, but some other Kippers were milling about the place. Time seemed to be moving faster than the counts at Clacton and Rochester, thanks to the drama unfolding across the country.

The first result, Houghton & Sunderland South, was declared at 10.49 p.m. Labour increased its majority, but UKIP snuck into second – although still 12,938 votes behind the victorious Bridget Phillipson.

Further results showed the Tories weren't just clinging on to some seats, but increasing their support. Nuneaton, held up as a seat Labour had to win to show Ed Miliband had Middle England appeal, stayed Tory, with Marcus Jones more than doubling his majority.

The first huge shock/not shock of the night came in Paisley and Renfrewshire South, Scotland. The SNP surge had been long predicted ever since a huge increase in support after the 2014 independence referendum. Labour were set to be wiped out in Scotland, but it was still something of a surprise when shadow Foreign Secretary Douglas Alexander lost his seat to the SNP's Mhairi Black, a twenty-year-old university student.

At 2.39 a.m., the first of the seats UKIP had a chance of winning was declared – Castle Point, where the party had launched its general election campaign three months earlier. In 2008, it was home to UKIP's first ever MP, Dr Bob Spink. The former Tory only stayed with the party for seven months, quitting in November 2008 to sit as an independent until the 2010 general election.

Could Castle Point splash the first fleck of purple on the UK's electoral map?

No, Jamie Huntman came second to the Tories by 8,934 votes.

More results from across the country poured in, including Scottish Labour leader Jim Murphy losing his seat in East Renfrewshire to the marauding SNP.

At 3.32 a.m., the result for Hartlepool was announced, the constituency from where Farage had predicted a UKIP uprising against Labour in the north of England. Labour's Iain Wright held onto the seat, but Farage was proved marginally right, as UKIP stormed from fourth place in 2010 to second in 2015. Philip Broughton was just 3,024 votes behind the winner.

Ten minutes after the Hartlepool result, the Great Grimsby declaration was made. This was seen as another northern seat that the People's Army might be able to win. Alas for UKIP, its candidate, the former Tory Victoria Ayling, came third – behind the Conservatives and the victorious Labour Party.

Kippers around me were looking downcast. They were making gains in some areas, but not enough to win any seats. As the pundits took in the defeat of Lib Dem Cabinet minister Ed Davey in Kingston, another result flashed up that indicated UKIP may not win any seats in the north of England.

Heywood & Middleton, scene of the October by-election that saw UKIP come within 618 votes of beating Labour, declared at just before 4 a.m. Labour had not only held the seat, but increased its majority to 5,299. UKIP candidate John Bickley actually increased his number of votes from 11,018 to 15,627, but the higher turnout than the October election had ultimately benefited Labour.

Where UKIP was expected to lose, it was 'losing well', but where it had a chance of winning, it was struggling to get over the line.

By now, the atmosphere in the room was one of shock, as more and more Lib Dems lost their seats, Labour failed to pick any up and the Tories were edging ever closer to the 326 MPs it needed to command a complete majority in the Commons.

Farage was nowhere to be seen, and word reached us from the counting hall that the result was not expected until well after 6 a.m. now, most likely nearer 7 a.m. I realised I was getting nothing good from being in the Winter Gardens, so decided to walk to the hotel that Farage was staying in.

It was 4 a.m., and once I made my way out of the vicinity of the Winter Gardens, the streets were my own. I briskly walked towards the Walpole Bay Hotel, just under a mile away from the count. The sea was on my left, and the light of the half-moon gave the horizon a silver glow. I felt like I was retreating from the war room, where messages of defeat after defeat were trickling in, to instead hunker down in the bunker of the army commander.

Christopher Hope, Laura Pitel and John Stevens were already at the hotel. Also there was Mary Turner, a photographer who, like me, had been following Farage throughout the election. We had shared many a car journey, whinge and moan over the past month. They were sitting on comfy leather chairs in the bar, watching the election coverage on laptops and iPads. Farage was in bed, but UKIP donor Arron Banks was sitting with the hacks. Across every spare chair and sofa lay a different cameraman or photographer trying to get some sleep before the long day ahead of them. The welcoming hotel staff brought out pots of tea and coffee for us as we took in the changing electoral landscape.

Downstairs, numerous members of the People's Army were watching a large TV. Many of them were slumped back on chairs, trying to keep their eyes open. Others had given up on staying awake and were curled up under blankets on yet more sofas. Another room had the remnants of a buffet and, amid the scraps of bread, cheese, crisps, salad and other food, were about a hundred champagne flutes arranged on three tiers of trays in the middle of the table. The fact they were untouched made them stand out even more against the scraps of food.

I wasn't the only hack who noticed the champagne glasses, and Stevens snapped a picture of the set. Apparently, us hacks had been told not to take any pictures downstairs, and when the People's Army discovered Stevens had taken some snaps, we were all banned from going down there for the rest of the night.

I didn't realise such an edict had been issued, so was surprised when I was stopped from going down the stairs to use the gents' toilets by one of Farage's security team.

'Why can't I go down there?' I asked.

'Because John Stevens is a cunt,' was the reply.

'Yes, but that doesn't answer my question,' I quipped back.

Another security guard standing a few feet away looked at me and repeated: 'John Stevens is a cunt.'

The problem was they were the only gents' toilets in the hotel, and I'd been drinking a lot of tea.

I tried again ten minutes later when yet another of Farage's personal bodyguards was positioned at the top of the stairs.

'Sorry, you can't do down there,' he said.

'Let me guess, because John Stevens is a cunt?'

'That's right.'

I wandered the rest of the hotel trying to find another toilet, and it was only then I realised what sort of place I was in. The Walpole Bay was less a hotel, more a setting for a *Doctor Who* episode. The

Edwardian building doubled up as a museum, with every nook and cranny stuffed with objects and items from the period. What made it chilling was the sudden appearance of fully clothed mannequins hidden around certain corners, or a giant cot filled with dolls of all shapes and sizes in one of the corridors. Every time I found a door marked 'Toilet' I opened it to discover it was actually another exhibit, so round and round I would go, opening more doors, climbing more stairs, seeing more mannequins and dolls and toasters and spinning wheels and then some more mannequins until all these items and my lack of sleep made me feel like I was on an old-school carousel and I was standing still but being spun around and around and around while everything danced before me.

Eventually, I gave up looking and used the ladies' toilet on the first floor.

At 4.17 a.m., UKIP finally had something to celebrate. Douglas Carswell had won Clacton. It was the first time the party had ever won a seat in the general election, and technically counted as a gain from the Tories based on the 2010 results. His majority, which stood at 12,404 in October, had been dramatically reduced to just 3,437. Regardless, it meant that UKIP would have a representative in the House of Commons after the election.

Fewer than ten minutes later, the Kippers in the bar with the hacks and downstairs in the basement were not celebrating. The Thurrock result came through. Tim Aker, who had been tipped by so many to win the Essex seat, including me, finished third. Tory MP Jackie Doyle-Price not only clung on, but increased her majority from ninety-two to 536. 'Parachute Polly' Billington, the Labour candidate, came second, just 438 votes ahead of Aker. UKIP were within 974 votes of winning Thurrock, but that was scant consolation to the People's Army.

Moments later, and the declaration in Twickenham revealed the Business Secretary Vince Cable had lost his seat. Us journalists shouted with such surprise as we watched the result announced that someone from the hotel came over to politely but firmly remind us there were guests trying to sleep.

The Croydon North result came through at 4.52 a.m. Alas for Winston McKenzie, he had failed to win any kind of election for the eleventh time, coming third: 9,250 behind the Tories and 30,614 behind Labour.

An old dawn broke over Margate at about 5 a.m., and Kirsten Farage was up well in advance of her husband. An hour later and us hacks sat down for a buffet breakfast in the hotel, still waiting for Farage to emerge.

Word reached us that the South Thanet result, which was originally expected for 6 a.m., would be another two hours at least. For us, the waiting continued, but for Lib Dem's Chief Secretary to the Treasury Danny Alexander, it was over. Another huge scalp taken by the SNP.

At just gone 6 a.m., it was announced that Respect MP George Galloway had lost Bradford West, and at 6.55 a.m. another seat that UKIP had been polling well in, Great Yarmouth, was announced. The People's Army had fallen short again, coming third, and 8,819 votes behind the Tory victor.

If I was going to get any return on my bet of three UKIP seats, I needed both Farage and Reckless to come out as winners. But, by 8.15 a.m., it was all over. Reckless lost Rochester & Strood to the Tories. Kelly Tolhurst, who he had beaten in November, had the last laugh, winning back the seat for the Conservatives with a majority of 7,133. Reckless polled only slightly fewer votes than he had in November – 16,009 against 16,867 – which suggested the UKIP vote had held up. But the increased turnout from 50.6 per cent to 66.5 per cent saw support for Tolhurst rise from 13,947 to 23,142.

'Hallelujah. Mark Reckless out. Don't let the door hit your fat arse as you leave' was the verdict of Tory MP Claire Perry on Twitter.

As the clock ticked on, we all gathered at the bottom of the marble staircase, waiting for Farage to descend. Mary Turner had been in the spot for hours, realising what a brilliant photo it would be. Even when we all rushed back into the bar to watch shadow Chancellor Ed Balls lose his seat at 8.20 a.m., Turner held firm in her spot as we shouted the drama back to her.

At about 9 a.m., Farage emerged. He looked surprisingly rested, and claimed he'd had a wonderful night's sleep. As he made his way through the media scrum to get into his Land Rover, he was asked about the night's yield of just one UKIP MP.

> I have to say I think there will be lots and lots of UKIP voters out there very angry that they are not going to be represented and I think our system is bust. However, we've got a Conservative majority government by the looks of it, which means not terribly much is going to change.

'How about here in South Thanet, how do you feel?' asked Stevens.

'I think there's a massive turnout and I think that must be to the advantage of the Conservatives, and I felt that yesterday at Broadstairs seeing them all queueing up, I thought, "Wow, they've got their vote out in a big way."'

He went on: 'The big factor is fear of the SNP, there isn't much doubt about that.'

Hope asked him if he was still going to step down as UKIP leader if he had indeed lost the South Thanet vote.

'Are you calling me a liar?' was his response.

He was asked if he could be persuaded to stay on as leader.

'I have never ever broken my word before so I am very unlikely to start now,' he said before getting into the Land Rover and speeding away.

We made our way down to the count, expecting to see Farage there, but he had gone off for breakfast before travelling to the Winter Gardens. Tory candidate Craig Mackinlay arrived first, walking through the tired journalists and worn-out activists like a man who had enjoyed a wonderfully deep sleep. Those with Tory rosettes offered him their congratulations and when I asked him if he thought he had won he simply replied: 'Rejoice.'

When Farage did arrive, he gave a TV interview as he walked down the long road to the venue's entrance, in which he talked about the party's future.

'I think what you'll see UKIP become is a very young and very active political force, so yes, there will be disappointment, but as far as the UKIP story is concerned, we are just going to begin a different chapter,' he said.

'Will UKIP need a different type of leader to effect that change in the demographic from this election?' he was asked.

'Well, we've seen the voter demographic change in this election, so the answer is "not necessarily", but I'll talk to you about that afterwards,' Farage replied with a slight grin.

His arrival into the Winter Gardens itself was typical of the whole campaign: a media scrum with his team of bodyguards pushing everyone out of the way. Farage went into the counting hall, which was in a separate area to where the declaration was to be made. I stayed in front of the stage from which the result would be announced as I wanted to make sure I had a good spot. Chris Bruni-Lowe, Farage's data man, tapped me on the shoulder.

'We've lost by about 1,700 votes,' he said.

Minutes later and Farage and all the other candidates lined up on the stage. The UKIP leader stood in between Labour candidate Will Scobie and comedian Al Murray. Both men were over 6 ft tall, making Farage look even smaller than his 5 ft 8 in. It was 10.36 a.m., and returning officer William Alexander stepped up to the microphone to deliver the results we had waited hours, days, weeks and, for some people, years to hear.

'Nigel Askew, We Are The Reality Party: 126.' Polite applause.

'Ruth Angela Bailey, Manston Airport Independent Party: 191.' Polite applause, a few cheers.

'Graham George Birchall, Party for a United Thanet: sixty-three.' Polite applause.

'Robert George Bowler, commonly known as Abu-Obadiah Zeba-diah, Al-Zebabist Nation of Ooog: thirty.' Cheers, applause, cries of 'ooog ag-bar' from his supporters.

'Ian Driver, the Green Party: 1,076.' A few claps.

'Nigel Paul Farage, UKIP: 16,026.' As soon as Farage's name was mentioned people in the crowd started hissing and booing. Some were wearing Labour rosettes, some were anti-UKIP protesters who had got into the count thanks to Abu-Obadiah Zebadiah inviting them as his guests. Farage said 'thank you' to those applauding him.

'Craig Mackinlay, the Conservative Party candidate: 18,838.' Loud applause and cheers broke out in the audience. Mackinlay threw his head back, let out a big sigh and rubbed his hands together. Far-age clapped a few times, and said the word 'close' to himself twice. Al Murray hammed it up for the cameras, adopting a look of utter surprise.

'Bye, Nigel! Bye! We told you so!' some anti-UKIP protesters began shouting.

The returning officer carried on reading out the results, but my attention stayed on Farage. He seemed to shrink before my eyes. This man who, for two years, I had seen winning applause and admira-tion in town halls across the country, who had persuaded two Tory MPs to risk their careers and join his party, who had survived a plane crash, a car crash and cancer with a devil-may-care attitude, suddenly seemed very small, very vulnerable. And very lonely.

When it came down to it, no matter how big his People's Army was, he was on that stage facing the jeers from his opponents and the humiliation of defeat on his own.

In his acceptance speech, Mackinlay claimed the people of South Thanet 'decided they don't just want an MP who will protest angrily from the sidelines'.

In a reference to his former membership of UKIP – Mackinlay was stand-in leader in 1997 after Dr Alan Sked quit – he said: 'Just as I realised some time ago in my own political journey, people here have shown that there is no need for Nigel Farage and there is no need for UKIP.'

Farage stood like a statue with his arms at his side throughout Mackinlay's speech, but leapt up to the microphone in a flash when the victor had finished speaking:

> The definition of whether you are having a good day or a bad day – and many of you may think I'm having a bad day – but let me tell you, five years ago on election day I was in intensive care after an aeroplane crash, so compared to that this feels pretty damn good. I do congratulate the Prime Minister, he secured a Tory majority, something no one thought possible. And there was an earthquake in this election, and it happened north of the border, it happened in Scotland, and I think what you saw were a lot of voters so scared of that Labour/SNP coalition that they shifted to the Conservatives. That included some of the people here that voted UKIP last time round.

He ended his speech with a call for 'real, genuine, radical reform' to the UK voting system, and added that while he felt disappointed professionally, 'on a personal level, I feel an enormous weight has been lifted from my shoulders, and I have never felt happier. Thank you.'

With that, he left the stage, not sticking around to hear the speeches from the other candidates as is customary. UKIP's director of communications Paul Lambert came up to me and said: 'Botany Bay Hotel, now.'

The resignation.

I grabbed my bag and ran out of the Winter Gardens to try to find a taxi. Running beside me was Mary Turner and, without saying a word, we both ran to her car. She sped off while I navigated, and within ten minutes we were parked up outside the Botany Bay Hotel, situated atop beautiful Kent cliffs with the English Channel as the backdrop. Within a matter of minutes, my tired eyes had gone from the artificial light and heavy atmosphere of the Winter Gardens to fresh sunshine, blue sky and a glittering sea.

Camera crews, journalists and photographers all arrived on the scene within minutes. Farage came over to the press pack and positioned himself to deliver his resignation speech.

He started by echoing the words he had just delivered in the Winter Gardens, reflecting on his plane crash five years ago, bemoaning the unfairness of the first-past-the-post voting system, highlighting voters' SNP/Labour fears.

> I said as this campaign went on that if I didn't win I would stand down as leader of UKIP, and I know that you in the media are used to party leaders making endless promises that they don't actually keep, but I'm a man of my word. I don't break my word, so I shall be writing to the UKIP national executive in a few minutes saying that I am standing down as leader of UKIP. I will recommend that pro tem they put in place as acting leader Suzanne Evans, who I think has emerged from this campaign as an absolute tower of strength within UKIP. She works in London, she's based in the London office and I think that's the right way for us to go.

There it was. Farage quits as UKIP leader. Who would take over? Would the party survive without him? What would he do next?

But Farage hadn't finished talking.

> I haven't had a fortnight's holiday since October 1993. I intend to take the summer off, enjoy myself a little bit and not do very much politics at all, and there will be a leadership election for the next leader of UKIP in September and I will consider over the course of this summer whether to put my name forward to do that job again.

What? WHAT? WHAT?!?!

Farage wanted to come back! He had just quit, but was already planning his return! I couldn't believe what I had heard. I suspected Farage would seek to make a comeback after the summer, knowing that he couldn't leave the party alone, but I honestly did not think he would quit and then announce he might return in the same speech!

After fielding questions about his resignation and potential comeback, Farage departed.

Christopher Hope, Laura Pitel, Mary Turner, John Stevens and I were struggling to get our tired minds around what he had said. We decided the best thing to do was get a cab to the railway station, get some sleep on the train and think about it when we got to London.

In the cab, Hope and myself both got a text from Sarah White: 'Just you three meet us at the Northwood in 5. No one else!'

We weren't sure who the third person was, but ordered the taxi driver to take us to the Northwood social club in Ramsgate.

Hope and I made our apologies to Pitel, who was in the cab with us but not invited, and went inside. At the bar was Raheem Kassam, Sarah White and Chris Bruni-Lowe. Outside having a cigarette and talking on his phone was Farage. The third person to get the text was Paul Francis from the KM group of newspapers, which included the *Kent Messenger*.

Once Farage had finished his cigarette we were led outside and granted the final interview he would give as leader of UKIP.

He looked relaxed and happy – genuinely like a weight had been lifted off his shoulders. Sitting in the beer garden, drinking ale and smoking a cigarette with a smile on his face, this was the Farage I had met in Hoddesdon two years previously.

We started with the interview. Why did you leave the door open for a return?

> I am not closing it completely because to do that in life is moronic. I am no longer leader of UKIP, the burden is lifted

off my shoulders. I am happy. I have the summer off to think
about my life. I will think: 'Do I really want to do this again?'

What would you do instead, go back into metal trading?

'I am too old for that. What I am good at is spotting trends in
public opinion. If I hadn't got that then UKIP would not be able to
fly. There are commentators who present radio shows. I am going
to rethink my life.'

What will you do over the summer?

'I want to spend some time seeing the children, catching a few fish.'

Who do you think should lead UKIP?

Suzanne is highly competent woman, who I am recommend-
ing to the party. Any leadership election involves a debate
about the party. Post the election and post 4 million votes
there is a lot more that unites them than divides them.

I don't know who will stand. Douglas has said he didn't want
to do it in the past, and maybe Douglas doesn't want to do it.
I'd always thought the next UKIP leader would have to be an
MP but Nicola Sturgeon has blown that theory out of the water.

Will you carry on as an MEP?

'I am going to go to Brussels next week and sit down and talk to
them and find out what they want. I have to be mindful of that referendum [on Britain's EU membership].'

Have you spoken to Mark Reckless today? If so, what did you say?

I said that I was sorrier for his result than I was for mine,
because Mark is an incredibly noble and brave man. He took
a massive risk with his career to try to change things, to try
to do good as he saw it and I felt very, very sore for him.

When did you know you had lost the South Thanet election?

I knew the result yesterday lunchtime. I could see the wards in
Broadstairs were 80 per cent turnouts, with people queuing for
[an] inordinate amount of time to vote. I talked to lots of them
down in the street and they just said: 'Look, Nigel, we love
you but we can't have Nicola Sturgeon running the country.'

He added: 'I'm an honourable man, I keep my promises. I said I
would go if I lost. What's done is done. I'm relieved.'

With that, the interview was over. We all shook his hand. Then we
all hugged Sarah, shook the hands of Raheem, Chris Bruni-Lowe,
UKIP party secretary Matt Richardson and even all the bodyguards.

A taxi picked us up and took us to the station. On the train back to
London I reflected back over the past two years. UKIP had dominated
my fledgling career as a political reporter. Despite their many, many faults,
gaffes and shortcomings, I had enjoyed covering them, and enjoyed following Farage from a pub in Hoddesdon to a clifftop in Kent to a social
club in Ramsgate. I had watched closely as this little party had grown
into a powerful force in UK politics, but, at the last battle, the People's
Army were ultimately defeated. For all the hyperbole, grandstanding and
posturing, just one UKIP MP would be sitting on the Commons' green
benches when Parliament reconvened in ten days' time.

I felt privileged that I had been there to witness Farage's failure – a
moment I would never forget. The life of a journalist is often a frus-
trating one, constantly behind the events and trying to piece together
what happened afterwards.

As I was writing this book, Bloomberg's Robert Hutton sent me
some words by the great journalist Alistair Cooke: 'Only by the
wildest freak is a reporter, after many years on the hop, actually present at a single accidental convulsion of history. Mostly, we write
the coroner's inquest, the account of the funeral, the reconstruction
of the prison riot, the trial of the spy, not the hatching of the plot.'

I had been there. I had Followed Farage until the end.

Hadn't I?

PART 3

DEFEAT

'The only person that's ever plotted against Nigel Farage's leadership is Nigel Farage himself.'

Suzanne Evans, Wednesday 20 May 2015

CHAPTER 15

OH! WHAT A LOVELY WAR

FRIDAY 15 MAY 2015, 9.01 A.M.

'WHERE ARE YOU?' SAID Farage.

'East London,' I replied.

'Get on the Central line to Bond Street and meet me in the office. Quick as you can.'

He hung up the phone.

I ran into my bedroom, threw on my suit, said goodbye to my pet cat Charlie and rushed to Mile End Tube station. I was there within ten minutes and boarded a Central line train to Bond Street. A week ago I was getting ready to hear the confirmation that Farage had lost his battle with South Thanet, and less than an hour later I had been standing with him on the cliffs as he announced his resignation as UKIP leader.

Had it really been a week? I thought to myself as I got out my notebook and flicked through the reams and reams of shorthand notes I had made since then.

Where to start?

Farage's resignation was seen by many UKIP activists and voters as a huge blow to the party. Under his leadership, the party had won 3,881,129 votes last Thursday – an increase of 2,961,658 on the 2010 general election. Despite only having one MP, UKIP came second in 125 seats all across England and Wales, only failing to come in the top two positions in any constituencies in Scotland and Northern Ireland. The party was in the strongest position it had ever been.

But at the top of the party, there was a sense of frustration. Farage hadn't told anyone of his plan to consider standing again in September, not even sharing it with his closest advisors as they discussed where he would make his resignation statement over breakfast before the South Thanet result was announced. Many felt he was foolish to promise to quit as leader if he didn't win his seat, but even more foolish to cast doubts on his resignation by openly contemplating if he would stand again in September. How could Suzanne Evans, his anointed successor, lead the party until the election knowing he may come back? Would anyone even dare challenge Farage in a leadership contest?

A senior official in the party told me the day after Farage stepped down that he shouldn't try to come back. 'We've reached peak Farage, not peak UKIP,' the official said.

Farage's advisors tried to persuade him to change his mind about quitting entirely, and he had been bombarded with thousands of messages from supporters urging him to reconsider standing down even before he addressed the media atop the Kent cliffs.

Talk in UKIP circles over the weekend was dominated by whether he would stand again as leader in September, and whether anyone would challenge him.

I used the time to speak to various people in the party about where they thought the campaign had gone right or wrong. It was obvious the Kippers were falling into two camps. The first was that the campaign had been a huge success because the core vote had held up, giving UKIP similar levels of support it had achieved at the previous year's European election.

A Kipper who worked on the Farage campaign in South Thanet said:

> We couldn't have fought a better campaign. Twenty-five public meetings, we did about twenty direct mailings, we must have done about forty different leaflets, we had about thirty ad trucks down there, we had every billboard in the constituency, we owned the Manston Airport issue, we owned the green belt housing issue.

The Kipper compared it to the failed 1964 US presidential election campaign of Republican Barry Goldwater – 'a glorious disaster'.

I asked the Kipper if he thought there had been any mistakes in the campaign.

'If you really want what went wrong: flying Nigel up to Grimsby to meet Joey Essex on a boat.'

The second camp in the party felt the campaign message had been too narrow, focusing on firing up the people who were already going to vote UKIP, instead of trying to attract floating voters.

Douglas Carswell was firmly in this camp, and told me:

> People say we did really well in getting 4 million voters. That's an achievement, but not quite a remarkable achievement. I don't think we were positive enough. I think we were talking about all the things that got us going. For every ten people only three voted for us. We have got to recognise what it is about us which made the seven out of ten not vote for us. What did we offer a mum in her thirties or forties in Kent?
>
> UKIP has only ever won three parliamentary contests. Having been intimately involved in two of the three, I think I have some things to say about winning over voters. It's all about values. It doesn't matter if voters agree with what you are saying if the way you say it makes them question your

motives. That's why the 'shock and awful' approach was so awful. Simply awful.

Disputes over the tone of the campaign had begun at the beginning of the year. Carswell and party chairman Steve Crowther were put in charge of producing the billboard posters that would be unveiled throughout the election.

A source told me: 'Carswell and Crowther took them on this fairness, corporate taxes bent and all the adverts read "unreal" in big bold letters, and then it would say "corporates only pay this amount of taxes" and they went down this road.'

The more hawkish members of Farage's team, including Raheem Kassam, Chris Bruni-Lowe, and UKIP party director Steve Stanbury, were tasked with coming up with a set of posters more in keeping with those that had been used during last year's European elections.

In April 2014, UKIP produced a poster featuring an escalator going up the white cliffs of Dover with the slogan: 'No border. No control.' For the general election, they used the same image, but this time there were three escalators.

'Unfortunately at the beginning there was such a long period of time when we were going down this wrong route that we didn't really have time to ramp up messaging slowly,' said someone involved with the campaign. 'We had three phrases at the beginning planned; by the time we actually implemented what we wanted we only had one phase left so they all had to go out at the same time. That's why you saw we rushed poster truck launches, day by day.'

It was clear that Carswell's attempts to broaden UKIP's appeal were not going down well with the hawks around Farage.

'Yes, the Carswells in the party wanted to go for a broader vote,' said one:

> I had seen and taken the lessons from, and I thought Douglas had too, the 2010 Tory campaign where they went for hugging

huskies and hoodies and all that. I thought, 'Do you know what? I don't want to get into that territory at all.' We got four and a half million votes in the Europeans, let's get those guys back out again and we'll take seats and we'll increase our vote share to four and a half million, that sort of thing. Again, without the SNP stuff we would have absolutely got four or five seats. No doubt.

The splits on campaign strategy were clear, but as the weekend after the election drew to a close, they had remained relatively hidden from public view.

But, come Monday afternoon, UKIP's civil war started to go very public indeed.

An email popped into my inbox at 3.41 p.m. titled: 'STATEMENT UKIP URGENT':

> Steve Crowther, Chairman of UKIP: As promised Nigel Farage tendered his official resignation as leader of UKIP to the NEC. This offer was unanimously rejected by the NEC members who produced overwhelming evidence that the UKIP membership did not want Nigel to go.
>
> The NEC also concluded that UKIP's general election campaign had been a great success. We have fought a positive campaign with a very good manifesto and despite relentless, negative attacks and an astonishing last-minute swing to the Conservatives over fear of the SNP, that in these circumstances, 4 million votes was an extraordinary achievement.
>
> On that basis Mr Farage withdrew his resignation and will remain leader of UKIP. In addition the NEC recognised that the referendum campaign has already begun this week and we need our best team to fight that campaign led by Nigel.
>
> He has therefore been persuaded by the NEC to withdraw his resignation and remains leader of UKIP.

Farage hadn't gone. He was still leader. He had unresigned.

I, like most people I know in the media, burst out laughing. How ridiculous! All that talk of not wanting the party to be a one-man band, of looking forward to a break away from politics, of having no 'credibility' as a party leader outside Westminster. What a joke!

Rumours started flying that Farage had never actually formally offered his resignation, and that he had sat in on the NEC meeting in UKIP's London headquarters while his future was being discussed to put off any dissenters.

One member of the NEC told me what happened:

> He tendered his resignation, but the NEC begged him to stay and asked him to reconsider. That went on for ten minutes. He said: 'I want a holiday, I need a break. I would like to put this person as interim leader.'
>
> All the ducks were in rows [for his departure]. However, although that had all been confirmed that morning, some had a change of heart. All the teams meant to fall into place didn't and it left a dilemma.
>
> Farage was surprised, he had more support than he thought, there had been 1,600 emails and calls asking him to stay. I think that he was probably taken aback by that. The vote was then held on whether the NEC was going to accept his resignation. He was in the room, but he had a right to be there.

Despite the vote being unanimous, I asked the NEC member if he felt there were some who would have spoken out against Farage staying as leader if he had left the room.

'There were about three people who felt that UKIP needed a change, but they would have lost the vote,' said the source.

I spoke to a long-standing UKIP MEP after the news broke who was dumbfounded by Farage's unresignation. 'I don't understand it all. He just does what he wants when he feels like it. We have to move beyond the Nigel Farage personality cult and not just make things up on the spur of the moment in front of the TV cameras.'

Farage's surprise move may have been hogging the headlines, but another meeting that took place that day was about to set in motion a chain of events that would lead to a purge at the top of the party.

UKIP party secretary Matthew Richardson, one of Farage's key advisors in Kent, held a meeting with the party's only MP, Douglas Carswell. He presented Carswell with a plan to use the public funds he was set to receive – so-called 'Short Money' – to employ fifteen members of staff. The money is designed to help opposition parties with their parliamentary activities. UKIP qualified for more than £650,000 a year, as the formula awards £16,689.13 for every seat won at the most recent election, plus £33.33 for every 200 votes gained by a party.

Carswell was furious. He had long campaigned for a reduction in the cost of politics, and he was being asked to use public money to effectively keep Farage's advisors on the payroll. If he had gone ahead with the proposal and employed fifteen staff, his back room would have been bigger than that of the Leader of the Opposition. He told Richardson he would not take all the Short Money available, and would instead claim half of the funds to finance an appropriate team to help with his constituency and parliamentary duties.

With the meeting over, Carswell only found out about Farage's unresignation when Laura Pitel from *The Times* stopped him in Parliament and showed him the news on her Twitter feed. A shocked Carswell immediately emailed UKIP HQ setting out his objections to the Short Money plan in writing. He then went off to take part in a long-planned post-election conference organised by Conservative Home, the TaxPayers' Alliance, Business for Britain and the Institute of Economic Affairs.

The news of Farage's unresignation had broken just hours before, and the press at the event were keen to get the reaction of the party's only MP. Having already spoken out about the tone of the election campaign, many suspected Carswell would not be happy about the return of the man behind it.

The *Huffington Post*'s Ned Simons asked: 'Douglas, were you surprised that Nigel Farage unresigned himself today? And given your comments about the tone, is he the best person to lead UKIP and the Eurosceptic movement going forward?'

Carswell replied: 'Ned, I'm delighted that you've asked a question about the subject we're discussing. I heard about the unresignation on, I think, Twitter or whatever. You'll need to ask me about it later. I'm not going to talk about that now.'

Unfortunately for Carswell, also present at the conference was Bloomberg's Rob Hutton, he of the 'Malala' tweet in Clacton that had clearly embarrassed the Ukipper.

Hutton and Carswell barely spoke any more, what with Carswell banning him from the post-by-election press conference and then blocking him on Twitter. Hutton spotted that this was his chance to reacquaint with his old nemesis and chased him down the stairs as Carswell tried to leave at the end of the conference.

'Are you still in UKIP?' asked Hutton.

Carswell didn't answer. The silent treatment continued.

With Carswell refusing to publicly back Farage, together with his email stating his intentions not to let the party get its hands on the Short Money, the briefings against him from those close to the leader began the next day.

Journalists, including myself, were tipped off about the Short Money row, but were told Carswell had wanted to keep it all for himself and had gone 'ballistic' when told by Farage's advisors he couldn't.

One source close to the Farage camp told me: 'He wanted to be leader. He was "fucking this" and "fucking that" during the meeting. He thought he was taking over.'

Further briefings from people close to the UKIP leader said Carswell would be letting down the 4 million people who voted UKIP if he didn't take the money and use it to represent them.

With the briefings against Carswell getting louder and more intense – there were even claims he was going to quit UKIP, head back to the

Tories and trigger another by-election in which Farage would stand against him in – other Kippers took to Twitter to defend the Clacton MP.

'Whoever is briefing against @DouglasCarswell does not have UKIP's best interests at heart. Idea he would do anything "improper" is absurd' wrote Patrick O'Flynn.

'Those briefing against @DouglasCarswell must stop. He is a man of integrity and honour and that is to be respected' said Steven Woolfe.

Defeated Thurrock candidate Tim Aker tweeted: 'Congrats @DouglasCarswell on your re-election. Followed your advice and nearly made it. Essex will #gopurple.'

The next morning, Carswell broke cover and appeared on BBC Radio 4's *Today* programme to give his side of the story:

> Well, there are one or two rather excitable staffers in UKIP who came up with a proposal that involves hiring fifteen extra people, and, you know, I would just point out that I'm not an American senator. I doubt very much that even Ed Miliband when he was Leader of the Opposition would have had fifteen staff in his office.
>
> I would much rather deal with this now than in a year's time face awkward question from journalists like you, phoning up and saying, 'Why on earth are you spending the best part of a million pounds running an office?'
>
> UKIP's meant to be different, and UKIP is going to be different, and I think we need to make absolutely clear that when we spend money we're doing it because it's the right thing to do, not just simply because the money's there.

He added: 'I'm confident, absolutely certain, that Nigel will see the good sense of this.'

Later that day, Carswell and Farage met for talks about how to use the Short Money, but no agreement was made.

Any suggestion the row was dying down was completely blown

out the water on Thursday 14 May. Tensions between those in UKIP HQ and Farage's team in Thanet exploded into the open thanks to comments made by O'Flynn in an interview with *The Times*.

The UKIP economics spokesman, who had been the party's campaign director during the election, claimed Farage had become a 'snarling, thin-skinned, aggressive' man, far removed from the 'cheerful, ebullient, cheeky, daring' politician of the past.

O'Flynn laid the blame for Farage's transition squarely at the door of his advisors Raheem Kassam and Matt Richardson. Although he did not mention them by name, there was little doubt as to his target as he criticised a 'Tea Party, ultra-aggressive American influence'.

He urged Farage to 'clear out' these 'aggressive' and 'inexperienced' aides and adopt 'a much more consultative and consensual leadership style'.

Referring to Farage's unresignation he said: 'What's happened since Thursday night/Friday morning has certainly laid us open to the charge that this looks like an absolutist monarchy or a personality cult. I don't think that even Nigel would say it's been the most glorious chapter of his leadership.'

The comments provoked uproar in the Farage camp, with many convinced O'Flynn and Carswell were working together to overthrow the UKIP leader. UKIP donor Arron Banks, one of Farage's biggest supporters, told me: 'It's all related to Carswell. They want to be the voice of the "no" campaign in the referendum.'

He went on to say that O'Flynn could never be leader as his TV appearances are 'like watching paint dry'.

Bringing Carswell's close friend the Eurosceptic Conservative MEP Daniel Hannan into the mix, Banks added: 'People like Hannan and Carswell are paper Eurosceptic tigers. Nigel is a big beast in the jungle.'

By lunchtime, Richardson, whose contract expired at the end of June anyway, offered his resignation to the party in light of O'Flynn's comments. Unlike Farage's, his was accepted.

But Richardson's departure was not enough for some, and former

UKIP treasurer Stuart Wheeler took to the airwaves to call on Farage to step down.

'If he wants to put himself up in an election then he has every right to do so, though I personally would prefer someone else,' said Wheeler.

Claims of a coup led by O'Flynn were getting stronger, provoking outrage among UKIP members who adored Farage.

The former *Express* journalist tried to pour cold water on the rumours in an interview with Sky News:

> If anyone thinks that I am planning some kind of coup against Nigel they could not be more wrong. He is my political hero and will remain so.
>
> He has done an amazing thing, I have been a loyal supporter of his leadership all the way along but … a couple of people in his inner circle – for want of a better term – they are wrong 'uns.

Speaking to me two days later, O'Flynn revealed his motivation for making the comments:

> The unresignation made it look like a personality cult and didn't present the party in a very good light. Then there was the aggressive approach to our only MP over the Short Money. I was worried we were in danger of losing our only MP. That was against the party's interest.
>
> I regret getting sucked into that sort of, what was presented as a personal attack. I was attacking the advisors but also criticising Nigel over the 'I will resign/I will not resign' episode. It was in the book [*The Purple Revolution*] and it led to a senior member of the party – not me – to quite legitimately think of the fact there could be a leadership contest. Two or three senior members of the party were treated pretty shoddily.
>
> I have always tried to be a supportive and helpful advisor.

Turning to Farage's advisors, the 'wrong 'uns' as he had called them, O'Flynn said:

> It's massively important UKIP is seen not to have these links
> or support with right-wing American politics. I am not fla-
> vour of the month with party members. This episode of the
> last few days has been helpful for Nigel in terms of dem-
> onstrating the overwhelming support in UKIP. The party
> membership is overwhelmingly with Nigel's leadership.

He scoffed at suggestions his intervention was part of an attempted coup, especially one that involved placing Tory MEP Daniel Hannan ahead of Farage in the Better Off Out campaign in the EU referendum.

'If anyone has the idea that Daniel Hannan can communicate with ordinary voters in the way that Nigel can is completely wrong,' he said.

Despite the attack from the party's general election campaign manager, Farage stayed silent throughout the day. He was due to appear on that evening's *Question Time*, and told me he was going to keep quiet until then.

The UKIP press office fired into action, and throughout the day statements of support for Farage were pumped out from deputy leader Paul Nuttall, former party leader Lord Pearson, and donors Alan Bown, Ko Barclay, Richard Desmond and Paul Sykes. Together with the already declared support of Banks, Farage clearly had the backing of those who bankrolled the party.

At 7 p.m., Raheem Kassam, who was on holiday in America, popped up on Sky News to respond to O'Flynn's description of him as a 'wrong 'un'.

'An elected MEP should not be behaving like that,' said Kassam, live from New York. He quashed speculation he had been sacked that day, saying his contract was due to expire at the end of the month and he was on leave until then.

Kassam announced he was 'moving back into journalism for Breitbart

London, and if Patrick O'Flynn thinks that he's seen aggressive-style tactics before, he ain't seen nothing yet'.

Sky News presenter Adam Boulton asked Kassam if he had put pressure on the NEC to reject Farage's resignation. He denied the allegation, and said, 'The first I heard of it was a big round of applause coming out of the UKIP boardroom.'

Before concluding the interview, Kassam lobbed a few more grenades in the direction of O'Flynn. Boulton asked him: 'Are you saying there should be no place in the party now for Patrick O'Flynn?'

'That's absolutely what I'm saying,' said Kassam:

> You cannot go to a national newspaper and air internal party grievances as an elected party representative of the party. It's wholly unprofessional and I think Patrick should absolutely consider his position. I have no problem with him as a bloke, he's a nice chap, he has some good ideas, but unfortunately, over the past twenty-four hours, he has shown himself to be utterly unprofessional and undeserving of holding that title and holding a spokesman role for the UK Independence Party.

He ended the interview by casting doubt on O'Flynn's political leanings, something that would further push the party activists behind Farage and against any coup.

'I think his heart is generally in the right place. I'm not sure he's necessarily a Kipper through and through, but if he believes he is then I think the party should give him the benefit of the doubt.'

Even by UKIP's standards, it had been a hell of a day. Open warfare had broken out. O'Flynn had risen to the bait of all the backbiting against Carswell and only succeeded in turning the guns on himself.

But there was still more to come, as Farage appeared on the BBC's *Question Time* show that evening. He would have the last word of the day.

'Is there a place in today's politics for snarling, thin-skinned and aggressive leaders?' was the first question of the show.

'No, course there isn't! I mean, snarling, aggressive, angry leaders wouldn't get very far, would they?' Farage joked as he began his
response:

> I was disappointed that a member of our team said this but,
> look, in general elections you are under a huge amount of
> pressure particularly. It's like a boiler room, a pressure cooker,
> and I'm sure the others [on the panel] would agree, and we
> maintained discipline as a party extraordinarily well during
> this general election compared to the past.
>
> The election's over, people are letting off steam and we've
> seen one or two people fighting personal wars against each
> other. What I would say is this: I think what people are look-
> ing for in politics is people that are assertive, people that
> are not afraid to tell the truth, even if they know it may not
> always be popular. Leaders that have actually had a job in
> the real world, and got some experience of life, and lead-
> ers that are in politics out of conviction and not just for a
> career. Whatever my faults are, and perhaps they're many, I
> am in politics because I believe in what I say and I want this
> country to change.

Question Time chairman David Dimbleby pushed Farage on why he
promised to stand down, only to retract his resignation three days
later.

> I did resign, is the first point to make, and I said if I didn't
> win, I would resign, and I had to offer that resignation for-
> mally to our elected national executive of the party who just
> point-blank refused to accept it and showed me online sig-
> natures of thousands of members saying I simply shouldn't
> go, I mustn't go. So I went and sat in a darkened room and
> thought: what do I do? And actually what amazed me was

for the national executive of any political party to be unanimous was in itself pretty remarkable and I felt quite frankly moved by the strength of their appeal and I said, on the basis of that, I will continue.

Particularly as the one thing I have striven for in twenty years in politics from a tiny party to what is now quite a big party, I've always pushed for this country to have a referendum on our membership of the European Union and now would have been, in retrospect, the wrong time to go.

Farage rejected the suggestion of holding a leadership election to 'clear the air', saying there was vital work to do on getting the 'No' campaign ready for the European referendum.

'We can't afford as a party that wants Britain to be free to waste three or four months of our time having a leadership contest where, frankly, we know the result already,' he said.

Farage did try to make peace with Carswell by saying the party would not be accepting any of the Short Money.

One audience member summed up the views of many people perplexed by the whole debacle.

'Like most politicians you've said something and gone back on what you've said. Surely you're in the Nick Clegg group now?'

As you can see, I had a lot going through my mind as the Tube whizzed me into central London for my interview with Nigel Farage.

CHAPTER 16

FARAGE EXPLAINS IT ALL

FRIDAY 15 MAY 2015 – UKIP HEADQUARTERS, MAYFAIR, LONDON – 10.15 A.M.

NIGEL FARAGE SAT OPPOSITE me, taking drags on a cigarette.

We were in his office, and there was no smoking ban in this section of his world.

Before I could even get my Dictaphone out, he started talking, so I began scribbling down his words in shorthand.

'The first big game is who leads the "out" campaign in the referendum – who's the hero?' he said. 'There's a high priest of Euroscepticism who thinks quoting large amounts of Shakespeare will help connect with people. The posh boys are going to talk about trade when you've got an open goal with immigration and should use that.'

Farage was keen to outline his take on the week's events. For him, it all came down to the European referendum. The 'high priest of Euroscepticism' was no doubt Tory MEP Daniel Hannan.

The word being put round about Farage, according to the man

himself, was 'toxic'. Seeing as he had just helped the party win almost 4 million votes, Farage did not see himself that way.

The second factor at play, according to Farage, was the huge pressure coming from Brussels on Westminster politicians to stay in the EU:

> They are caving already. They are going to rush the referendum. It will be next year. The same day as the Europhile areas of London and Scotland vote in their elections.
>
> [European Council president Jean-Claude] Juncker and [Antti] Timonen, his sidekick, who is a very smart man – I say it's *The Pinky and Perky Show* – they will bend over backwards to make cosmetic concessions. But if [German Chancellor Angela] Merkel goes for treaty change it will be pulling the strand out of the jumper.

He referred back to the 2008 Irish referendum on the Lisbon Treaty, and said that when he arrived in Dublin airport and drove into the city: 'Every single billboard was "What Europe's done for us".'

I drag him away from the European issue and try to take him back a week to when we were all standing on that clifftop in Kent.

'I did mean what I said on Friday morning, I did genuinely walk in there [he gestured to the UKIP boardroom where the NEC met on Monday] saying, "Goodbye, I'm off for the summer." I could have made my life a bit easier.'

At that point his phone rang. It was Christopher Hope from the *Telegraph* asking him about more anonymous Ukippers expressing their unhappiness with his behaviour in the past few days:

> I've had enough of all this internal bickering, there will be no more of it, and if that means I have to move into a slightly autocratic mode and say that, if anybody is caught briefing behind each other's backs after what we've gone through for

the past two or three days, they will be removed. I've no idea
who it is but enough's enough...

While he was talking, I took my chance to look around the office. A
messy desk, an ash tray, some prints of newspaper cartoons depict-
ing Farage sweeping away the other party leaders. Exactly what I
had expected.

There was also a copy of the gay lifestyle magazine *Attitude* on Farage's desk. I did not expect that. I contemplated making a joke about
whether his passion for coming out of Europe was masking another
sort of 'coming out' but decided now was not the time.

'I'm sorry, it's like being back in [an] '80s trading room,' said Farage as he hung up the phone. 'I love to be busy, I can't stand not [to
be], it's why I never watch television.'

'Yes, I noticed that when out on the campaign trail in Ramsgate
before one of the public meetings. You didn't have anything to do for a
few minutes and you didn't know what to do with yourself,' I replied.

> I'm hopeless. I've got to be engaged! Either working hard
> or playing hard. The idea of R & R – forget it, it's just of no
> interest to me at all. R & R for me is going to Cornwall and
> climbing a dangerous cliff. You've got to have risk, you've
> got to have excitement. Managed risk obviously, but yes, an
> element of risk in what you do is very exciting.

'Is that why you said what you said about standing down if you didn't
win in South Thanet?'

'Yeah, of course.'

'Is that your biggest political regret?'

> No, you say what you say. I could have played the card
> more cleverly on Friday morning. If my intention had been
> the outcome that we've had this week, I could have played

the card cleverly, but, to be honest with you, I just thought, 'That's it – I'm out.'

There was a second argument that convinced me, of course, and it wasn't just the passion and emotion of the NEC and people bombarding me saying, 'You mustn't go, don't think this is a failure.' All sorts of people said that to me, including our backers. It was also the sense that if I hadn't been around, would we have been getting a referendum? It's happening, and what if it isn't next May?

'Surely you could have been that strong "out" voice but not been leader?'

Yeah, but it would have been difficult because actually it would have put us, from 7 May until 22 September, which is when the ballots would have come back in, we would have looked a bit out of the game.

Now Augusts aren't traditionally busy but it seems to me that things are moving quite quickly. So that was the other thing that convinced me. But do I regret it? There's no point spending your life looking backwards.

You've got to look forwards, and if I look back at all my failures I would curl up in a ball.

I took Farage back to the first time we met in Hoddesdon in 2013, and asked if he remembered it.

He nodded:

When you saw me I was towards the end of a fortnight's tour. I had been all over Britain in that bus, which had broken down, but the black cab had kept going. There was no heating in it and I had Ray Finch [now an MEP] driving it; he must be one of the worst drivers in the world.

I then took him through all the people I had met on my journey following him, finally putting to him some of the questions I'd been
looking to ask for months.

I started with UKIP founder Dr Alan Sked. At the mention of his
name, Farage rolled his eyes.

'He gets dragged out all the time,' he said:

> He's somebody who intellectually was clever, but couldn't
> drive a motor car, couldn't boil an egg and should have done
> a deal with Jimmy Goldsmith, and didn't, and three of us,
> who were senior members of the party after the '97 general
> election, said, 'This is ridiculous, we have to do something
> about this,' and he's been bitter and twisted for eighteen years.

'Having met him, I can see why you may have been attracted to his
way of thinking,' I said.

'I was very attracted to what Alan was doing, I thought it was a very
brave thing for someone in the academic and intellectual world to do.'

'He said you didn't have any policies of your own, and you wanted
to buy them in from right-wing think tanks. Is that true?'

Farage threw his hands up in the air:

> I was twenty years ahead of my time. Why go through the
> agonies and expense of setting up policy units when all over
> London and Washington and all over the free world there
> are people doing this? If you believe in free enterprise, the
> Institute of Economic Affairs pump out a pamphlet every
> couple of months; if you believe the British education sys-
> tem is broken and needs fixing, join Civitas for thirty quid
> a year – it's all out there. So I was way ahead of my time on
> that. So no regrets about that.

He paused before adding: 'I wouldn't necessarily have said

"right-wing", I would have said "think tanks", but whatever, that's a moot point.'

'What about the suggestion you were drunk by 9 p.m. every night?'

At this, Farage smiled slowly, leaned forward and said:

> There was one day when the NEC meeting was at seven in the evening and I had been at Lord's for the first day of the Test match since 9.30 that morning, so I might have been refreshed – that was quite possible.
>
> But, look, in my job we had lunch every day so evening meetings weren't really ideal, but so what? He thinks that's terrible, but that was my life.

Moving on, I asked him about his former aide Annabelle Fuller.

'Was it difficult for you when she left? You had been together for a long time.'

'A hell of a long time,' he said firmly:

> And we'd been through a lot of abuse together. A hell of a lot. Never-ending sniping, a bit like Raheem. Anyone that gets close to me gets the bullet and it's unfair. Annabelle, again, in her own way, tremendous political brain. Frailties, personal frailties. But then when I worked in business I employed waifs and strays. I picked people out of the gutter who had been thrown out by the corporates for not quite fitting in, and one or two of them absolutely flourished under me because I was very tolerant of their eccentricities and their faults. But I gave them a chance to get on and do things and I think in politics, in a way, perhaps I'm similar.

'Were you sad when she went?'

'It was horrible. It was very difficult. We are still in contact. In the end it just became impossible, as it has for Raheem.'

I moved on to Godfrey Bloom, and asked if he did indeed cry when he sacked his friend and former flatmate from the party in 2013.

'Well, I'm not going to say yes or no to that. Godfrey Bloom was somebody with whom I had an extraordinary amount of fun.'

Farage reminisced about the pair's tours of the Western Front as part of their shared interest in the First World War: 'I missed the fun that we used to have, yes.'

Bloom had been on the airwaves the day before we met calling on Farage 'to move over' from UKIP leader. I read him some of the comments Bloom had made to me over our lunch in Yorkshire and asked if they hurt:

> No, not any more. Godfrey changed, Godfrey changed. Godfrey had treatment when he was very ill and he used to laugh his way out of crisis and then he decided after he would fight his way out of a crisis and it didn't work.
>
> Bongo bongo we just about lived with, but you have to remember, two weeks before that conference, Nuttall and I took him for a dinner in Strasbourg. It was a little Jewish restaurant – I quite like Jewish food actually – a little Jewish restaurant in a quiet part of Strasbourg where we knew nobody important would go to a place like this, just people like us who enjoy normal things. That evening degenerated with each bottle. There was a terrible row, and both Paul and I said to each other the next morning, 'There's a terrible train crash coming.'
>
> That annual conference we spent a fortune on. Doing a big conference in London costs six-figure money. We had spent a fortune on [it], we had the best ever plan, we were unveiling domestic policy.
>
> Housing, the idea of setting up a sovereign wealth fund, lots of really good stuff. It was interesting: two of Murdoch's directors were sitting in the audience and I saw them a few

months later and [they said], 'We sat there and thought, "Bloody hell, this party is really going somewhere."'

He lit another cigarette and recounted the moment he was told his old friend had hit Michael Crick:

> I'm in the Westminster Arms, oblivious to what is happening, thinking I must have a fag and a pint. I'm suddenly jumped by Sky News saying, 'How do you feel, Mr Farage, about Godfrey Bloom hitting Michael Crick?'
>
> I said: 'It's very tempting.' There was like an hour of total madness.
>
> The 'sluts' comment – come on, Godfrey, we're not in the Officers' Mess, it's not 1968. Bashing Crick, yeah, we all get provoked. We all feel like it, I feel like it sometimes. I can quite see how celebrities coming out of nightclubs, punch photographers – I can understand why, but you don't do it.
>
> The low point was the interview with the ITN guy. The ITN guy said: 'You hit Michael Crick.'

Farage adopted an angry, Bloom-style voice: 'Any more cheek from you, young man, and you'll get the same!'

> By this point it had gone mad, literally gone mad. He had destroyed the conference at which we had people like Lord Digby Jones speaking. That was a big coup for me, to get Digby, only just stepped down as a Labour trade minister, to get Digby to speak at a UKIP conference about why there was a big world out there and we didn't need the EU was, I thought, a very significant moment for us.

Moving on, I asked about the Clacton by-election. 'Was that the high-point in your UKIP career?'

'No, Rochester was the high point. Well, Clacton was the high point at that moment in time, although almost usurped by the remarkable events in Greater Rochdale that night.'

'Do you not think you should have gone up to Heywood & Middleton in those final few days and tried to rustle up a few more votes?' I asked.

Farage shook his head: 'I think when somebody has put their neck on the line, that is an act of bravery that cannot go unsupported. Had I spent the last fortnight in Heywood it may have been different, but how could I?'

'The next morning the papers were dominated with your comments about migrants with HIV. Was that the first sign of a difference between you and Douglas?' I asked.

No, Douglas and I have a different view on the question of immigration and that's not exactly a trade secret. We have very similar views on the European project and what it means for democracy, what it means for Britain's place in the world and he's got a Commonwealth background.

So when I talk about the Commonwealth and he talks about the Commonwealth, the bigger, extended, English-speaking family that's out there in the world, we are very much at one. Where we are also very much at one is on political reform, very much at one. Now that's a higher point on the agenda.

We don't see eye to eye on the importance of immigration as an issue and there's a sort of classical liberal, libertarian, Gladstonian wing of the party who don't see that as being as high a priority as I made it over the past two years.

But that's the point about leadership. You can try and please everybody and say nothing or you must say, 'I'm going to make a decision here and chart a course' – and that's what I did.

Farage told me unveiling Mark Reckless at the Doncaster confer-ence in 2014 was 'the most exciting moment of my career in UKIP'.

'I had it all carefully planned. I'd even looked at the Velcro of the curtain. I do delegate, but I do trust myself not to breach my own secrets. I sent the security team off to an address in the Midlands to pick up an unnamed gentleman from an address in a car with dark windows. I sussed it all out.'

'What about O'Flynn's "Wag Tax"? I asked. 'You didn't know about that until we told you about it after your speech, did you?'

He admitted he didn't know anything about it, despite asking for 'a full briefing note of all the speeches that were going to be given'.

He then laughed and said: 'Apart from mine, [for] which there isn't one. I get up in the morning and think, "Fuck! What am I going to say?"'

I asked if he had got the idea for the 'tanks on the lawn' part of his speech from *Telegraph* journalist Matthew Holehouse after he had said it at the previous night's media drinks. 'Did that plant the phrase in your head?' I asked.

'It did, I think,' Farage replied. 'I had used it before once on the Tories. Holehouse said that, I thought, 'Oh, I like that.' No line is so good you can't nick it. I gave that speech in Doncaster very much off the cuff.'

Time was running out, but I had so much more to ask Farage. 'Rochester was tough but it was a fantastic result, very, very excit-ing,' he said as I asked him about that by-election battle.

'Were you worried you might lose?'

'I was worried until 7.15 p.m. the day of polling day when I took Bruni-Lowe out the back and said, "Right, what's the game?",' he said. 'By then we got to the stage where we had the numbers, the pledges, the systems – we had become a proper electoral mission for the first time properly. We had test-marketed it at Clacton. Chris said, "I know we're fine."'

I mention the name 'Winston McKenzie' and Farage starts to smile:

I love Winston. I'll never forget that night, live down the line with Dimbleby giving it this [Farage started shadow boxing]. Just so funny. He just loves me. There's never a day when I don't get messages from Winston, never ever a day.

I had to put Jim in charge of the Commonwealth brief, because you've got to have an elected person doing it, but I like him very much.

Now it was time to turn to the election campaign, and the first person I had to ask about was Raheem Kassam, a man so despised in the party that high-profile Kippers like Patrick O'Flynn had started an all-out war in a bid to get rid of him.

'Raheem is brilliant. He will do tremendously well,' was Farage's first thought on the subject.

After lighting another cigarette, Farage carried on:

He had been covering UKIP for Breitbart so he had been turning up for meetings, so he was a face I was bumping into. I went to the States, spent some time with him and I could see he was bright. I read his stuff, which was good, and he seemed very, very keen to do it.

I never ever ever ever from that conversation thought this was a long-term job. I thought for him it was an exciting project to jump onto, from which to move on and do other things, and so I never saw Raheem and myself working together in five years' time.

'Did you think he was, or had the potential to be, divisive?' I asked.

'No, but I can see why he is,' Farage replied. 'If he thinks people are useless he tells them. I wonder where he gets that from!'

'Did you become thin-skinned, snarling and aggressive?' I asked.

Farage paused for a while, thinking, and then with a smile said: 'Not thin-skinned!'

'What about the complaint about the BBC?' I said.

'I didn't put that in, did I?' he replied.

'Was it a good thing to do?'

'I think what was allowed to happen was outrageous,' Farage said:

> If you believe in the Representation of the People's Act, that shouldn't have been allowed. At the time, we were fighting the BBC on bias, and with some justification, so one of the lawyers did it. I didn't sit here and ponder for hours, 'Should I do it?' I was busy: 'Yeah, alright, OK.' I think the BBC's treatment of UKIP in the campaign was disgusting at every level. Treated on the ten o'clock news every night as about as important as Plaid Cymru, that's what we're basically saying. Mocked on every satire left-wing show that the BBC has.
>
> Am I thin-skinned? No! I can mix it with the best of them, of course I can, but I thought we reached a point where something had to be said.

The line coming out from those in the Farage camp over the past week had been that it was the threat of an SNP/Labour coalition deal that had left UKIP with just one MP, not the narrowness of the party's campaign message. I asked Farage if he thought he had talked up the SNP threat too much.

'No, I think in a funny sort of way it harmed our vote in the south and helped our vote in the north. But did it hurt us? Yes, yes it did.'

At that moment his mobile phone beeped with a text message. He read it out: '"Chuka [Umunna] out of [Labour] leadership" – bugger, bugger. He was the dream. Too much ambition.'

Turning back to the campaign, he said: 'We had a lot to say on a lot of issues and we didn't fully get the chance and that was disappointing. I found the earlier bits of the campaign tough. I wasn't in the best state.'

I asked if it was because he was going out too much in the evenings.

Farage shook his head: 'It's because I wasn't looking after myself properly. I wasn't doing any of it [physio]. I should be doing exercise every day and I should be regularly going to the hospital and having treatment. It's not hard. I'm a bloke! So I was a bit crocked.'

I decided this would be a good time to ask him whether he regretted the moment that appeared to have crystallised the split in the party on campaign tone – the HIV comments in the TV debate:

> I don't regret it at all. Even if some people here [UKIP HQ] do, even if some of the party do. I'm sorry, it's true.
>
> The *Mail* polled it heavily and, in their editorial, for almost the first time in the history of the *Daily Mail*, they said, 'Mr Farage has a very serious point here which everyone has turned their backs on.' And having spent last night in an Accident and Emergency unit after *Question Time*, seeing the horrors of what was going on in there...

'Why were you in A&E?' I asked.

> 'It wasn't happening to me, but I had to leave *Question Time* as quickly as I could for reasons that weren't particularly funny. Not a very good night. But I was in a war zone last night in what you would have thought was a very respectable part of this country. People with stab vests on guarding the doors, guarding the wards. Lack of beds, people being put on the floor. I came out last night and I said [to the person I was with], 'You know everything I've said about a rising population and the impossibility of our resources to cope, we've just seen it tonight.'
>
> Do I regret it? No, I don't.

He was defiant. 'How about attacking the audience in the second TV debate?'

'I was absolutely right. Nobody else would do that. At that moment in time, maintaining our core vote was our priority. We were under attack, we were beginning to slip in the polls. Everyone was talking us down, every interview [was], "Well, you're collapsing in the polls, Mr Farage."'

It was as if I were talking to Kassam, not Farage. I asked him why he decided not to visit the pub in Grimsby where the landlord had produced a special beer for him.

'Because they'd have beaten me up,' he said, matter-of-factly:

> There was an aggressive left-wing mob from Sheffield, the same people who had come after me in Rotherham, they would have done me physical violence. That would have been great, wouldn't it? Oh yes, the broadcast would have loved it. They were in touch with these people everywhere I went. That's what they wanted, I wasn't going to give it to them.
>
> I felt very sorry for the publican, he had produced that beer – very sad – but that's how life's changed. And that's why I couldn't do now what I did in 2013. I couldn't just tour the country. Take me back to 2013! In terms of the job and in terms of the enjoyment of doing it and in terms of the thrill of feeling you were trying to build this revolution, that was fantastic. It was the sense of freedom, not needing to be shepherded around everywhere. Not facing physical assault, that sort of thing, that's a big change.

This seemed a good time to ask him what he really thought of my profession. Farage was constantly sniping about the media's treatment of UKIP, but deep down I suspected he quite liked journalists. He said:

> I think I'm more trusting of human beings, including journalists, than almost anybody you've ever met. An old friend

of mine – he was my agent – he was the first ever UKIP press officer, he was my agent in 1999 for the European election, George Franklin-Ryan.

Dear old George, who is now elderly, retired, living in Ramsgate, funnily enough. Well, somebody wrote a book about me a few years ago and he interviewed George, who'd known me very well in the early days of UKIP. Very bright, very political, been a Tory activist all his life and George said of me: 'Nigel trusts everybody, until they let him down and then he never speaks to them again.' There's a lot of truth in that.

I told him what Stuart Wheeler had said about him having a succession of 'new favourite people', and asked if that was true.

No, because what you have to do is embed people into organisations. It's a fundamental misunderstanding of people who say that. They just don't get it. If you invite somebody into a club, and the rest of the club treat them like a new boy and they are not actually embedded into a club, then the chances are you lose them, and people don't get that. Once they are in the club, I've got to get somebody else in. Is that cynical? No. Not really. It's called building an organisation.

'Are you a good manager of people?' I asked.

It depends how much time I've got. If you speak to my former employees who worked for me in the City – although most of them have died of cirrhosis by now – if you talk to the people who worked for me at Farage Futures, I am personal friends still with all of them – all of them. A wide range of backgrounds. The oddball who used to work for me is a socialist, but all of that's irrelevant. I'm in touch with all of them. They all worked for me, and we're all friends.

Was I fair with them, financially and everything else? Yeah, I wasn't a greedy boss; I paid people fairly; I let people have holidays, lunches, enjoy life – but if we're busy we work our arses off. It's very difficult to judge me as a man-manager of a political party, I'm supposed to be the leader, I'm not sup-posed to be the manager, and I get judged too often as the manager and that's completely unfair. I can't do everything.

Seeing as Farage mentioned cirrhosis, I ask him the question I've always wanted to know the answer to: 'Do you think you're an alcoholic?'

'No,' he said instantly. 'I've written about this, I've talked about this. No, I'm lucky, some people are. Some people aren't.'

'Some people who drink less than you could be considered to be,' I suggest.

'There are people out there who drink three pints of beer and they're all over the shop, out of control,' he replied.

'Have you ever used alcohol as a crutch?'

'I'm a happy drinker, not a sad drinker.'

'So it's never been, "I'm feeling depressed, give me a beer, give me a gin and tonic"?'

'No, it's, "Wahey! Here we go! Let's go and party!" And I'm told that's the right way to be with it.'

'You gave it up for a month in January – you didn't miss it?'

'No problem. The first two weeks were easy. Last two weeks were hard because I had so many social engagements to go to. I was sur-rounded by people talking bollocks and I'm sure I'm not talking that. No, I'm not [an alcoholic], fortunately, I'm lucky really.'

'Wasn't your father an alcoholic?'

Farage nodded.

'Did that affect your relationship with alcohol at all?'

Not really. Obviously you're aware that people can go over the line and there were times in the City when I thought, 'I'm pretty close to that line, we really better start thinking about this.' Particularly with the 11.30 sharp that was part of the daily routine. You do begin to think, 'I better watch this.' But then there were always so many people who drunk more than you did, there was great comfort in this. I remember when I employed a bloke who drunk one and a half to two bottles of whisky a day. One of my friends, Tony, he said, 'The good news, Nigel, is we won't feel guilty at all any more.'

'I've seen you do public meetings. Do you think you could do them as well without the beer?'

'Oh, yes, I do.'

'So, it's not performance-enhancing?'

Nothing to do with it. I joke about it, but it's nothing to do with it. The only difference is if you're giving an after-dinner speech then you're with a group of people who have had gin and tonics and white wine and red wine, to be stone-cold sober and give an after-dinner speech is a huge mistake, because you're just not on their wavelength. In terms of public performances, no. Do I have a drink before I go on *Question Time*? Yes. How many do I have? One, maybe two.

I decided to move off the drinking and on to the personal nature of the job. 'People do say nasty things about you. Does it hurt you at all, or does it bounce off?'

'I know, they're bound to. It doesn't really. It depends who says them.'

'Do you read what people write about you? The political commentators?'

I used to. I stopped about a year ago. I still flick through, have a look and see the cartoons. I accept that a) it's a rough game, and b) I'm taking on the establishment, and they will necessarily make it more difficult for me across the board than they do for anybody else and, see, the British public have got a reasonable sense of fair play.

My time with Farage was almost at end, so I decide to go for the *Desert Island Discs*-style last few questions.

'What do you want your legacy to be? Britain out of the EU is a key one, I imagine?'

'Yes.'

'Lord Farage?'

Oh, God, no. That doesn't interest me at all. Do you know I've never had a business card with my title on it? I haven't even got a UKIP leader's business card. I'm not interested in stuff like that, I'm not interested in titles. I never wanted to be leader of UKIP, really, I was the most reluctant ... I had to be dragged into doing that. I could have done it years earlier and I didn't want to do it. I'm not into titles.

In terms of legacy, when I'm dead, I would like my children to be proud of me. What more could I hope for? And they might say: 'Well, he wasn't a dad we saw that much of, but at least he did something and changed things.' It's rather like your father was in the war for six years – many came back from the war and the kids didn't recognise them. I would like them to think that I'd achieved something and, you never know, I just might.

'You probably have, haven't you?'

'It's nowhere near enough yet.'

'You've got the referendum?'

'Maybe that's just the beginning.'
'In ten years' time will you still be doing this?'

> There will be other issues, there will be other things the establishment is wrong on which need changing. I'm quite good at looking ahead in terms of where social change is going to come and where moods change. I can already see what the next general election is going to be fought on. I'm not going to tell you, but I know what it is. I know exactly what it will be.

'The health service?'

> No, it will be a very, very big existential question about our civilisation, and who we are as a country and what the West is. We are headed for real, real problems. We could win the European battle but still lose the kind of society that I would like to see.

'Losing the tolerant, open society?'
'Yes.'
'Too much political correctness?'

> We'll all finish up living in gated communities. Those with money will live in gated communities and the rest will starve. There's nothing on the agenda here which is going to narrow the wealth gap. Absolutely nothing, and my joy all through my life – whether it was at school, or on the metal exchange, or in politics – I've always loved cross-mixing with all the social classes and all the different types of people. It's what I'm best at and I fear our society is moving away from that. The power of the corporates and just watching Britain become this low-wage economy I don't like. I like pubs where all

classes go in and mix and drink together and have a right
laugh, and that's disappeared.

And on that happy note, Farage got up and we walked out of his
office together. Before we had taken the twelve steps to the main
office door, he was on his phone again. I briefly shook his hand and
stepped out onto the sunny Mayfair street.

I could have talked to him all day; there was so much still to ask
him. For all the in-fighting in UKIP, he seemed happy and relaxed.
Why wouldn't he be? He was back as leader of the party that he simply couldn't leave. If he was no longer leader of UKIP, who was Nigel
Farage? An absent father; a big-time drinker whose friends were now
on mineral water; a seven-times failed parliamentary candidate? But
with UKIP he was the leader of 4 million voters; the bogeyman of
the pro-Europeans; the darling of the patriotic working class.

Nigel Farage resigning as UKIP leader on the Kent cliffs would
have provided a cleaner, more rounded ending for this book.

But leaving him in his smoke-filled office to deal with an internal
power struggle of his own making is a far more appropriate way to
stop following Farage.

EPILOGUE

G ODFREY BLOOM WAS RIGHT. In Yorkshire, on that cold, bright January day, he told me Nigel Farage gets rid of the alpha males in the party. 'Primeval' was his word.

Four days after I interviewed Farage, Patrick O'Flynn and Suzanne Evans were gone from the UKIP front bench.

O'Flynn stepped down as economic spokesman and issued a statement that read like something a North Korean dissident might say in the hope of being spared the firing squad:

> I would like to express to colleagues my sincere regret at going public with my frustrations about the turn of events following polling day. And more than that, I would like to apologise directly to Nigel for the phrase 'snarling, thin-skinned and aggressive'. This was a fragment of a wider passage about perceptions and is not what I think of him. Nonetheless, I should have known better than anyone what use would be made of phrases that were both unfair and unkind.
>
> I am proud of what we achieved in the general election and am only sorry to have succumbed, as Roger [Helmer] put it, with such impressive understatement, to public remarks that were 'unhelpful'. I think it appropriate to stand down as economic spokesman, which I have done. I hope in the months ahead to be of use to the great campaign to persuade

the British people to leave the EU, which is, after all, what brought me into politics in the first place.

Farage decided to spare his life, saying O'Flynn 'came in person to tell me he had realised that he had made a mistake and, being the honourable man that he is, tendered his resignation as UKIP economic spokesman. I accepted his resignation with some sadness, not least because he is very able and has been a great asset to the team. He continues to be a committed UKIP member and MEP.'

Evans, whom Farage had anointed as temporary leader when he initially resigned, was also part of the cull. Despite producing an excellent manifesto, her contract as UKIP's policy chief was not renewed.

The two people who had stood with Farage as the manifesto was unveiled in Thurrock were no longer at the top table.

The UKIP civil war was over.

But there was still one outstanding question in all of this: who was Brendan O'Brien, the man who had gone off on that anti-Islamic rant at me in Margate and then mysteriously appeared at Farage's book launch?

I discovered he was an aeroplane display pilot who ran a company called O'Brien's Flying Circus, but I could find no link to UKIP. I trawled through the Electoral Commission records to see if he was a donor, but I couldn't find his name. It seemed no one in the party had heard of him.

Twelve hours before my book deadline, it was suggested to me he may be a patron of the party – a group of people so secret not even Farage's top team knows who is on the list.

In return for a donation of £1,000 a year, patrons get honorary membership to the party, invitations to dinners hosted by Farage, speaker events, policy forums and a reception at their annual conference.

Patrons also get enrolled 'in the party network, providing opportunities to meet and debate with like-minded people around the country'.

And to make it all just that bit sweeter, patrons get a Cornish pewter lapel badge and 'Cranks & Gadflies' tie.

I found O'Brien's number and called him up. He remembered me, and I asked him if he was a patron of UKIP.

'Yes,' he replied

'For how long?'

'About four years,' he said.

I emailed the UKIP press office the transcript of my conversation with O'Brien in Margate, asking for confirmation he was a patron, and what the party made of his views. I didn't get a reply from them, but I did get a mysterious email from a 'Capt. Boogaloo' a few hours later.

The subject line read: 'I live in east London, and live with thousands upon thousands of Muslims'.

That was a quote from me in the transcript I had sent to UKIP.

The email read:

> GREAT – LET'S DO IT! Thanks for the call earlier today – how's my old chum 'Mrs Palmer?' [A reference to me being a 'wanker', I think.] You still don't get it – do you! You have been set up pal – SCAMMED! Well, more fool you. Also, what appalling writing and you a journalist?? You will have to do better than that or become a laughing stock! We WILL have the FULL transcript – VERBATIM!
>
> You also omitted, which I will not, my personal position as a committed humanist [he didn't mention this to me either time I met him] – which is: Irrespective of your race, creed, colour, age, gender, political persuasion – nay even, your personal proclivities and propensities – if you are a player – welcome, if you are a plonker – ADIOS.
>
> Above all else, I espouse EQUALITY OF OPPORTUNITY for all – not the nonsense of egalitarianism!
>
> Definition of plonker in English: noun, British, 1, informal A foolish or inept person.

If you live by the sword Owen you must be prepared to
die by the sword – THE SAME GOES FOR THE PEN!

Educate yourself in the very broadest sense – not just in
the details of the OED and SOED so that you can at least
give accurate substance to your ramblings but so that you
don't fall headlong into the bottomless abyss as you teeter
on the periphery of the great existentialist vacuum, where
every thing is nothing, and nothing is everything! This now
has NOTHING to do with UKIP!! It is just YOU and ME
– no backers, no parties, no Huffs or Puffs!

If such exists – may God have mercy on you – because for
sure, I won't. Capt. Boogaloo.

Slightly odd, I'm sure you'll agree. I replied asking him in what way
I had been 'set up', and got this email back:

I GUESS WE WILL MEET ON THE OTHER SIDE OF
MIDNIGHT – YOUR HELL OR MINE – WE SHALL
SEE – BUT REMEMBER THIS WELL, SO AS YOU
STRUCK THE FIRST BLOW, SO SHALL I STRIKE THE
LAST! THIS IS JUST ABOUT YOU AND ME NOW –
NO ONE AND NOTHING ELSE.